The
Magic
Room

The
Magic
Room

*A Story About the Love
We Wish for Our Daughters*

Jeffrey Zaslow

GOTHAM
BOOKS

GOTHAM BOOKS
Published by Penguin Group (USA) Inc.
375 Hudson Street, New York, New York 10014, U.S.A.
Penguin Group (Canada), 90 Eglinton Avenue East, Suite 700, Toronto, Ontario M4P 2Y3, Canada (a division of Pearson Penguin Canada Inc.) • Penguin Books Ltd, 80 Strand, London WC2R 0RL, England • Penguin Ireland, 25 St Stephen's Green, Dublin 2, Ireland (a division of Penguin Books Ltd) • Penguin Group (Australia), 250 Camberwell Road, Camberwell, Victoria 3124, Australia (a division of Pearson Australia Group Pty Ltd) • Penguin Books India Pvt Ltd, 11 Community Centre, Panchsheel Park, New Delhi—110 017, India • Penguin Group (NZ), 67 Apollo Drive, Rosedale, Auckland 0632, New Zealand (a division of Pearson New Zealand Ltd) • Penguin Books (South Africa) (Pty) Ltd, 24 Sturdee Avenue, Rosebank, Johannesburg 2196, South Africa

Penguin Books Ltd, Registered Offices: 80 Strand, London WC2R 0RL, England

Published by Gotham Books, a member of Penguin Group (USA) Inc.

First printing, January 2012
1   3   5   7   9   10   8   6   4   2

Copyright © 2012 by Jeffrey Zaslow
Photograph credits: pages viii, xvii, xviii, 7, 14, 37, 45, 55, 183, 232, 282 copyright © Kelly Lynne Photography; pages 12, 146, 158, 258, 260 courtesy of Danielle K. Wenzel; page 27 courtesy of Meredith Kaufman; page 34 courtesy of Roxanne M. Maitner; pages 48, 172, 180, 274 courtesy of Lynn Hansen; pages 72, 216 courtesy of Laura Pardo; page 88 courtesy of Courtney Schlauel; pages 90, 97, 116, 121, 127 courtesy of Michelle (Shelley) Becker Mueller; pages 103, 106, 244, 250, 269 courtesy of Julie M. Wieber; pages 132, 140, 267 courtesy of Ashley Bradenberg; pages 195, 197, 200, 209 courtesy of Carol L. Otto; page 237 courtesy of Ben Friedkin; page 264 copyright © Kelli Wiseman, Clever Creations Photography; page 277 courtesy of Megan Martin
All rights reserved

Gotham Books and the skyscraper logo are trademarks of Penguin Group (USA) Inc.

LIBRARY OF CONGRESS CATALOGING-IN-PUBLICATION DATA
Zaslow, Jeffrey.
The magic room : a story about the love we wish for our daughters / Jeffrey Zaslow.
p. cm.
ISBN 978-1-592-40661-6
1. Mothers and daughters.   2. Fathers and daughters.   3. Parent and child.   I. Title.
HQ755.85.Z37 2012
306.8740973—dc23   2011027157

ISBN 978-1-592-40661-6

Printed in the United States of America
Set in Simoncini Garamond with Kabel and Coronet Display
Designed by Elke Sigal

While the author has made every effort to provide accurate telephone numbers and Internet addresses at the time of publication, neither the publisher nor the author assumes any responsibility for errors, or for changes that occur after publication. Further, the publisher does not have any control over and does not assume any responsibility for author or third-party websites or their content.

For my daughters, Jordan, Alex, and Eden,
and for your daughters too . . .

Contents

Becker's Bridal, a mainstay on Fowler's Main Street since 1934.

Introduction

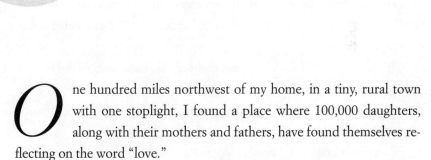

*O*ne hundred miles northwest of my home, in a tiny, rural town with one stoplight, I found a place where 100,000 daughters, along with their mothers and fathers, have found themselves reflecting on the word "love."

It's a place where, every day, parents can't help but be enveloped by a swell of emotion as they think back to the love they felt when their daughters were little girls. They think ahead, too, contemplating the love needed to carry their daughters onward from here. These parents know the disappointments and betrayals associated with the word "love," especially these days. They know the losses that define life. Still, most make their pilgrimage here with a sense of hope and optimism.

For the daughters, usually women in their twenties, this is a place that makes clear they are at a crossroads. They have so much on their minds—"love" being at the forefront, usually—but they also can be distracted, impulsive, naïve, and fearful. Each of them has a story that brought them here. Not all will find happiness after they leave.

I never knew that all of this emotion was so well concentrated in one spot, a ninety-minute drive from my house in suburban Detroit. But once I started coming here, to watch and listen, I often found myself caught up in the swell of my own parental feelings, as the father of three daughters. For all of us who desperately wish that our girls will go through life safe, happy, and surrounded by love, time spent here offers visceral reminders of the challenges our girls face, of the ways in which sadness is so often intertwined with their joy, and of the sweet possibilities that await them— or that may be beyond their grasp.

What is this place?

Put simply, it is a room . . . in a building . . . in this very small town.

The town is Fowler, Michigan, a middle-class community with 1,100 residents—and 2,500 wedding dresses.

The building is Becker's Bridal, the largest business in town, and home to all those dresses—a "blizzard of white" squeezed tightly on three floors of crowded racks.

And the room? That's up a short flight of stairs and over to the left, on the second level of Becker's. Each wall of the ten-foot-by-eight-foot space has a floor-to-ceiling mirror designed to carry a bride's image into infinity. They call it "The Magic Room," and with good reason.

From the outside, the store looks like an old bank. That's because the two-story, heavy stone structure was built a century ago to house People's Bank, until the bank went under during the Depression. What was once the bank's vault—cleared out of the few stacks of money that remained— is now the Magic Room, a place with soft lighting and a tiled, circular pedestal. This is where brides are taken when they finally decide which of the 2,500 dresses could be "the one."

Becker's sits at the south end of a tired-looking two-block Main Street. The family owned store, led in an unbroken chain of ownership by four generations of Becker women, has been a mainstay at this location since 1934. Over the years, the store has served more than 100,000 brides, many of whom traveled here from across the Midwest. It is a place rich in history, visited by young women who usually know none of it.

Thanks to Becker's Bridal, the town of Fowler has more wedding dresses per capita than any other municipality in the United States, or perhaps in the world. But not many people outside of Michigan have heard of this place, or know anything about the women of Becker's—a daughter, her mother, her grandmother, and her great-grandmother—who built and nurtured the store, guiding all of those brides into all of their dresses for seventy-six years.

As for the Magic Room, the saleswomen at Becker's don't use the word "magic" lightly when talking about it. They routinely watch brides and their mothers melt into tears in this room as they reflect on all the moments in their lives that led them here. After seeing their daughters on that pedestal, fathers are often overcome with emotion too. They excuse themselves, leaving the vault and then the store, so they can compose themselves. Fathers can be seen pacing up and down Main Street in Fowler, blowing their noses and wiping their eyes.

We live in an age when TV reality shows—*Say Yes to the Dress, Bridezillas*—have drawn attention by showcasing the frenzied pursuit of the wedding dress. These programs are framed like sporting events, with brides bickering and dickering and racing toward a finish line marked by their selection of a dress.

Some of this goes on at Becker's, too, of course. But I came here not just to write about wedding gowns and what they represent. I also wanted to understand the women wearing them, their fears and yearnings.

I resolved to pay less attention to brides I met whose motives seemed somewhat frivolous, the ones more focused on their dresses than their upcoming marriages. Instead, I wanted to find brides and their families whose paths here were not necessarily easy, but who have given great thought to the love that guides and connects them.

I guess I wanted to stand in the Magic Room with these families whose stories touched me the most, and while there, contemplate my feelings for my own daughters.

⌒

For a decade now, I have written a column for *The Wall Street Journal* about our most emotional life transitions. That's my beat. Before this job,

I spent fourteen years as an advice columnist. (In 1987, I won a competition to replace Ann Landers at the *Chicago Sun-Times*.) And so I long have been drawn to stories about love, especially the bonds between parents and daughters. My three daughters are now ages twenty-one, nineteen, and fifteen, and I know they will need love in their lives—from me, my wife, each other, and someday I hope, from their husbands and children.

As my girls have grown up, I've always tried to pay attention to the detailed ways in which other parents express affection for their daughters— the ways they sought to reassure or encourage them. As a father, I was often guided by the readers of my columns, and the thousands of letters they sent my way. Their stories remain with me, and have helped me find my bearings in the Magic Room.

There was the judge in Illinois who told me he grew up in a home where everyone always said "I love you." Because of that, he found it easy to say those words to his own children. One Friday night in 1995, as his eighteen-year-old daughter headed out the door with her friends, he said to her, "Remember I love you." She replied: "I love you too, Dad." She died hours later in a car accident, and the judge told me how grateful he was that his last words to her were a reminder of his love.

The judge's wife wasn't raised in a family where affection was articulated so effortlessly. And so the words didn't come as easily to her. She was in the other room that day, and wasn't fated to have a final loving exchange with her daughter. She told me she didn't need to say "I love you"—her daughter knew she was loved—and yet a part of her ached because she wishes she had said it.

Again and again, people have explained to me the ways in which "I love you" can be said to daughters without saying it.

A woman once wrote to me to explain that when she was growing up, her mother never asked her to wash dishes. Even if she offered to help, her mother wouldn't let her near the sink. "As long as I live," her mother told her, "I want to do this. After I'm gone, many dishes will be left for you, and I hope it warms your heart to remember that I always did them for you." Since her mother's death, this woman often thinks of her, happily, when she washes dishes. "She was setting this up," the woman told me. "She wasn't always in good health, and she knew the time would come."

I've seen how people's love for their daughters can be strengthened in times of adversity.

I was moved by conversations I had with an eighty-one-year-old reader whose sixty-year-old daughter had Alzheimer's. She spoke of changing her daughter's diaper, just as she had sixty years earlier. "When I push her in her wheelchair, I think of how I pushed her in her baby buggy," she said. This mother had always assumed that when she got old, her daughter would lovingly look after her. "But feeling sorry for yourself, that's bad news," she said. Her story taught me about accepting fate, pushing on, counting blessings. She spoke of telling her daughter "I love you," and her daughter looking at her blankly, through cloudy eyes. That was OK. "I'm lucky to have my daughter in my life," she said.

Over the years, I've written about the ways in which love still can be expressed, even when our daughters leave us weary or disappointed. (One exasperated mother told me that she often ends her phone conversations with her argumentative college-age daughter the same way: "I love you, but I'm hanging up now.") I've also seen how parental love can be burdened by regret, and how a mother's or father's worst behavior can do terrible damage. I've thought of these stories too as I've gotten to know the families who journeyed into the Magic Room.

I once spent a day with female inmates at a maximum-security prison in Illinois. One woman was serving a life sentence for her role in the murder of her mother. But that day, she was focused on her nine-year-old daughter. As part of a prison literacy program, she was reading good-night books into a cassette player, after which the tape would be mailed to her child. The book project was created to remind children of incarcerated parents that "love can travel through prison walls." This inmate read her daughters titles including *Goodnight Moon* and *Guess How Much I Love You*. "You want to be there when your child is sick or needs comforting," she told me. That wasn't possible, of course, but by reading good-night books, "I can give her the love in my voice."

I've remained haunted by the young adopted woman I once interviewed who had finally found her birth mother. During their tearful reunion, she asked about her birth father. She hoped to hear a love story: perhaps her parents had been too young to marry and made the hard choice to give her up for adoption. Turned out, that wasn't the story. "Your father was a stranger with long blond hair," her birth mother said. "He asked for directions, then raped me." The young woman swallowed the news. "Now I know," she said. She came to accept this startling revelation. The rape had given her life.

Though I've written mostly about strangers, much of what I learn leads me to think about my own daughters. When my kids were younger, I once joined a hundred dads in a high-school auditorium near my home. It was a gorgeous Saturday morning, the sort of autumn day that called out for fathers and sons to toss footballs. But we were indoors, asking ourselves hard questions about our relationships with our daughters.

How do I look at women? Do I comment on their weight or attractiveness? What message does my behavior send to my daughters?

The session, part of a fathering conference, was a reminder that these are precarious times for parent/daughter relationships—especially girls' bonds with their fathers. Reams of research show that girls who are close to their dads are less likely to be promiscuous, develop eating disorders, drop out of school, or commit suicide.

Like the other fathers, I winced as the session leader told us that most of our daughters would be lifelong dieters, have a negative body image, and be emotionally scarred by bullies. A dad's job, we were told, is to remind a daughter of her strengths, and to guide her into womanhood. We were encouraged to start by developing small rituals that reinforced the message: "Dad loves you." My youngest daughter, then eight years old, had recently broken her leg, and needed me to carry her up stairs. I decided to kiss her lightly on top of her head as I lifted her, and she'd been smiling luminously in response. When I began putting notes in her lunch bag, wishing her a good day at school and telling her I was thinking about her, she surprised me by saving every note in a box in her drawer.

After I told that story in my column, I heard from daughters, young and old, offering their own recollections, and warnings, too. Some women described the damage that results when parents don't show love. "My father never told me I was pretty," one woman wrote. "He never said he loved me, so when the first knucklehead came along and said it, I jumped right in." Another woman, now in her forties, told me that a part of her is still "an awkward twelve-year-old, wishing my dad would say, 'I love you, too,' when I said, 'I love you, Daddy.' But he didn't and still doesn't."

I've seen how tightly women hold on to their happiest recollections from childhood. One woman in her fifties told me about a memory of being eight years old. She had fallen asleep during a family car ride and woke up as her dad was carrying her into the house. In her grogginess, she had this wonderful feeling of being loved and secure. "My dad had me safely in his arms," she told me, calling the moment "a treasured memory."

As I've collected these stories throughout my career, I've also seen how parents with daughters focus on the future. From the time our daughters are born, we can't help but think about the men they might marry. We all have our laundry list of qualities for potential sons-in-law—that they respect our daughters and provide for them, that they will deeply love our daughters and the children they raise together.

I've heard from men who seem to know what love is all about, and they go beyond the clichés. When all of us think about the mates we want for our daughters, these are the sorts of men we envision.

I once asked readers to send me their definitions of love. One man replied with a story about a cruise he had taken years before. He was out on the ship's deck, looking out at the ocean, when he spotted a school of dolphins.

"They were racing alongside the ship," he told me, "against the backdrop of the most beautiful rainbow I had ever seen."

So why did this scene define what love meant to him?

It's because, even years later, when he thinks back to that breathtaking moment, he feels more sadness than happiness. "I'm sad," he told me, "because my wife was not there to see it with me."

That's the sort of love we wish for our daughters. Men who will feel that way when our daughters are not with them.

⌒

My wife, Sherry, knew I had been searching for a way to write a book about how all of us can best show love to our daughters today. I wanted to look at cultural touchstones, and to offer a well-reported sense of what the words "I love you" feel like in our changing times. Sherry and I talked about where such a book might be set. Maybe I could visit maternity wards, dance studios, daddy-daughter date nights or spas where mothers and daughters go to bond. There were plenty of possibilities.

But then Sherry thought back to her happiest memory of spending time with her own father.

Before we got married in 1987, Sherry was living in Detroit and I lived in Chicago. Our wedding would be held in Buffalo, New York, Sherry's hometown. She planned to fly into Buffalo a couple days before the wedding, but by the time her wedding gown alterations were finished, it was too late to ship the dress. She didn't want the gown getting wrinkled in the plane's baggage compartment, and it seemed silly to ask about buying a seat for it in the cabin.

And so her father offered to drive 320 miles from Buffalo to Detroit to pick up Sherry and her wedding dress, and to turn around and drive 320 miles back. Sherry was touched by his willingness to do that, and she calls the six hours she spent in the car that day—with her dad and her dress— one of the happiest memories of her life. It was a selfless, loving act by her dad, and it turned into a special chance for him to talk to her about his love for her, and about his hopes for her marriage to me.

"There's something about a wedding dress . . . ," Sherry said to me.

And that's when I first considered the idea of setting this book at a bridal shop, of giving voice to a handful of memorable women on the brink of commitment.

I was willing to go anywhere in the country to find the right store and the right stories, and I began exploring potential options. As things turned out, I didn't have to search too far or too long.

When I first drove up to Becker's Bridal, I was aware only that the store was a popular stop for brides-to-be from central Michigan. I didn't know its history. I knew nothing about the family that ran it. I certainly didn't know about the Magic Room.

But on the very first day I visited Becker's, I truly sensed that this was a place that could illuminate the most poignant aspects of a woman's journey to the altar. I just knew that the story I wanted to tell about all of our daughters was here—in the walls, in the mirrors, on the racks, and especially, in that small, simple room at the top of the stairs.

The Magic Room

Shelley in front of the store with a dress over her shoulder

Chapter One

The Mirror

*I*t's 9:20 a.m. on a Tuesday in July, and Shelley Becker Mueller, owner of Becker's Bridal, stands at the store's back door, jiggling her key in the lock. It's the same routine her mother followed for decades, and her grandmother before that.

Shelley steps through the "employees only" entrance, a cup of coffee in her hand, flips on the light switch, and heads into the back office to plug in the commercial vapor iron. That's always the opening ritual, since the iron takes a half hour to warm up and will be needed right away.

The phone is already ringing—no doubt it's a bride or her mother with an alteration issue—but Shelley's not ready to answer it just yet. Whoever it is can call back after the store opens at ten. No one's walking down any aisles before then anyway.

Shelley stops at her desk, puts down her coffee, and looks at her appointment book. Twenty-one brides will pick up their dresses today, and she quickly makes sure their gowns are on the final pressing rack in order of their appointment times. She then heads out onto the sales floor and stops in the seventeen fitting rooms, one by one, to see whether any gowns

1

or crinolines, tried on the evening before, need to be returned to their racks. Today all she finds is a stray bra.

No new brides-to-be have arrived yet. But the old brides, they're all still here; 100,000 of them.

Shelley can feel the presence of all those brides partly because, to the right of the front counter, there's a large, ninety-year-old mirror in a weathered wooden frame. Guarded on either side by two mannequins in wedding gowns, the mirror has been in the store since the very first dress was sold in 1934. Most every Becker's bride has stood in front of it, usually with her mother looking over her shoulder.

Some cultures think that a mirror captures your soul, and Shelley believes it too. She considers mirrors a reflection of the past; after we look in them, our spirits remain there with everyone else. When tourists walk through Monticello, Thomas Jefferson's home in Virginia, they stand in front of a mirror used by Jefferson himself; their souls mix with his. In the same way, every Becker's bride who looks in the store's old mirror is connected to every bride who came before her. Every mother-of-the-bride communes with all the mothers before her. Every father with all the fathers. That's how Shelley sees it, and it gives her comfort.

Now forty-five years old, Shelley has been looking in this mirror since she was a little girl. Over the decades, she's seen ten thousand versions of herself in it—as a toddler just learning to walk, as a fourteen-year-old girl working here on the floor, as a nineteen-year-old bride wearing the store's priciest wedding dress, and as a middle-age woman now in charge of everything. Lately, for all sorts of reasons, she's been getting more sentimental about the mirror. When she stands in front of it and she's not crazy-busy catering to a customer, she sometimes takes a moment and wonders about the lives reflected in it: What became of all those brides who smiled at themselves, or wiped away happy tears, in front of this mirror? How many children and grandchildren did they go on to have? Whose marriage made it and whose did not? How many of those brides are alive today?

Shelley knows how life goes. An unknown number of the brides who looked in this mirror ended up estranged from their parents, or they died young, or they were inexplicably loyal to scoundrels who abused them. Others lived to be old women, their marriages growing richer each year. A few lived long enough to see great-granddaughters buy their dresses at Becker's.

The mirror also reminds Shelley of the store's founder, her grandmother Eva Becker, the no-nonsense businesswoman who oversaw employees and customers with a firm hand. What would Grandma Eva, who stood in front of this mirror with thousands of brides, think of the way Shelley is running the place?

Shelley truly feels that Eva is somehow here in the store, watching. Some of her saleswomen suspect the place is haunted. They often hear odd creaking noises, or boxes in the upstairs storage area will topple for unexplained reasons, as if someone were up there pushing them over. Items such as car keys and bridal accessories will disappear, only to mysteriously reappear on the front counter the next day. When the saleswomen tell brides about "The Ghost of Eva," they're mostly kidding. Still, Grandma Eva, whose unsmiling 1922 wedding photo hangs near that old mirror, remains a formidable force here, thirty-four years after her death.

The old mirror used to be on a freestanding base in a corner, but after Shelley took over the store from her mother, she moved it near the counter, so that every visitor couldn't help but pass it. She likes the idea of connecting today's brides with those who came before. Most of the women who bought dresses at Becker's in its first half century stayed married—just look at the low divorce statistics then—so Shelley figures it's good karma to have today's customers see themselves in this mirror. Maybe some old-fashioned values will rub off on them. Shelley recently had the names of her great-grandparents, grandparents, and parents stenciled at the top of it, with the years they took over ownership of Becker's—1899, 1928, 1974. When she leaves the business, maybe her name will be stenciled there too, with the year she bought the business from her parents, 2005.

On this morning, Shelley takes just a few seconds to look at herself in the mirror. She gives herself a half-smile. She's five-foot-ten and strikingly attractive, but more than that, she dresses as if she means it. She's in a sleek black dress with the highest of high heels, and wears three strands of baubles around her neck (large pearls and rhinestones) and five bracelets (layers of crystals and more rhinestones). She looks unlike any other woman in Fowler, Michigan—a simple, mostly blue-collar town where no one dresses too fancy, especially this early in the morning. Her grandmother had been something of a fashion diva when she ran the store, always wearing a hat with feathers in it. Shelley reasons that it's a new, showier age, and she wants to make a statement, too. Others have certainly noticed that she's single-handedly trying to deliver a stepped-up style here on Fowler's drab Main Street. A few roll their eyes a bit. Most like it. Everyone notices. Several people in town describe her the same way: "She's like Sandra Bullock, all dressed up in that movie *The Blind Side.*"

Shelley is also able to pull off a haircut that reminds others in Fowler of Fleetwood Mac singer Stevie Nicks, circa 1982. It's a twenty-first-century streaked blonde shag, and it works for her.

Just as Shelley moves on from the old mirror, the back door opens. It's her twenty-four-year-old daughter, Alyssa, the fourth-generation Becker to work at the store. Alyssa, who isn't as determinedly stylish as Shelley, likes to kid her mother about her outfits, her heels, her near-perfect figure. "Hi, Barbie," she says to Shelley as she puts on her name tag.

Shelley doesn't mind her daughter's playful digs. She's thrilled that Alyssa, a recent graduate of nearby Central Michigan University, is with her every day. After spending time in both Paris and New York, Alyssa has decided that, at least for now, she wants to work here, in tiny Fowler, in the family business. Given that Shelley spends her days watching mothers and daughters laugh, cry, and annoy each other, it's nice to have her own daughter close by. They commiserate about the mother/daughter relationships all around them; it gives them a sense of how they're doing.

A large part of Shelley hopes that Alyssa will stay at Becker's Bridal forever, and that she'll take over the store one day. And yet Shelley also knows how confining this small town can be, and how much of the world you miss if you spend all your time here. Alyssa is a gifted writer with a sense of humor and a lot going for her. Shelley's dreams for Alyssa vary by the day, even by the hour. Sometimes she wants to hold her tight, sharing life here at Becker's. Sometimes she wants to set her free.

Today, Alyssa is especially chirpy. The phone has been ringing, and Alyssa tells her mother, "Don't worry, Barbie, I'll get it" while Shelley finishes her final morning rounds. Shelley heads up the six stairs just around the corner from the old mirror and walks into that special room on the left, the Magic Room. One of her saleswomen straightened it out and vacuumed the night before. The soft lights in the room are set perfectly. The emerald-green carpet looks clean and fresh. The pedestal shines.

"OK, the place looks presentable," Shelley thinks. She returns to the back office to turn on the store's music system. Sinatra is up first. Michael Bublé and Harry Connick Jr. will follow. It's music to buy wedding dresses by.

A couple of Shelley's employees arrive at the back door. Mona, a fifty-five-year-old veteran saleswoman, is all smiles, as usual. She's one of the secret weapons at Becker's, a good-humored dynamo who allegedly has the uncanny ability to look into a bride's eyes and know exactly which of the 2,500 dresses is right for her. (She also looks at the bride's figure, of course. But the eyes tell her more.)

Bill arrives right behind Mona, adding another upbeat presence to the morning. He used to manage Main Street Pizza across the street, until Shelley convinced him to work for her. Bill is the back-office organizer, but he also greets customers with great energy. Because brides these days watch bridal reality TV shows, they expect men working at a bridal shop to be gay, like the men on TV. Bill, a married father of two, has come to realize that women are more comfortable with him if he sounds like "Franck," the flamboyant Martin Short character in 1991's *Father of the Bride*. No one is in the store yet, but Bill warms up for the day by getting into character for Alyssa and Mona: "Oh my gosh, darlings, let me see you both. Turn around, gorgeous, just gorgeous!"

At this moment, about a dozen brides-to-be and their mothers are already on their way to Becker's. For those from out of town, the drive here can be a time for bonding and reminiscing. Those traveling from the west pass through miles of cow pastures and cornfields. Those coming from the east see hundreds of acres of mint fields. There are long empty stretches on the way to Fowler—not a gas station, not a house—so almost all of the out-of-town brides and mothers will have the same request when they arrive at Becker's: "Where's the bathroom?"

Shelley's ready for them. She looks at the clock. It's exactly 10:00 a.m., and two brides-to-be and their mothers are waiting on the sidewalk outside the front door. She unlocks the door and smiles. "Good morning! Welcome to Becker's. Nice to see you."

"Do you mind if we use the restroom?" one of the mothers asks.

"I'll go with you," says her daughter. The other bride and mother join them.

After the restroom visits, Shelley directs the two brides and their moms to the front counter to fill out the sign-in sheet. That's when the brides-to-be, wearing their street clothes, pass the old mirror for the first time, oblivious to it. Soon enough, they'll add their reflections to the white and ivory procession that has been captured in that mirror six days a week for seventy-six years now. If they try on a dress and fall in love with it later this morning, an invitation will be issued.

"Come on up the stairs," Shelley will say. "Let's see what you look like in the Magic Room."

You can see why they call it the Magic Room.

Chapter Two

Danielle

Women are surprised by the thoughts that come into their heads as they approach the Magic Room. Some brides say they flash back to the days they played dress-up as little girls; they instantly regress to age eight or nine. Others say they don't even recognize themselves. It's almost like an out-of-body experience: Who exactly is that woman in the mirror? And then there are the brides whose minds go totally blank. All they see is the dress. It's hard to even speak.

The brides' mothers have flashbacks too. Usually, of course, they think of the day they first saw themselves in their own wedding dresses. But they also have more wistful thoughts. They remember the words their late parents said to them when they tried on their dresses. Or they think of fiancés who loved them once, but turned into husbands who no longer wanted to be married to them.

Danielle DeVoe, a twenty-five-year-old social worker, is excited but not overtly emotional as she walks up the stairs at Becker's in a sparkling, off-white wedding dress from Casablanca Bridal. "I think this is the one," she says, almost to herself, smiling. All around her are mothers and daugh-

9

ters fussing over dresses, with Shelley directing them into fitting rooms, but Danielle is focused, head forward, on a mission.

Unlike the other bride-mother pairings here today, she has come with her grandmother, Cynda, who holds back tears as Danielle steps into the Magic Room.

In this moment, Cynda finds herself thinking of Danielle's birth in 1985, and the beautiful white dress with pink rosebuds that she wore home from the hospital. It looked almost like a miniature wedding dress.

Cynda had bought that dress within hours of Danielle's birth. Her daughter, Kris, didn't know if she was having a boy or a girl, and when Danielle arrived, Cynda decided that a new little girl needs to step into the world in a special dress. She had asked Kris, "Would you mind if I bought her the outfit she'll wear home?"

"Sure, Mom," Kris had answered.

Cynda always considered that purchase to be her first loving act as a grandmother. Now, twenty-five years later, she had asked Danielle if she could buy another landmark dress for her—her wedding gown.

"Sure, Grandma, I'd be honored," Danielle had said. And so they made their way to Becker's, where it appears they've found the winner.

"It's the most gorgeous dress in the entire store," Cynda says as Danielle turns around and around, studying herself in all the Magic Room mirrors. The ivory dress is the perfect color, given Danielle's dark brown hair and big brown eyes.

Cynda leans against the mirrored east wall of the Magic Room, and in her mind, clear as can be, she sees that little homecoming outfit she'd bought in 1985, a dress barely bigger than the palm of her hand. She smiles at the memory, blinks, and then she's lost in a rush of thoughts, contemplating the twenty-five years that led to this wedding dress, and the beautiful grown woman modeling it. "Danielle, you look stunning, honey," Cynda says, trying to keep her mind from wandering back through a lot of heartache.

Cynda's daughter, Kris, had been just nineteen years old when she gave birth to Danielle, who would be her only child. Kris had gotten married right out of high school to a man who seemed incapable of being responsible. He was constantly disappointing her—he even went AWOL the night Danielle was born—and the marriage ended badly after just two years. Cynda has heard Danielle speak of both her mother and her father with a clear-eyed directness. "My mom raised me as a single parent," Danielle tells people, "after I saw my biological father abuse alcohol, drugs, and my mother."

The divorce had left Danielle and her mother as kindred souls. Kris was such a young mother, and yet, because of their circumstances, both she and Danielle felt mature beyond their years. Cynda would watch them together and marvel at the ease with which they connected. They'd sit together around a campfire and talk for hours—an eight-year-old kid and her twenty-seven-year-old mother.

Perhaps because Kris had picked a man who treated her so poorly, and had a marriage that failed, she began giving advice at an early age. "You have to love yourself first," she'd say to Danielle. "You have to take care of yourself first. You can't love someone else until you love yourself." Above all, that was the love she wished for her daughter.

Kris had great affection for children, and after getting her degree in child development, she went on to operate her own preschool. The children called her "Miss Kris." "I've got thirty kids," she'd tell Danielle, "but of course, you're my favorite."

Danielle loved helping out at the preschool. The kids were four and five years old, and Danielle was just eight or nine, but she looked after them in the sweetest, most maternal ways; the kids followed her around like a line of ducks.

Her father had made attempts to stay in touch with Danielle, but his addictions left him unreliable much of the time. He'd promise to pick her up for a weekend visit, and she'd always pack her bags and be set to go fifteen minutes before his scheduled arrival time. She'd sit in the living room, bundled in her winter coat, her suitcase at her feet, always at the ready. Half the time, he wouldn't show up. For Kris, it was hard to watch her pretty little girl waiting thirty or forty minutes, then unbuttoning her coat, tears in her eyes, and carrying her suitcase back into the bedroom.

When Danielle was seven years old, in 1992, she asked Kris if she could dress as a bride for Halloween. So Kris found her a long white dress, a veil and a large bouquet of fake flowers, and Danielle went door-to-door as a bride without a groom.

Seven-year-old Danielle wearing a wedding dress for Halloween

Cynda is thinking of this too as she watches Danielle, all grown up, studying herself in the Magic Room mirrors.

Outside of the doorway, a bride and her mother wait patiently for Danielle to step off the pedestal and surrender the room. Danielle knows her time is up, but it's hard for her. "I don't want to leave," she says, "I don't want to get out of the dress."

"You'll wear it again soon," her grandmother reassures her.

As Danielle finally takes leave of the Magic Room, she and Cynda talk about the alterations needed, and whether her fiancé, Brian, ought to see the dress before the big day. They do the math, figuring out how many weeks until the wedding. It's happy small talk. Neither of them mentions Kris, and how desperately they wish she was here with them. That's not something they can talk about easily.

Shelley doesn't ask why Danielle is with her grandmother and not her mother. She has learned over the years that every bride has a story, and that some stories are revealed slowly, or not at all.

"You looked gorgeous in that dress," she says when Danielle reaches the front counter to put down her deposit. "It's a great choice for you."

Becker's Bridal, home to more than 2,500 dresses

Chapter Three

Sweethearts and Girlies

W hen Shelley was a young girl in the early 1970s, she'd head over to Becker's to watch her mother and grandmother at work, and she'd often hide behind a rack of dresses. She could be there forty minutes, sitting on the floor, pressed against bridal gowns or bridesmaids dresses, just listening. Her little face sometimes peeked out, but usually, none of the brides knew she was there.

Shelley would study all of those young women, many still in their teens. Most seemed pretty to her, but not the way brides are these days—sexy and self-assured, with tanning-salon tans in the dead of winter. Back then, most brides had the same flip in their hair, the same pale skin. They wore glasses, not contacts, and few came in wearing a lot of makeup. (Grandma Eve frowned on makeup because it came off on the dresses. Those wearing too much makeup were asked to put Saran Wrap–like shields over their faces when they got into their gowns.)

The brides tended to be farm girls or the daughters of auto workers. They hadn't traveled much, didn't expect much, and ended up taking whichever dresses their mothers or Grandma Eva thought they looked best in. The store had only a couple hundred gowns back then, and Eva didn't have patience for those who wanted a lot of options. Today, a bride can try on thirty dresses. In her time, Eva liked to offer three choices, maybe four, after which, she'd say something like, "Well, I think the first one looks best. Don't you?"

"Yes, I guess I think you're right," a bride would answer, and a bride's mother would say, "The first one was lovely, wasn't it?" And the sale was set.

Some mothers wouldn't even wait for Eva to venture a verdict. They did all the deciding and didn't engage in much discussion with their daughters. "That's the one. We'll take it," Shelley would hear a mother say, and unlike today, the brides didn't often argue about it. They smiled, kissed their mothers, and said thank you.

Shelley began to see that brides had a sense of destiny when it came to their selection of a dress. Again and again, she heard brides say that a dress had "talked" to them. Talked to them? They meant that a dress had announced itself as "the one," somehow calling out from its place on the rack in a voice only the bride could hear. Shelley did wonder about these "talking dresses," which always seemed pretty silent to her. But in time she came to understand the power of a wedding dress.

She also learned the saleswomen's secret language. If they liked a bride, they'd refer to her as "girlie." They'd say, "Girlie, that looks beautiful on you. Oh, girlie, it's perfect!"

If a bride was being difficult, they'd call her "sweetheart." That was code to let coworkers know who they were dealing with. "Would you help this young sweetheart find a veil?" Grandma Eva would say to a saleswoman.

As Shelley sat in her hiding place, she often had the same questions in her head: "What does all of this mean? These girls are standing here in these dresses, they're getting married, but what's really going on? How did they fall in love? Are they in love?"

Her mother and grandmother didn't offer her any explanations. They were there to sell dresses, not to talk about love.

Saturdays have always been the busiest day at Becker's because brides and their parents don't have to go to work or to church. On some Saturday mornings, when the store hosts trunk shows from major designers, the line of brides and their entourages can stretch around the block before the store even opens.

And so for decades, young men in Fowler have cruised Main Street in search of roaming bands of bridesmaids. The brides are already taken, of course, but the unmarried bridesmaids they bring with them are fair game. There's usually more girl-watching than successful flirting, but in a tiny town without much entertainment, it's a scenic view.

Ken Hafner, born here in 1942, has watched bridesmaids parade down Main Street since he was a boy. "You'll see ten of them walking to the store," he says. "It's good for the town. They eat. They buy gas. They're great to look at. Well, most of them."

Shelley's daughter, Alyssa, convinced her twenty-four-year-old boy-friend, Cory, to work at Becker's part-time doing accounting tasks. His friends think he's got the life, hanging out with beautiful young women all day. They don't realize he's stuck in the back office, adding up sales-women's commissions. His friends will see a couple of attractive women on Main Street and they'll text Cory: "Sexy blonde just entered store with two friends. Is she a bride or bridesmaid?"

"Don't know," Cory will text back. "I'm in the office."

"Need to know," comes the reply. "Find out!"

Though lovely women of all sizes and shapes come in here every day, plenty of Becker's brides look nothing like the models found in bridal magazines. "I try to tell my friends that," says Cory, "but they seem to only notice the prettiest girls." (It may be true that all brides, like all babies, are beautiful. "Maybe on their wedding days," says Cory diplomatically. Not necessarily on their shopping days at Becker's.)

Given the large bridal business on Main Street—and the fact that the extended Becker family runs a men's store and a furniture store—locals have long referred to Fowler as "Beckerville." Some say it with affection. Some don't. And either way, there's an uncertainty in town about just how to reconcile, or to celebrate, the presence of Becker's Bridal. A suggestion, years ago, to make a wedding gown the town symbol never got much traction. It would have been nice if pennants featuring wedding dresses were hanging from the town's lampposts; fewer brides and their mothers, driving by on Michigan State Road 21, would end up missing the place.

Shelley appreciates it when locals say they're grateful for the business her brides bring to town. For instance, bridal parties account for a large chunk of the business at KJ's Café, the restaurant next door. If brides weren't walking around on Main Street, Fowler would look pretty empty, like any other dying rural town.

Locals also say that when they travel elsewhere in Michigan, and tell people they're from Fowler, they're often told, "Yeah, my ex-wife got her wedding dress there." Or: "Both of my ex-wives got their dresses there."

It's hard to find anyone here who doesn't have a connection to the store. Most every woman in Fowler—like her mother, grandmother, or great-grandmother before her—bought her wedding dress at Becker's. Visit any attic in town and you're likely to find an old gown with a Becker's tag in it. The dresses are mostly modest numbers—Becker's current prices range from $680 to $2,600—though more extravagant dresses are sometimes ordered, usually for more-affluent customers visiting from larger cities. (The average bride in the United States now spends $1,056 on a wedding dress, up 34 percent from 1999. Shelley credits the bridal shows on TV, which focus on the upper-end gowns, convincing viewers of all income levels that every bride deserves a pricey dress.)

Fowler still holds tightly to its German Catholic roots, and pretty much all 1,100 residents know each other. As grinning residents like to tell outsiders, "Fowler is a town where, even if your wife divorces you, at least she's still your cousin."

It always has been a quintessentially Middle-American community; a good number of its sons and daughters now serve in the military. Many residents work at auto plants nearby, while others drive a half-hour south to Lansing or East Lansing, where they hold white-collar jobs at Michigan State University, or government jobs at the state capital. And then there are those who choose to commute two or three minutes to work by taking a job at Becker's, which now has twenty-two employees.

Eleanor Klein is the current record-holder for most time served as a Becker's employee. Grandma Eva's niece, she got the job in 1935, when she was fifteen, and went on to work at Becker's for seventy-two years. Now eighty-nine and retired, she's understandably wistful about the old days. Shelley turns to her for insights and gut checks, because decade after decade, Eleanor has watched the changes in brides, parents, dresses, and marriages.

From the 1930s through the 1950s, most brides had no jobs and no money of their own. Parents paid for wedding gowns. By the time Eleanor left the store in 2007, brides were doing almost all of the deciding, and often paying for dresses themselves. "These days, the brides tell their parents what they want instead of vice versa," Eleanor says.

Wedding gowns are now far more risqué, of course. "Mothers used to say, 'That's too naked!'" Eleanor explains. "I used to have to set lace in places where there was bare skin. Now almost all the brides want bare skin. Some want to show the whole body."

Becker's brides used to be smaller than they are today. The average bride now is a bridal size 14 (which translates to a street size 8 to 10) and many have size 10 feet. Years ago, brides were less muscular. They didn't exercise and lift weights. They didn't eat the way Americans eat today. That's why most brides today can't wear the dresses their grandmothers bought at Becker's.

Eleanor considers her early years in the store to be more fulfilling. When she sold a dress, she explains, "I'd feel as if I accomplished something. You sent a bride off into marriage, and it was for life. In the later years, you knew so many of the marriages weren't going to be forever." She'd sell a dress and wonder: Were they getting married with the idea that they could just get married again someday? About a third of Becker's brides today are divorced, buying a dress for a second or third wedding.

Shelley shares Eleanor's concerns, and yet the machinery of Becker's Bridal constantly rumbles along; there's no time to hit the Pause button. Like her grandmother and mother before her, Shelley oversees a military operation, always strategizing ways to get through each day as waves of new brides show up, while those who've already bought their gowns return for second fittings. There isn't time to ask, "Do you love him?" or "Is loving him enough?" And truly, Shelley knows, it's not really her place.

Our culture today focuses on individualism, on satisfying personal needs and finding mates to make us happy. More than their mothers and grandmothers, many women today expect romance to be the main fuel for their marriages. But researchers are now discovering that intensely romantic couples are actually more likely to engage in conflict and get divorced. In 2010, the University of Virginia's National Marriage Project released data showing that people who define marriage mostly as a "romance" seem more apt to put their own needs over the needs of the partnership. The bonds in their marriages can be exciting and fulfilling, but they're more fragile, and 1.5 times more likely to end in divorce. Couples tend to do better if they focus more on the shared responsibilities of child-rearing, fiscal prudence, and being there for each other. Bottom line: Couples are more successful in marriage if they see themselves as helpmates rather than soul mates.

Researchers are also finding that the most successful couples don't necessarily solve their problems—they outlast them. They call this "the marital endurance ethic." In fact, a University of Chicago study found that 80 percent of couples who were "very unhappy" and agreed not to divorce described themselves as "happy" five years later. Of those who divorced, only half were happy five years up the road.

At Becker's these days, many brides seem enthralled by the romance of marriage, but they can be clueless about the mechanics and annoyances of marriage. The result, it seems, is more relationships ending short of the altar.

Becker's brides are told that wedding-dress sales are final, given the alterations required. That explains why there's a room, beyond the view of buoyant brides, dubbed the Dress Cemetery. It's a sad, crowded place where dresses are piled up after engagements are broken or brides-to-be are abandoned by grooms with cold feet. Sometimes, women return years later to reclaim their dresses, usually before marrying different bridegrooms. The rest of the dresses remain here for years, waiting for customers who never come back for them.

Lately, more wedding gowns than ever are ending up in Becker's Dress Cemetery. As Shelley puts it: "The world feels more unsettled, money is tighter, weddings are being canceled, and some brides are just unsure of things." Day after day, Shelley sees parents who don't understand their daughters, who don't have a sense of their yearnings, who can't fully communicate with them. She sees daughters who don't have a great deal of self-knowledge: They think they know the kind of wedding dress they want, but they don't have a clear sense of the kind of life they want, or the kind of man who might best accompany them.

Indeed, inside this bridal shop in this tiny town, Shelley is able to speak to a global sense of uncertainty. Without the aid of research studies, she knows things. She knows what commitment means to all different kinds of people. She knows about promiscuity and serial monogamy, and how that leads into marriage today. She knows the joys and terrors that brides are feeling. And she sees how women are drawn these days to all of those TV bridal shows; they've led to an epidemic of interest in brides, their behavior, and their dresses—though not necessarily an interest in thoughtful musings about the concept of marriage.

Every day, Shelley sees examples of our changed culture, and she notices inconsistencies. "I'd like a white dress, and my mom says the sleeves need to cover my arms," a first-time bride tells her. "I want to dress modestly. My family is religious, and I guess I am too." The young woman and her boyfriend already have a toddler, who is zipping around the store while she shops. Shelley dutifully looks for the requested modest dress with long sleeves, making no judgment about the bride's decision to put maternity before marriage. If a mother says a bride's fiancé (and live-in lover) shouldn't see her bare arms until after they're married, well, she'll accommodate that.

Some of Shelley's customers say they've found inspiration in the movie *Bull Durham*, which celebrated the notion that a wedding dress needn't reflect a woman's past. A character in the film had slept with a baseball team's starting lineup. "Do you think I deserve to wear white?" she asks the woman altering her bridal gown. "Honey," comes the answer, "everybody deserves to wear white."

At Becker's today, 25 percent of first-time brides already have children. Another 7 or 8 percent are pregnant, looking for a wedding dress with room to expand. "When I started here at age fourteen," Shelley says, "maybe one out of three hundred brides would be pregnant. And very few had children before getting married for the first time."

Certainly, many Becker's brides are still taking the old-fashioned route; marrying young and then starting families. But others are adhering to trends playing out nationally. Americans are having children out of wedlock at eight times the rate they did in 1960. More than 40 percent of those born in the United States each day are the offspring of unmarried women; that compares to 2 percent in Japan.

Meanwhile, more women are marrying later—or not at all.

The annual number of weddings in America, which peaked in 1984 at 2.48 million, has declined every year since then. In 2009, there were only 2.08 million weddings recorded. Those in the large "echo boom" generation—the children of baby boomers—are now of marital age, but they are less eager to marry than the generations before them. For women, the average age of first marriage has risen to twenty-six years old from twenty-one in 1970. For men, it has risen to twenty-eight from twenty-three.

In the wedding business, it used to be an accepted fact that nine out of ten Americans would marry at least once by age forty. Bridal shops could assume that a woman who isn't shopping for a dress today will need one eventually. (In 1980, the percentage of forty-year-olds married at least once hit a high of 93 percent. Now, it's 81 percent, and is expected to fall further.) How many of today's unmarried twenty- and thirtysomethings will someday marry? When Shelley talks with other bridal-shop owners at design showcases in New York, the state of the unions in America is a perennial topic. Assumptions that were once taken for granted have been thrown away.

There are many reasons for young people's reluctance to marry today.

There's no longer much stigma for those who live together or have children outside of marriage. And millions of echo boomers have seen their parents' marriages fail, which gives them pause. Yes, they appreciate that their grandparents understood the idea of couples suffering through difficult times, hoping things would get better. But there's no going back to that. Tolerance for imperfect relationships has gotten so low that giving up early seems to be the American Way. (Forget the seven-year itch. University of Minnesota researchers have found that more divorces now happen in the fourth year of marriage than any other.) It's not really a surprise, then, that some echo boomers are deciding to skip the wedding, which makes the inevitable breakup less complicated.

Marriage is just "not as necessary as it used to be," a 2010 Pew Research study concluded. The study found that 39 percent of survey respondents believe that marriage is "becoming obsolete"; that's up from 28 percent who felt that way in 1979.

That sounds like a harsh statistic. And yet here Shelley is, day after day, catering to the 61 percent who still believe in the possibilities of marriage. These customers tell her in words and actions that their dreams are still alive, even if their dreams are not the same as their mothers'. Shelley also has plenty of customers who might define themselves as the 39 percenters; they wonder (or worry) about marriage becoming obsolete. But they're here too, trying on dresses, hoping they'll buck the odds. "I still believe there's magic in the institution of marriage," Shelley says.

There's an old Jewish saying: "Every time a marriage takes place, a new world is created." Each day at the store, Shelley witnesses pieces of those transitions from old world to new in the interactions of the brides with their parents—and in the chatter about the brides' fiancés, and their plans for the future.

Shelley's a driven saleswoman, yes, like her grandmother. But she's a romantic, too, and she tries to wish a good outcome for every woman who walks through her door. She says she wishes for peace and happiness in each new world she helps create.

In her own life, Shelley has seen how love can fade, and how children can be hurt by a troubled marriage. She doesn't talk about her life or marriage when she's dealing with brides. It's almost a relief that they're usually too hyperfocused on their own issues to ask Shelley any questions about herself. But when she thinks of the path her own life has taken, her wish for each of these brides is that their journey will be easier.

Chapter Four

Meredith

*B*efore arriving at Becker's on a Thursday evening, Meredith Maitner had visited other dress stores, including David's Bridal, the three-hundred-store chain that claims 35 percent of America's bridal business today.

Meredith is thirty-nine years old, marrying for the first time, and David's had not been an easy experience for her. "I had to share a pedestal with a girl half my size and half my age," she says.

The prices at David's were lower than elsewhere, which was a plus. But Meredith didn't receive much attention, and there certainly wasn't a special room with soft lights and an air of magic. "Just a big mirror and that pedestal," she says again, for emphasis, "and you had to share it with little skinny girls. It was kind of awful."

Meredith is a woman with a full laugh, an easy sense of humor, and a willingness to discuss her long path to the Magic Room. Blond, buxom, and sophisticated, she also exudes a Midwestern softness that allows her to place her life until now into a meaningful context. She'll turn forty right before her wedding day.

"Growing up, you see there's an order to things," she explains. "You go to grade school then high school then college—and then you get married. That's what my parents did. That's how I thought the world worked. And I somehow got off track."

Sixteen years ago, on the day before Meredith's twenty-fourth birthday, her mother had called her. At one point while they were talking, her mom nonchalantly said, "You know, the night before I turned twenty-four, I was getting married." Meredith certainly knew that her mom and dad—a first-grade teacher and a school principal, now both retired—had gotten married the evening before her mom's birthday. All her life, her parents' anniversary was August ninth; her mom's birthday was August tenth. But for her mother to pick this moment, the day before Meredith turned twenty-four, to make this comment, well, it felt like a judgmental slap in the face.

"That kind of stings," Meredith said to her mother.

"It made me feel like a failure," she now recalls. "I know my mother was just making conversation, but the message was: 'When I was your age, my life was progressing. I was getting married. And you're not.' It could be she was just marking time: 'This is where I was on my timeline. You're not in the same place on your timeline.' Or it could be that there's something in everything that mothers say."

Parents don't always realize how their nonchalant observations sound to adult children. (Meredith's story brings to mind research done by Jane Isay, author of *Walking on Eggshells*, about the delicate relationships between adult children and their parents. "A parent's voice, even when whispered, is louder than anyone else's voice in their grown kids' ears," Isay says. She counsels parents to temper criticisms: "The idea that your kids need you to tell them what's wrong with them is a canard. They know what's wrong with them. What they want from parents is support for what's right with them.")

Meredith's mother knew as soon as she spoke those words that she shouldn't have said them. "It kind of came out," she says. "I didn't

Meredith in 1992, at age twenty-one, as a young career woman in Japan

mean to sound as if I was asking 'What's the matter with you? Why aren't you married yet?' I was talking about how my life followed a different path."

Meredith's path diverged as she was finishing college and noticed a flyer on a bulletin board, looking for young people to go to Japan and teach English as a second language. On a whim, she applied, and lived there for a glorious year. She embraced the culture and expat life, and had fun socializing with Marines stationed there. She realized she wanted a career in international business, and when she returned to the States, she first worked for a company that owned theaters and radio stations. Then she moved to a national footwear company in Rockford, Michigan, where she has spent fourteen years, traveling the world—to England, Russia,

Turkey, Germany—as director of planning and operations for three brands of shoes. Along the way, she got her master's degree.

While her professional life progressed, she had a mixed record in her love life. She dated some men who were nice but there was no chemistry. She was bored with them. She dated others who weren't greatly interested in her. And she also was involved with a couple of guys she refers to as "my horror stories."

She dated one man for three months who was in public relations. Things seemed to be going well. He met her family; they liked him. "He was doing and saying the right things," she recalls. "And he was spending a lot of money on me, always picking up the tab for dinner, drinks, whatever."

Then she discovered he had stolen her Social Security number and used it to get a credit card under his first name and her last name. He charged $5,000 to the card before he was caught. The romance turned into a police matter. Prosecutors charged him with identity theft and filing false information with a financial institution, both felonies. Meredith told the court she wanted no contact with him, and has never seen him again.

There was another man she dated for a year. They lived together, but he was often depressed. One morning they got in an argument after Meredith told him he needed to take better charge of his life and finances. Later that day, he took several boxes of sleeping tablets in a suicide attempt. Meredith discovered him when she came home from work. She called 911, frantically giving the story: "He's having seizures on my couch!" The call got disconnected. She had to call back and start over.

Her boyfriend was asleep for four days and hospitalized for a week, but he survived. After he spent another week at a mental health center, Meredith took him home to her apartment. She helped him put together a résumé, typed his cover letter, boosted his spirits, and then she helped him find a job in California. He moved out there on the day before her birthday, and she was relieved to see him go.

"I started doing background checks on every single guy I dated," Meredith says, wearily. "I checked the police and court websites. I could see if they've been divorced, arrested, gotten speeding tickets, everything."

She ended up dating another man—"a decent guy"—for four years, but he wouldn't commit. Six months after they broke up, he was engaged to a woman much younger than Meredith.

Through the years, there were times when Meredith loved being single and independent. But she was frustrated, too. She recognized that she wasn't single because she preferred it that way. She was single because she wanted to find someone, but couldn't.

She found it helpful to focus on the positives. "I could have dinner when I wanted, see friends when I wanted. I realized I would rather be home, drinking wine and reading a good book, than being on a date with a jackass."

Her mother started to look at the matter philosophically. "As the years went by," her mom says, "I thought maybe it's not God's will for her to be married. Maybe she's supposed to be single. A lot of single people are very happy. And you hear so much about divorce. Maybe it's good that she didn't get married and then divorced."

⁓

Meredith realizes that she arrived at her chronically single status via her own unique set of circumstances. And yet, over the years, when she would share her story with women she'd meet, her experiences sounded familiar to a lot of them—including those two or three decades older than she is.

The women from the generation ahead of Meredith say they were the first to be branded hopelessly single—as a group. And what they went through has been instructional for Meredith.

In 1986, when Meredith was fifteen, *Newsweek* magazine caused a stir with a story titled "Too Late for Prince Charming?" For unmarried women over age thirty, the story contained bad news, and America took great pity on them.

The article showcased a study by Yale and Harvard researchers suggesting that thirty-year-old white, college-educated single women had only a 20 percent chance of finding husbands. At age forty, the probability fell to 2.6 percent. Using hyperbole and humor that became infamous then, and sounds far more awful today, *Newsweek* said those forty-year-olds were "more likely to be killed by a terrorist" than land a mate.

Meredith was finishing up tenth grade that summer. It didn't occur to her then that she would one day fit exactly into this demographic. And so she didn't pay much attention to all the hand-wringing over that study, the countless articles and talk-show debates, the tearful conversations between single women and their mothers.

Looking back, Meredith identifies in some ways with the unmarried older women of that generation. They feared being alone. They questioned what they did "wrong." They listened to downbeat voices in the culture designed to make them feel insecure.

In 1986, insecurity had been especially rampant. Gail Prince, a Chicago dating coach quoted in that *Newsweek* piece, now recalls that many women found the Harvard-Yale study "perversely reassuring," because it suggested that societal issues, rather than their own inadequacies, were behind their struggles to find men. In *Newsweek,* Prince had advised women "to carry conversation openers, like a feather boa or a copy of *Sports Illustrated.*" Such ploys would feel hokey by the time Meredith reached her thirties, in the new century, but they are a reminder of the urgency with which people back then were seeking direction. (Some would argue that the urgency remains today, only in different forms. "Conversation starters" now are risqué photos posted on Facebook, or online "pokes" meant to lure men into poking back.)

In any case, the *Newsweek* statistics would later be challenged by a US Census Bureau demographer, who calculated that those thirty-year-olds actually had about a 62 percent likelihood of finding a husband. For forty-year-olds it was 20 percent. But the Harvard-Yale study's core message—that educated, career-focused women risk spending their lives alone—continued to reverberate as Meredith entered her thirties.

So what became of those unmarried, college-educated forty-year-olds from 1986? They're in their mid-sixties now, and census data shows that less than 10 percent of them have never been married. *Newsweek,*

Harvard, and Yale got it wrong. Meanwhile, new research suggests that women today who are highly educated are actually more likely to get and stay married.

Of course, for Meredith in her late thirties, these relatively upbeat statistics could give her hope, but they didn't tell the full story. She saw that traditional forces, so much stronger years ago, have less power to create a marriage today. Religions used to push people down the aisle through guilt, threats of damnation, and calls to behave responsibly. Now religions don't exert the same kind of pressure. Parents used to insist that their sons do the right thing and marry the girl. Parents aren't as insistent anymore.

And so, in the end, studies, statistics, changes in social mores, and screaming media reports couldn't explain everything, or help Meredith. As she saw it, the facts were very simple: She was one woman. She needed to find one man. And it wasn't happening.

Eventually, Meredith told her parents that she'd given up on love. Twenty-five years of dating had not produced a life partner. "It's likely I'll never have a husband," she said, "and so I need to take care of myself well. That's my goal." She could afford to buy herself jewelry, and she did so. "The thing about necklaces and bracelets is that you'll have them forever and they'll fit you forever, even on fat days." She tried to embrace the idea that she didn't need a husband. "It's nice to believe you can do it alone."

As for the possibility that she'd never have children, she became philosophical: "My brother and sister-in-law have always been good about letting me love their kids, and so I'm very close with my nephews and my niece. I love them so much. And if I don't have children of my own, I'll love them even more."

To her credit, Meredith's mother found ways to focus on the silver linings. "I felt selfish in a way," she says. "If she wasn't going to get married, we'd get to spend more time with her." Meredith and her parents planned regular international cuisine nights. After work, Meredith would pick up unfamiliar dishes from all kinds of offbeat restaurants and bring them to her parents' house. They celebrated Ethiopian Night, Turkish Night, Indian Night, and more.

Perhaps life might have gone on like that, pleasantly, but then one evening Meredith went to a Polish social hall during Pulaski Days in Grand Rapids, Michigan. The annual citywide event is a celebration of Revolutionary War hero Casimir Pulaski, who died in battle in 1779, at age thirty-two. A Polish immigrant, the father of the US Calvary, and a friend of Ben Franklin's, he's celebrated by American Poles as a freedom fighter. They salute him with a good deal of drinking, polka-dancing, parades, and pageants.

Meredith had finally sworn off dating (it had been seven months) but agreed to join friends at this Polish hall, where she ended up sitting next to a friend of a friend of a friend, a forty-two-year-old man—a freelance illustrator and graphic designer—who also had never been married. His name was Ron.

She thought he was sweet, funny, and attractive—they conversed so easily with each other—but she assumed he was "totally gay." He had two earrings in one ear and one earring in the other. "There was the whole artist thing," she says, "plus he wore Doc Martens. And he was very attentive to me." She hadn't seen such attentiveness from a straight guy in years. She also wondered how, if he wasn't gay, he'd made it to age forty-two without being snatched up. She was taken with his big brown eyes, his full head of hair, his straight white teeth.

Ron, meanwhile, thought Meredith was attractive too, and he enjoyed listening to her banter with others at the table. She got in an argument with someone about which port was America's busiest. (Meredith was right: Los Angeles/Long Beach.)

At the end of the night, Ron asked one of Meredith's friends for her number. Though he waited two weeks to call her, once he did they were locked into each other.

Ron told her about his own journey into her life. "I once had a good woman at the wrong time," he explained, "then I had the wrong woman at the right time, and now I think I've found the perfect woman for all time."

Meredith ran a police check on Ron, and thank goodness, found only parking tickets. A year after they met, he asked her to marry him and she accepted.

"It's better to be an older bride," Meredith now says. "I know who I am, I know what I want in a man, and I know enough to set that aside and accept that what I need in a man is the better thing to have."

For Meredith's mom, it's a great relief, and a great joy, to be here at Becker's. They've come, along with Meredith's sister-in-law, to look through the offerings at a Maggie Sottero trunk show. Shelley's staffers try their best to figure out the right dress for her, but what they don't know is this: Meredith has already found a gown, days earlier, at another store and is almost ready to buy it. She has come to Becker's just to make sure. In her head, she justifies letting the saleswomen here spend a couple hours helping her. She isn't 100 percent sure of that other dress. As she puts it: "My heart's open. Maybe it's like dating a few more guys before realizing you're with the right one."

There's one dress she looks sensational in, and that's the one she decides to wear into the Magic Room. It's strapless and low-cut, with a sexy corset. "I look so fricking hot in this dress," Meredith says to her sister-in-law. "It's like movie-star glamorous. Look at my boobs hanging out!"

She studies herself in the mirrors that carry her off into infinity. "It's like a whole bunch of me's looking fabulous!" She smiles in the mirror for a few more beats, while her sister-in-law takes photos. A part of her would love to wear this dress. Then Meredith says, "You know, it's awfully va-va-va-voom. I don't want Ron passing out right there in the church." She makes a decision: "I just don't feel like a bride in it. I feel like a movie star walking the red carpet in Hollywood."

She heads to the lower level, by the fitting rooms, and tries on more dresses without success. Finally, she shrugs and says, "I guess that's all for tonight."

She walks past the old mirror, over to the front counter, and one of Shelley's saleswomen writes down her measurements, contact info, and wedding date. Meredith thanks her for her time, takes one last glance at the sexy dress, and as she's leaving, her mother tells her, "That may have been everything we didn't want in a wedding dress—strapless, with all that lace and those horizontal stripes—but I've got to tell you, you sure looked gorgeous in it. Just gorgeous."

Sometimes mothers know just the right thing to say.

Meredith in the Magic Room with her too-sexy dress

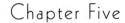

Chapter Five

Grandma Eva

S helley likes that Becker's Bridal is located in an old bank. The century-old structure is solid, like a good marriage should be. That's meaningful to her. She likes that the word "BANK" is prominently carved in large block letters in the gray stone at the top of the building. That's a reminder to Shelley that she comes here to make money to support her family, that this business is the family's bank. There's also the recognition, both mystical and meaningful, that the bank's vault once held people's most precious material possessions in safe deposit boxes. Now parents are bringing something even more precious into the Magic Room—their daughters.

As a child, Shelley saw the word "BANK" at the top of the building, but she never asked Grandma Eva for an explanation. And so Shelley doesn't really know how Eva felt about her store occupying this space. Was it a reminder to Eva of the Depression-era losses the town suffered there? Did she like the powerful and stately shadow it cast as the most prominent structure on Main Street?

There are still a handful of Fowler residents, now in their nineties, who remember the day in 1932 when People's Bank went under. Banks were failing everywhere, and adjusters came to Fowler to calculate how many pennies on the dollar depositors would receive. They went into the vault, on the second floor, and seized what little cash was left there. Some people got nothing. The man who for decades owned the restaurant next door to Becker's Bridal was one of them. He lost his entire fortune at the bank. "I was twelve years old at the time it went under," he likes to tell people. "I'd been a hardworking paperboy, and I had twelve dollars and fifty cents at that bank. Never saw a penny of it."

Though he has played his loss for laughs over the years, he and other old-timers also speak of how the bank failure devastated Fowler. Many in town lost their savings, farms, and businesses. One Fowler farmer was so distraught at having lost $5,000 that he went into his barn, threw a rope over one of the beams, and hanged himself.

A dry cleaner occupied the former bank for a short run, and then Eva moved her shop from across the street into the empty building. At first, she used the bank vault for storage. It was an odd space—a heavily fortified room surrounded by concrete walls, supported by two-foot-thick concrete slabs in the basement. Wedding dresses didn't seem to belong in a room designed to protect stacks of money. It wouldn't be until after Eva died that Shelley dreamed of turning the vault into the Magic Room.

Now that the store is hers, Shelley is more curious about the history of this building, and about Eva's role as family matriarch. She'd like to better understand exactly how this business remained in her family's hands, in this location, for seventy-six years. She thinks about how every generation of Beckers made sacrifices on the home front—missing moments in their children's lives—to keep this store running. Eva's work ethic was passed down to her children and grandchildren, but there was a price they all paid. Sure, there were plenty of fulfilling moments over the years, and they made a comfortable living, but the Beckers didn't get those 100,000 brides into their dresses without enduring their own scars and disappointments.

A lot of today's Becker family dynamics can be traced back to Grandma Eva. In 1922, at age twenty-two, she married Frank Becker, the oldest of

nine siblings, and joined a family with a long history in the retail business. Like most people in town, the Beckers were faithful German-Catholics, and their church was central to a serious, God-fearing life. There were expectations in Fowler: You prayed, worked hard, and had a lot of children—and you made sure that they worked hard and prayed too.

Eva's in-laws had operated a general store on Main Street since 1899, selling feed and seed to farmers, and fabric and dry goods to others in town. As would be the rule for generations in the family, everyone was expected to pitch in, and so Eva and her husband Frank worked at the store, eventually taking it over.

It was in 1934 that Eva dipped her toe into the bridal-gown business. She had driven six hours to Chicago to pick up goods for the store, and decided to bring back a wedding dress from a wholesaler. Her first customer was a local girl named Helen Miller, and the dress was a high-necked, pure white satin number with leg-o'-mutton sleeves. Eva also sold Helen a pleated, halo-bonnet headpiece, with a floor-length veil.

The highlight of Helen's wedding reception, held in a local barn, was an impromptu performance by best man Clem Sohn, a twenty-four-year-old neighbor who had become famous in the early 1930s as an air-show daredevil known as "The Batwing Jumper." By studying bats, Clem had figured out a way to glide through the air in a wing-suit he fashioned himself using zephyr cloth attached to steel tubes. He traveled the world jumping out of airplanes and gliding like a bat until he was a thousand feet off the ground, at which point he'd open a parachute. He liked to tell the media: "I feel as safe as you would in your grandmother's kitchen."

At Helen's wedding, Clem jumped off the top of the barn in his bat suit while wedding guests cheered him on from below. (About three years later, a horrified air-show crowd of 110,000 in Vincennes, France, watched him desperately pull the ripcord of his emergency parachute. It never opened. Film footage of his death spiral, which was his 175th jump, is now on the Internet.) The oldest people in Fowler remember that it was Clem's Batman getup, not Helen's wedding dress, that was fawned over at her wedding.

Likewise, Eva's arrival in the bridal business was hardly noticed. The general store was better known for its pickles. But Eva continued to make out-of-town trips, bringing back dresses, and over time word spread to neighboring towns that she was the go-to woman for bridal gowns. Eventually, that became the focus of the family business.

Early on, Eva realized that gowns will always be changing, and so she'd better be aware of trends. When she started selling wedding dresses, they were still being fastened with a complicated line of hook-and-eye closures. But on shopping trips out of town, she began seeing more dresses with zippers, and she embraced the concept, bringing these modern dresses back to Fowler. Her brides were impressed by the glide of the zipper, and pleased with how easily they could get into and out of the dresses.

It was the heart of the Depression, and many in Fowler struggled financially. Their most indulgent form of recreation was to drive to Lansing and spend the night at a movie theater, where the characters on screen lived the high life. No men in Fowler casually walked around in tuxedos the way Cary Grant did in the 1937 film *Topper*. But weddings became the one opportunity that regular folks had to pretend that they, too, were dapper. And so they rented tuxedos, and the most daring bought wedding dresses from Eva that mirrored the slinky satin gowns worn by actresses such as Jean Harlow.

In the 1930s, wedding dresses were still expected to be multifunctional, rather than one-time-only fashion statements. A lot of women would wear their gowns at their weddings, and then months later, dye or hem them for other important occasions, or even as maternity wear. Eva would brainstorm with brides about how they could get another few uses out of a dress. That was part of the sales pitch.

Unlike today, when it's bad form or even bad luck to ask a bride to borrow her wedding dress, back then sharing was common. Eva lost business when one dress got passed around among friends, but it was a part of the business model she had to accept.

During World War II, when patriotism led people to cut back on ostentation, Becker's brides skipped long trains, sequins, and other embellishments. Then the war ended, and there was an unrelenting demand for ready-to-wear dresses to accommodate all the "rush weddings" between returning soldiers and their no-longer-patient sweethearts. Eva kept a steady parade of soldiers' brides marching through the store.

In the years that followed, with rationing over, shoulder pads got larger and so did wedding budgets. By the early 1950s, after Elizabeth Taylor's *Father of the Bride* arrived in Michigan theaters, brides started asking Eva for antebellum skirts and gowns that were as tight as possible in the waist.

Brides also came into Becker's chattering about Grace Kelly's 1956 wedding to Monaco's Prince Rainier. Thirty-five seamstresses and designers at MGM's wardrobe department in Hollywood had created her wedding gown, using one hundred yards of silk net and twenty-five yards of silk taffeta. The veil featured lace lovebirds and several thousand seed pearls. It was all good for Becker's. If Grace's father, Philadelphia millionaire Jack Kelly, could give his daughter away so gorgeously garbed, fathers in Fowler had to pay at least a few dollars more to make sure their daughters got a dress that was a step above ordinary.

It was in those years that the concept of daughters being entitled to fairy-tale ceremonies started to flourish. Dresses were less likely to be viewed as multipurpose garments, or something to be shared with anyone else. Weddings became less about two families gathered together and more about the bride. The bride became the star of her own fashion show, with her friends and loved ones as the audience.

Eva was happy that weddings were becoming commercialized pageants. She was selling more dresses and customers were spending more money. And she liked it when the weddings of the rich and famous captured people's imaginations.

In 1966, President Lyndon Johnson's nineteen-year-old daughter Luci got married wearing a staid gown that covered her entire body. She took her vows before ten equally unexposed pink-gowned bridesmaids, fifty-five million television viewers and seven hundred guests, including her sister Lynda's handsome young boyfriend, the actor George Hamilton.

The pomp-infused spectacle was good for business at Becker's, but Eva was also noticing signs of change. A *LIFE* magazine cover story called Luci Johnson's wedding a respite for the nation during "a summer of violence, frustration, and despair" over Vietnam and racial protests. Though central Michigan would hold on to its conservative values longer than other parts of the country, Eva suspected the shifting culture would reach her store. In 1967, forty-three people died during riots in Detroit. Hippies had begun advocating "free love," and feminists were suggesting that brides walk themselves down the aisle, rather than letting their fathers give them away like pieces of property. It was inevitable that some of Eva's potential customers would soon be forgoing her most ostentatious gowns, opting instead for simple peasant dresses bought elsewhere.

All she could do was remain tenacious with the customers who did come to her, reminding parents of the values their daughters would find in conventional weddings. She continued feeding her customers to the Catholic church a few blocks away, which kept uniting brides and grooms in traditional ceremonies centered on God.

Eva worked hard. And as always, Becker's survived.

When Shelley compares her grandmother's tenure to her own, she sees similarities, sure, but also societal sea changes. In Eva's day, most professional men didn't want professional women as wives, and in any case, few such women existed. Men married their secretaries, who then stayed home to care for the kids.

That was the American way, and women clung to the clichéd hope that a prince on a white horse would whisk them away from their ordinary lives. Shelley sees that a longing for this possibility still lingers today. Some of her middle-class brides were excited by the 2011 British royal wedding because they saw themselves in commoner Kate Middleton. Unlike in Europe, where young people rarely marry outside their class, marriage always has been one of the clearest paths to a higher status in the United States. "Marrying up" is made possible in part by our culture's fixation on attractiveness: men don't necessarily select trophy wives based on their pedigree or portfolios.

But as Shelley sees in her store, it is getting harder for someone from a lower economic class to find and marry someone from a higher class. "Assortative mating"—the human urge to pair up with someone who is similar to you—is on the rise in America, sociologists say. Those with college degrees are marrying people with college degrees at higher rates than ever. In Grandma Eva's time, male doctors married their nurses and receptionists. Now they're marrying their fellow doctors.

When Eva ran Becker's, almost all the brides were younger than their fiancés, and shorter, too. But in recent decades, the percentage of US brides who are older (and taller) than their husbands has risen steadily.

For Becker's brides today who are well educated with high-paying jobs, their self-sufficiency gives them power. They won't have to stay in a dead marriage. (That's one reason why 65 percent of US divorces today are initiated by wives.) But for brides at lower socioeconomic levels who marry their economic equals, things are more precarious and stressful. Unlike wealthy couples, it's harder for them to afford good child care, to hire housekeepers, to take parental leave, or to find jobs that let them telecommute. This all makes for more to worry and fight about, and given their dual roles at home and at work, women are especially burdened.

In Eva's day, most everyone headed to the altar; a lowly economic status rarely stopped couples. They'd find a way. But today, college grads are 16 percent more likely to get married than those with no degrees. As the previously mentioned 2010 Pew study summarized: "A marriage gap and a socioeconomic gap have been growing side by side for the past half-century, and each may be feeding off the other."

Some of these trends were first noticed by Grandma Eva as distant drumbeats. Now they affect how Shelley runs the business and interacts with brides, mothers, and grandmothers—all with different expectations based on where they fall on the timeline.

When brides buzz about Prince William marrying a commoner, on some level they're also contemplating their own lives. Even in seemingly frivolous conversations about a royal wedding, Shelley can trace the arc of the female experience, from Grandma Eva's time until today.

~~~

There aren't many people left in town who were alive during Becker's early days, and Shelley is drawn to those with firsthand recollections of Eva. When older women come into the store with their dress-buying grand-daughters and mention buying their own wedding dresses from an aging Eva, Shelley lights up. People say her grandmother was a tough business-woman. There was nothing touchy-feely about her. It reminds Shelley of how different the sales process is today. Unlike Shelley, selling wedding gowns in the modern age, Eva didn't spend much time complimenting brides on how beautiful they looked or sweet-talking their mothers. Eva's focus was on selling dresses, not catering to a bride's emotional state.

She didn't have much sympathy for broken engagements. "Our policy is very clear," she'd tell a mother-of-the-bride. "No refunds."

"But this was so unexpected. My daughter is so distraught. What can we do with a wedding dress when there isn't going to be a wedding?"

"There are no refunds," Eva would say. "That's our policy."

As Shelley sees it, despite Eva's clear lack of a soft spot, she was a trailblazer as a woman in the workplace. She not only kept the business afloat but expanded it at a time when women were almost exclusively in the home, especially in towns like Fowler.

She was a presence on dusty Main Street—a short, stocky woman with thick arms and thicker legs, wearing a white apron and that feathered hat of hers, always clutching wedding dresses as she walked to and from the bridal shop. Men took her seriously and admired her toughness; some said she was "a little Napoleon." Women respected her too. They figured Eva knew what was best for their daughters when it came to bridal gowns.

Eva had two sons. Her first, Luke, was born in 1923 and her second, Clark, was a surprise baby, born in 1937. Clark is Shelley's father and his unexpected arrival was not greeted with great enthusiasm by his parents. Eva—then thirty-seven years old—feared that looking after him would take time away from the store.

Clark is pretty straightforward in his descriptions of his mother. "She never showed much emotion," he says. "She ran the store six days a week. That was her focus. And my dad worked hard, doing the book work every night and on Sundays, too."

In the years that followed, Eva became determined not to let brides leave the store empty-handed. If a bride and her mother couldn't find a dress they liked, Eva would piece one together. When a bride didn't like any veils, Eva made her a new one. Eva traveled by herself to Chicago and New York to bring dresses back to Fowler.

Having logged seven decades at the store, Eva's niece, Eleanor, recalls her as a woman who worked herself hard, and was a taskmaster with employees. "If there was a wall to wash, we washed it," says Eleanor. When brides weren't in the store, Eva would give her saleswomen directions in German. It was a regimented operation.

Over time, Eva became more aggressive as a businesswoman, ordering so many dresses that her husband, Frank, feared the business could be crushed by debt. But Eva's ambition was overpowering, and boxes of wedding gowns kept arriving at the local train depot. Frank sometimes refused to sign for the packages. "We just can't afford to stock all of these dresses," he'd say apologetically.

"Just put the boxes over in the corner," the master at the depot would tell his underlings after Frank had left. "Eva will come down tomorrow, when Frank's not around, and she'll sign for 'em and take 'em with her."

Clark joined the business in 1959. He would have preferred working up the street, in the family furniture business. But that operation had gone to his older brother. So he was told he could work at Becker's Bridal, selling menswear at the back of the store. That was a flawed business plan. Not many men felt like walking through a bridal shop thick with chattering brides and their mothers. The place felt too feminine. So men went elsewhere to buy their suits and ties, and Clark's menswear business struggled.

The upside for Clark: working in the store allowed him to meet girls— bridesmaids, sisters of brides, window-shopping single girls—and one day a pretty young woman named Sharon walked in with her friends, just to look around. Clark took a liking to her and asked her on a date. They were married in 1962 and had eight children. Michelle—nicknamed Shelley— was the third born and the eldest daughter.

Sharon learned quickly that Eva was a tough woman, and would be a take-charge mother-in-law. "Everything was always done her way, and nobody argued with her," Sharon says. "Her husband was scared of her."

When it was time to pick out Sharon's bridal gown, Eva gave her three choices. The first was powder-blue. "It's nice, but I don't think I like it," Sharon volunteered.

"OK, try on this one," Eva told her. The second dress was satin, with Chantilly lace and a jewel neckline. "This is pretty," Sharon said.

"Good, then that's the one," Eva said. Sharon never even got to try the third dress.

Eva gave Sharon a cabbage-leaf headpiece. "This will work," she said. And that was that. Eva even picked Sharon's bridesmaids.

After the wedding, Eva took back the dress Sharon had worn, had it cleaned, cut the sleeves, hung it on a rack at the store, and sold it weeks later to another bride.

Eva's authoritarian ways were legendary in the family. When Shelley was three years old, she had long hair down to her waist. One day, while Sharon was out buying groceries, Grandma Eva took a close look at Shelley. "Your hair is too long," she said.

Shelley's seventeen-year-old cousin Beth was there too. "You need to cut this little girl's hair,"

Clark and Sharon at their wedding in 1962

Eva told the cousin. Eva got a pair of scissors and gave it to the teen, who did as she was instructed. "Keep cutting," Eva said.

By the time Sharon returned from the market, Shelley's hair was so short that she looked like a boy. Sharon was flabbergasted but said nothing to her mother-in-law. It was too late, and besides, there was no arguing with Eva. "Maybe that was the kind of mind-set it took to be a pioneering woman in the bridal industry," Shelley now says.

Clark, understandably, took a liking to Sharon's parents and siblings. Unlike the Becker family dynamics, which were so often business-focused, Sharon's family tried harder to embrace their home life. They measured happiness by the joy they found in one another, rather than the number of dresses sold in a given week down at the store.

It goes without saying that Eva was not a warm grandmother in the ways we like to think of grandmothers today. And yet Shelley, who was ten years old when Eva died, now feels closer to her than ever. Yes, Eva could be a tough, distant, formidable figure, but Shelley has a few sweeter memories of the family matriarch, and she holds them tightly. One day, at age eight or nine, Shelley was walking on Main Street and came upon Eva carrying a bridal gown. Eva switched the dress from her right to her left arm so she could reach into her pocket. She pulled out a dime.

"Here you go, girlie," Eva said.

It wasn't the dime that excited Shelley. It was the way her grandmother addressed her. It was that term of endearment she'd heard down at the shop.

These days, Shelley is often alone at the store, after hours, doing bookkeeping, and that's when she most feels her grandmother's presence. Shelley's daughter, Alyssa, was born eleven years after Eva died, and now that Alyssa is working at Becker's, Shelley feels that another generational bond has been forged.

"I'm grateful that it seems as if Grandma Eva is still in the store, helping Alyssa and me," Shelley says. "I feel she is showing her love now, through all her energy in the store. Sometimes when people are alive, they can't fully show the love they're feeling. Maybe for some people, like Grandma Eva, their love somehow comes afterward."

Chapter Six

Erika

*T*wenty-three-year-old Erika Hansen has come to Becker's with her mother, her three sisters, and her grandmother, and it's a very sentimental moment for all of them as she contemplates which dress to bring into the Magic Room. Erika's sisters surround her, fussing over each gown she tries on down by the fitting rooms, taking videos and photos, and talking all at once, issuing compliments and funny asides. Erika feels both excited and overwhelmed. She'd been here before, when her older sisters were on their own dress-buying missions. Now it's her turn.

"How will I know if it's the right dress?" she asks Mona, her saleswoman.

"You'll know," Mona tells her. "Usually, when you get into the Magic Room, and the tears come, that's the dress."

Her sisters know Erika is nervous about getting married, and about the whole pageantry of a wedding. They are here to remind her that it's not just about the wedding dress. It's also about the love she feels for her fiancé, Reuben, a former Marine who saw duty in both Iraq and Afghanistan.

The sisters have a great deal of affection for one another. You can see

Erika, far right, with her sisters

it in the way they stand so close together and brush the hair out of Erika's eyes. They have much in common, including a commitment to the sanctity of love and marriage that is rooted not just in their upbringing and their faith, but in their sense of themselves.

It's almost as if these very pretty, fresh-faced young women come from a different time, with different values, from almost all of their peers. All four sisters made a decision to save themselves for what they call "something very special." Each sister has embraced the beauty in an uncommon patience.

That's why it wasn't until just recently that Erika experienced her first romantic kiss. It happened on the day Reuben proposed to her. By her own design, she had waited a lifetime for that kiss.

Her sisters have similar stories.

Her oldest sister, Leanne, now twenty-six, received her first kiss on her wedding day, standing at the altar.

Her middle sister, Kayla, twenty-four, was first kissed on the day her fiancé and his platoon were deployed to Iraq.

Her youngest sister, Aleece, is twenty-two and has never been kissed. She vows to wait patiently until her time comes.

Here at Becker's, the sisters speak freely to Shelley, Mona, and the other saleswomen about their vows of purity—vows that go well beyond the doctrine of their Baptist church. When they were teens, their youth pastor routinely offered his thoughts about the stages of love, and the religious call to refrain from intercourse until marriage. But kissing? Cuddling? Maybe more? The underlying message was: We know you have urges, so be very careful and respectful. Other than intercourse, the girls learned, these personal decisions "are between you and God and your partner."

Erika's older sister, Leanne, was the first to consider the no-kissing vow, back when she was in fifth grade. She had read a young-adult book in which the heroine made a decision to save her first kiss for her wedding day. Leanne thought that sounded very romantic, and she made the same vow herself. She did this on her own. It wasn't that her parents were encouraging her. And one by one, her younger sisters took similar vows.

Here at Becker's, their mother, Lynn, an attractive fifty-year-old woman, is hanging back, letting her daughters talk. Then one of the saleswomen asks what she thinks of their decisions. "I teased the girls when they were little," Lynn answers. "I said, 'Save all your kisses for Mom and Dad and the man you marry.' I was kidding, and they knew I was kidding."

She may have been kidding, but she and her husband, Victor, could take things seriously, too. They tried to guide the girls in making good decisions, especially when it came to matters of sexuality. "We tried to train them. When they were wrestling with decisions, instead of getting close to the line, where you might cross over into a bad decision, it's best to stay as far from that line as possible. Our oldest daughter took that literally, and decided there would be no kissing. It became her soapbox, and that influenced her sisters. Honestly, it was totally them. They each made the decision and owned it individually."

Looking back at her younger years, Lynn describes her dating life as typical for the 1970s. "I loved kissing, and was nowhere near as chaste as my girls have been," she says. "When Leanne said she wouldn't kiss until marriage, I thought, 'Well, you'll never be able to make it,' but I didn't tell her that. I just said, 'It could be hard to do.' And I did challenge the girls as they got older. I didn't want them to think kissing was wrong. Every once in a while I'd say, 'You do understand that it's not bad to kiss, right?'"

The sisters each came up with their own slightly different standard. Leanne wanted to wait for marriage. Kayla wanted to wait until she knew she was in love, and had picked the man she'd marry. Erika decided it would be the day she got engaged. Aleece is still considering the exact circumstances that will feel right to her.

In one sense, it is hard to fathom that in 2010, young women such as the Hansen sisters exist. At Becker's, they seem completely refreshing. Shelley and her saleswomen have seen too many young women buying wedding dresses while pregnant. Some brides-to-be overshare their life stories, telling sordid tales of past relationships as they hope for better results with the new guys they're marrying. Just the other day, a woman was in the store shopping for a dress for her fourth wedding. She told Shelley with a half-smile, "I'm always the bride, never the bridesmaid."

And so Erika and her sisters seem so different from many of their contemporaries. There's a kind of serenity about them. They acknowledge that their choices may not be right for every young woman. But these choices are right for them.

And yet . . .

There are things that their mother, Lynn, doesn't talk about here at Becker's: hard memories that weigh on her, things the girls know about and also keep to themselves. Lynn grew up in a troubled home, and that has informed so many of her decisions as a mother. She wonders sometimes if maybe she's being too overprotective of her daughters. Maybe, in her love for them, in her visceral urge to maintain their safety, she's kept them too sheltered. Perhaps she's trying too desperately to keep them from enduring the heartaches that defined her young life. Could their vows about kissing be rooted, at least in part, to their understanding of their mother's upbringing?

The Hansens have been at Becker's for hours, since before the store opened. The day had begun with them standing outside the shop, surveying the tiny town, as they waited for Shelley to unlock the door. "You look at the building, and you wonder how they can possibly fit a couple thousand dresses in there," one of Erika's sisters told her. "Then you'll walk in, and they'll all be there, lined up and waiting for you."

Once in the front door, because the store wasn't busy yet, Erika's sisters had commandeered two dressing rooms, and kept finding dresses for her to try on. Some they thought could be contenders. Others they found so over-the-top or frilly that they thought it would be fun to see Erika wearing them, just because. Erika was game for all of it. "You're beaming in every dress you put on," her mother said.

Mona, their saleswoman, knew just how to keep the young women excited. "You know what?" she said at one point. "We just got some new dresses in. I'm dying to see what they look like on somebody. Would you try a couple on for me?"

Unlike most brides at Becker's, who never seem to consider their fiancés' taste in dresses, Erika was trying to keep in mind what Reuben might want to see her in. "He wouldn't want anything high-end or trendy," she told her sisters. "That's not Reuben."

As the morning wore on, Erika had gotten into and out of thirty or forty dresses. Some where lightweight: under four pounds. Others, like the thick satin number that weighed almost twenty pounds, were hard to walk around in. "I feel like I'm wearing a curtain," Erika announced at one point.

"We need to refuel," her mother said. "We're losing energy. Where can we get lunch?"

Mona sent them over to Main Street Pizza and promised that when Erika returned she could narrow the dresses down to a small handful. Then she could start thinking about looking at herself in the Magic Room.

Erika's sisters had taken photos of her in all of the dresses on their cell phones and a digital camera. They scrolled through them as they ate pizza, everyone weighing in. Some had lace. Some didn't. One had an elegant snowflake design. One, from Spain, was gorgeous but beyond their budget. All were completely modest.

Even though hordes of brides today want to look as sexy as possible in their wedding dresses, bridal-shop owners say there also has been a growing call for more modest bridal attire. Shelley has had customers who are Orthodox Jews, evangelical Christians, or Muslim. They need sleeves and higher necklines, with very little skin showing, but they still want to look glamorous.

When the Hansens got back to Becker's, they had narrowed their choices down to six. Mona pulled out some veils and mock bouquets and announced it was time. "OK," she said. "Let's try the Magic Room."

And so now here they are.

The first dress Erika tries on in the Magic Room is the one with all the snowflakes. Her sisters ooh and ahh, but that may be just a way to keep the energy level up. Someone asks, "What's next?"

Erika leaves and returns wearing the $2,300 gown from Spain. It's beautiful, she looks stunning, but the price makes everyone uncomfortable. And so Erika tries on the third dress, which offers a modern twist on a vintage lace dress. It's ivory, with ornate crystal beading on a satin band at the waist. The price tag: just under $1,000.

In the soft lighting, looking in those mirrors that go on forever, Erika suddenly has an image in her head: She's in this dress, standing at the altar.

"I think I'm going to cry," she says.

"Well, that's the sign," someone says. And then Erika is crying and her sisters are crying and her mother and grandmother, too. Then they're laughing. Just like that.

"I guess this is the one," Erika tells Mona. The fourth, fifth, and sixth dresses never make an appearance in the Magic Room.

Erika stands there on the pedestal for another half hour, turning left, then right, and then around and around. "I love it," she says. "I think Reuben will love it too."

Chapter Seven

The Mother-Daughter Business

*B*ack in the 1940s, it usually took a Becker's bride an hour to find and buy a dress. Grandma Eva would have only about fifty dresses in the store, and by the time sixty minutes had passed, the bride's parents were at the counter, paying cash for the dress.

In the 1950s and 1960s, Becker's offered a hundred or so dresses, and the process tended to take a couple of hours. For most brides, Becker's was the only shop they planned to visit, and they bought the dress on their first day.

In the 1970s and 1980s, there were a couple thousand different dresses at Becker's, and brides and their mothers often would show up with pictures torn out of bridal magazines, asking questions: "Do you have something like this, only with a lower neckline and short sleeves?" The process of trying on dresses could stretch to four hours, but again, saleswomen knew a sale was likely. More than 90 percent of the women who came to Becker's ended up buying.

By the 1990s, though, things had changed. Brides had it in their heads that they needed to hit several stores. Long shopping excursions became a

53

bridal tradition. A bride might try on dresses for several hours, then leave the store, never to be seen again.

"Can you write down everything about that dress for me?" they'd ask Shelley, and what could she do? She obediently wrote down the price, style, whatever they wanted.

These days, the search for a gown has become a weeks-long quest. "It's the great, fun, happy circus," says Shelley. And it's a lot more man-hours for her saleswomen.

Shelley hears brides on their cell phones, sitting in the fitting rooms. "I'm here at Becker's today with my mom, but I'm free Wednesday to hit the other stores with you," one says, not even in a whisper.

At Becker's, the first visit is usually one in which the brides bring their mothers, and these days, that can stretch to four hours without a sale. A few days later, they'll come back with girlfriends or sisters. Then maybe their mothers-in-law or aunts. Eventually, they'll show up with their mothers again, and maybe their fathers, but even then, with dads eager to pay and be on their way, a decision might be put off.

"They just don't want the fun to be over," says Shelley. "The shopping is the experience." She has had to hire more workers just to hold brides' hands and reassure them, dress after dress, that they look terrific. "Bridal has become such a time-intensive purchase," Shelley says. "It takes so much longer to close a sale." It can be frustrating for her salespeople, who sometimes resent all the work they put in without making a sale. But Shelley understands that brides don't want to feel bullied into buying a dress too quickly. And so she needs to orchestrate a delicate dance between brides and her salespeople to find the appropriate mix of anticipation, emotion, and commerce.

At bridal-industry trade gatherings, Shelley has heard all the alleged tricks of the trade: Don't start by showing a less-expensive dress; if a bride falls in love with it, she'll be less interested in buying a pricier dress. If a bride seems hesitant about getting married, her salesperson has to be reassuring about the institution of marriage and upbeat about wedding planning. "My wedding was the happiest day of my life," a saleswoman is supposed to say.

Shelley with her trusty measuring tape on a stack of outdated gowns

"I never felt more beautiful." A divorced saleswoman might seize on the happiest wedding story in her family. In attitude and conversation, bridal shop employees are told, they should give brides the message that the day they buy a gown is one of the most important days of their lives. (Indeed, Kleinfeld, the famous New York bridal store, sends letters to brides who make an appointment: "We believe the day you choose your wedding gown should be as joyful and memorable as the day you wear it.")

Consultants in the bridal industry also tell salespeople to watch the body language of a bride's entourage. Is there tension or affection between everyone? Is a bride dependent on friends' and relatives' approval or is she sorry she brought them? Can the entourage be deputized into advocating for a particular dress, so a sale can be closed? If so, engage them as allies.

Salespeople are encouraged to be on the lookout for the "'Oh, Mommy' moment." If a bride looks in a mirror and says, "Oh, Mommy!" that's when a salesperson should say, "Why don't we go downstairs to the counter and put a hold on the dress?"

Shelley isn't comfortable with such hard-sell efforts masked in nurturing empathy. She wants her saleswomen to be personable and helpful, but pushing customers into purchases can backfire. The "Oh, Mommy" moment can become "Oh, Mommy, don't make me wear this horrible dress they sold me!" And so she encourages her saleswomen to be positive and engaging, but to sell with subtlety rather than high-pressure tricks.

The jewelry industry has advertised that as a rule of thumb, a groom should spend two months' salary on an engagement ring. Shelley knows that this is no less self-serving than if the pickle industry announced that the rule of thumb is to spend two months' salary on pickles. Each Becker's customer has her own needs and price points, and Shelley has learned that it's counterproductive to not respect that.

Routinely, Shelley's saleswomen are called on to serve as referees between mothers and daughters. They partly blame TV reality shows; brides watch *Bridezillas* and assume that's expected behavior. "They think it's fair game to act that way," Shelley says. "Some women throw fits for no reason."

Especially during alterations, brides get testy when the smallest stitch seems wrong. Many want the dress curved at the bustline. "Go tighter, tighter," one says.

"We can't go any tighter," Shelley responds. "It will stress the zipper."

"I don't care about the zipper," the bride says. "I need it tighter."

"I can't do it," Shelley says. "It won't work. I'm sorry."

"Mom?!" the bride shouts to her mother across the room. "Can you come here and tell her I don't care about the zipper?"

Shelley smiles tightly and resists saying anything while the mother tells her, "She's not really concerned about the zipper. She needs it tighter at the bust."

Though a lot of brides are lovely and respectful, the stereotype of the dictatorial bride exists because it's often true. Part of it is the stress of all they need to accomplish before their wedding. But there's also more of a cultural sense of entitlement that seems to increase every year. A wedding has become the moment in a woman's life when she can vocally and endlessly obsess about herself, and no one calls her on it.

Shelley's mother, Sharon, says there was far less drama when she ran the place in the 1970s. Sales were sealed without much angst. "Mothers and daughters didn't argue the way they do today," she says. "There wasn't the cursing and disrespect. Back then, a bride was just tickled to get a dress. If a girl talked to her mother the way I see some girls talking in the store today, she'd have been slapped in the face."

Sharon attributes the changes not just to a coarsening of the culture, but to how families are structured. "Families are smaller now. Years, ago, in large families, there were lots of hand-me-downs. Kids were happy to get anything. Some parents today, in these small families, give kids everything they want." Mothers are more eager to please daughters nowadays, and less willing to cross them, Sharon says. "A mother might have two children, but only one is a daughter. And so she clings to her one daughter."

Watching mothers and daughters interact at Becker's today, you can see how they reflect the changes in the wider culture. When Grandma Eva was born in 1900, parents resisted showing too much affection to their children. Experts warned them that hugging or kissing kids spoiled them and spread diseases. Plus, because so many children died in infancy, mothers feared bonding with a child they might lose. A mother's primary responsibility was to keep her kids alive, not to nurture them.

When Shelley's mom Sharon was raising her in the 1960s, mothers were following Dr. Spock, who told them "you know more than you think you do. Trust your own common sense." His books led mothers to become more indulgent and fathers to become more involved. (In the 1970s, feminists complained about Dr. Spock's advice that fathers should compliment their daughters on their pretty dresses. He pulled the reference from his book, but fathers had already embraced the idea. It's a rare dad who visits Becker's and doesn't compliment his daughter on her pretty dress.)

In many ways, young women today are much closer to their parents than past generations were. Thanks to cell phones and texting, they're in constant touch—by the hour, by the minute—especially with their mothers. And there are factors beyond technology, too. Echoing Shelley's mom, researchers looking at this new "era of attachment" cite the influence of fewer daughters per mother. They also say that because young women are marrying later, there's more time to stay connected to their parents.

In past generations, women were usually on their second or third child by their midtwenties. They were nursing babies, straightening playrooms; they didn't have time to call their moms all day with incremental ruminations about their lives. In 1970, just 4 percent of women giving birth for the first time were over age twenty-nine. Today, almost a quarter of women are in their thirties when they have their first children, so they've often logged an extra decade bonding with their mothers—or arguing with them.

A large swath of brides today grew up coddled, with hovering parents who put great emphasis on spending time with them and saying yes to them. In polls, almost three-quarters of today's parents say they're easier on their kids than their parents were on them. One byproduct of that: Giving kids the soft life makes parents more popular. Nine out of ten young women today say they have a good relationship with their parents—that's up about 20 percent from the 1980s.

Parental coddling has changed how Americans today view themselves and their adult children. Most don't think adulthood begins until about age twenty-six, according to a National Opinion Research Center poll. This attitude is partially fueled by parents who don't know when and how to disengage. Temple University developmental psychologist Laurence Steinberg recently published a revised edition of his 1990 book, *You and Your Adolescent: A Parent's Guide for Ages 10–20.* Only this version defines adolescents as "ages 10–25."

But here's the odd thing: While young people are taking their time reaching adulthood, they're simultaneously leaving childhood more quickly. Fifty-five percent of parents believe childhood is now over at about age eleven, according to another survey. The signs are certainly there: Parents see their preteen daughters dressing provocatively and moving on quickly from the Disney Channel to the rawest MTV shows. Facebook, once restricted to college students, is now the province of thirteen-year-olds.

So if childhood ends at eleven and adulthood doesn't kick in until age twenty-six, where does that leave young women in the limbo years in between?

Well, a lot of them are at Becker's.

Every day, Shelley observes this changing dance between mothers and daughters. She sees moms who can't let go of their daughters, or their own youth. Some mothers, their bra-straps exposed, their outfits way too Olsen-Twins-chic for their age, talk of being their daughters' best friends. "People think we're sisters," a daughter will say, but Shelley can't tell if the young bride is happy about it. It can feel creepy.

Truth is, many daughters today want their mothers close and attentive, but they don't necessarily value Mom's opinions and input. Unlike previous generations of brides, young women today are more peer-focused. That's why so many of them arrive at Becker's with a flock of bridesmaids. Moms still weigh in, of course, and a lot of them take charge—or try to. But brides often assume their bridesmaids know best.

Certainly, in every generation daughters have found theirs mothers' advice outdated and ineffectual. These days, however, given how fast the world is changing, there's been a clear widening of the advice gap.

It's rooted in a devaluation of accumulated wisdom, a leveling of the relationship between old and young. "Age is no longer the qualifier for being the go-to person for advice," explains Jason Dorsey, a thirty-two-year-old cross-generational consultant who helps companies understand Generation Y, which he defines as people who are now ages sixteen to thirty-two.

Young people once had to rely on older people for basic advice. But now, if the young want to learn how to tie a tie, mix a drink, or plan a wedding, "we can go on YouTube and find a video," says Mr. Dorsey. "We don't call Mom and Dad." He warns that parental advice needs to be worthy, or young people tune out. "We have extraordinarily short attention spans and lots of distractions. If we don't like what you're saying, we can pull the world through our cell phones." (Indeed, brides at Becker's are routinely on their BlackBerrys and iPhones—cruising the Internet for shoes or texting friends with questions—while their mothers stand by, waiting to get their attention.)

Eighty-two percent of those now ages eighteen to twenty-nine believe there's "a generation gap" in America, according to a Pew Research Center poll. That's up from 60 percent in a similar poll in 1979, and even higher than the 74 percent registered in a 1969 poll, at the height of the youth rebellion movement. Back then, political and social issues created the gap between baby boomers and their parents. Today's youth cite generational differences in "perspective," "work ethic," and "technology"—which helps explain why they dismiss their elders' input.

At Becker's, for instance, more mothers lately have been telling the saleswomen that they tried to talk their daughters out of planning destination weddings. The moms argue that these weddings are inconvenient and expensive for guests, and they make the bride and groom seem self-indulgent. But on this issue, like so many others, parental advice often goes unheeded; the number of couples in the United States choosing destination weddings has quadrupled in the past decade, and now accounts for 16 percent of all weddings.

On the Becker's sales floor, Shelley encourages staffers to get a sense of each mother-daughter relationship and to recalibrate how they interact based on their observations. In years past, it was important for saleswomen to maintain eye contact with the bride's mother, and to be deferential to her suggestions. Nowadays, the bride is usually the boss.

Bill, the only man on the sales floor, finds that empowering today's brides is good for business. "I don't care what your mom thinks," he'll say to a bride. "I don't care what your mother-in-law thinks. I want to know what you think. Do you like this dress?"

"I do," a bride will answer.

"Perfect," he'll say. "That's all that matters."

And yet, despite such pronouncements, Bill also has a heart for the mothers, at least when they're buying their own dresses for their daughters' weddings.

He spends a lot of each day across Main Street, working in the Becker's storefront that caters to bridesmaids and mothers of brides. He finds that about 15 percent of mothers of brides are looking for dresses that are too revealing and sexy. He has to gently tell them that no bride wants her mother to look like an exhibitionist or a spotlight stealer. Some mothers get the message. Others don't care. They're the cleavage-spillers who think they look like their daughters' sisters.

But a bigger issue, Bill says, is that too many mothers in their late forties, fifties, and sixties—perhaps 35 percent of customers—"play themselves older than they really are. They're so focused on pleasing their daughters, so worried that they will pick something too sexy, that they end up floating over toward our grandmothers section. I have to tell them, 'I understand. You don't want to outshine your daughter. But you still want to look great. Look at your curves! You're beautiful! And my goal is to make you look even more beautiful, to accentuate those curves.'"

A lot of women blush when he speaks to them like that. "They haven't heard these kinds of compliments in a long time," he says. And he thinks he's on to something that can be beneficial not just to the older woman, but to their daughters as well.

These mothers may be waning beauties, but in this moment they can be role models for their daughters, showing them that it's possible to get older with confidence and a measure of grace. Many young women don't do a lot of thinking about what life will be like for them when they're older, but when they get there, they can't help but reflect on how their mothers found their way. Did their mothers age with self-assurance and a sense of adventure, or with feelings of dread and an urge to retreat?

Bill uses the term "conservative sex appeal" to describe what defines a perfect mother-of-the-bride dress in Middle America in the second decade of the twenty-first century. "There are certain shapes, styles, colors," Bill says. "I try to help them see the possibilities in themselves."

Bill often hugs mothers after they find the right dress, while their daughters, the brides, look on curiously. Some brides are glad to see their mothers getting attention and feeling special. Others are impatient. They want to get back to their own wedding needs and to-do lists.

For years, when Bill managed the pizza shop on Main Street, the only glimpse he had of mothers and daughters interacting was when they discussed what kind of toppings they wanted on their pizzas. Now that he's in the bridal business, Bill sees the complexities of the mother-daughter relationship.

He follows no formal playbook when he talks to older women as their daughters stand nearby, watching him. He just trusts his instincts. "We want everyone at the celebration to know where the bride came from," he'll say to a mother. "By showing off your own beauty, you'll be showing off the beauty of your daughter."

Most mothers smile at him, almost relieved, as they step away from the grandmother gowns and reassess their visions of themselves.

⌐

The Beckers are in the magic business, but they're still in the retail business, with all the attendant risks—from both mothers and daughters. One busy day several years ago, the most expensive dress in the store went missing; it had obviously been shoplifted. At first, speculation centered on the possibility that a bride carried it out in a garment bag, pretending she had just bought it. All the saleswomen were too distracted with other brides to notice. But then they recalled a bride who tried on a bunch of dresses, then left the store wearing a bulky, floor-length winter coat. Come to think of it, she did look much puffier in that coat when she left than when she came in. That may have been her getaway wardrobe.

What kind of woman would do such a thing? Did her mother help her plot her escape from the store? Shelley tried to picture a bride wearing a stolen dress down the aisle, smiling at all her loved ones (or her posse of accomplices). What sort of wife would she make? Would a marriage to such a woman last? Did her fiancé know what she had done? Had he lifted his tuxedo from a formal store?

And what about her wedding day? It was a stunning dress. Certainly, the bride's guests would have said to her, "You look so beautiful. Where'd you get the dress?"

Would the bride dodge the question or would she give an answer? "Becker's Bridal. They have quite a selection."

Somewhere, deeply imbedded in the old mirror by the front desk, is an image of that kleptomaniac bride. She surely passed the mirror on her way out of the fitting room in her bulky winter coat as she headed off into the night.

Perhaps the most challenging threat to bridal shops today is the competition from Internet bridal sites. "Some brides are taking three hours of our time, trying on dresses, and then they go online to save fifty dollars," says Shelley. On an average Saturday, fifty-five brides visit the store. "Usually ten or fifteen of them are using us, and then going on the Internet," says Shelley. "They lead us to believe they're true shoppers. But we see warning signs." Becker's saleswomen notice the glances brides will give their mothers, or the shared whispers when they think a saleswoman is out of earshot.

Some stores cut the names of designers out of the dresses so brides can't look them up online. Becker's has so many gowns that it would be too much work to remove every tag. They used to tell brides they couldn't take photos of a dress until they put down a deposit, but they gave up on that rule several years ago.

"Every bride has a camera on her body now," Shelley says. When brides are in fitting rooms, she often hears the clicking of cell-phone cameras. Brides photograph the tags, the inside of the dress—everything—so they can go home and figure out how to buy it less expensively.

Shelley has instructed her saleswomen not to confront these nonbuyers. "Smile through it," she advises them. "If we don't, they'll go online and say we're rude." These days, brides unhappy with the service they receive will often go on Facebook or WeddingWire.com to post one- and zero-star reviews. "We can't risk it," Shelley says.

After brides buy their dresses online and find they don't fit right, they'll sometimes bring them to Becker's, begging for help with alterations. "We have to say no," Shelley says. "It's hard enough keeping up with the alterations for customers who've bought from us." They try to send them away with a smile, so they're not attacked on WeddingWire for being unhelpful. The wedding industry in America has supposedly grown into a $40-billion-a-year business, but it gets harder and harder for Becker's to hold on to its slice of the sales.

Despite these challenges on the floor of the store, a part of Shelley enjoys watching the spectacle of the dress hunt. She's still touched when brides swoon over a dress, and she'll still choke up when a mother and daughter get teary and hug. "We're in the emotion business," she reminds her saleswomen at monthly staff meetings.

They're in the mother-daughter business, too, of course.

Shelley has spent her life watching how moms and daughters interact and express affection. She has heard the advice, good and bad, that mothers share with daughters, admonitions such as: "Never date a man who is prettier than you are, and never date a man who smells better than you do." (The lesson in that? Never listen to everything said by a mother who speaks in absolutes.) "Marry a man who loves you just a little bit more than you love him." (The problem with that: Love isn't a liquid that can be quantified in a measuring cup.) "The best gift you can give your children is to love your spouse." (Shelley saw truth in this, yes, but in her own life, knew this was a gift not easily delivered.)

In the back office one day, sitting with Alyssa, she speaks frankly: "I see mothers and daughters hugging and kissing and it makes me think I don't do that enough. I know I'm not expressive enough. I'm not cuddly."

"I don't need it," Alyssa tells her. "Really I don't."

"Well, I know you're seeing this all the time out on the floor, and I don't want you to think . . ." Shelley's voice trails off.

"It's OK. We're just not a huggy family," Alyssa says.

"That's the way it's always been, I guess," says Shelley.

In their years running the store, Shelley's parents, Clark and Sharon, were too busy just trying to make a living. They didn't have the time to make sure they were doling out public displays of affection to their kids. It didn't occur to them that Shelley was observing parents and daughters being affectionate in the store, and that maybe she'd be contemplating her own life.

And society was different then, too. Unlike today, parents didn't have a heightened sense of the need to say "I love you," or to share hugs. The media wasn't pounding out reminders that parents need to behave in loving, supportive ways.

And so Shelley and Alyssa are throwbacks in a way. Each day, they watch gushy mother-daughter bonding adventures unfold at the store. But by nature and upbringing, they're more reserved.

And Shelley understands and appreciates the family focus on business, instilled by Grandma Eva. She salutes her grandparents and parents for their efforts to keep this store going. She knows their story. Nothing was easy. And if there were trade-offs on the home front, well, that's what it took to keep Becker's Bridal in business.

Shelley recognizes how the history of Becker's hasn't just shaped the business she runs today: It also has shaped her as a daughter and as a mother.

After Grandma Eva installed Shelley's father, Clark, in the menswear business at the back of the store in 1959, he tried hard to make a go of it. But between 1963 and 1975, he and Sharon had eight kids, who kept arriving at eighteen-month intervals. Even though Sharon was working for Eva, it was tough to support all those children on the meager paychecks they were collecting at Becker's.

Eva had been promising Clark, starting in the early 1960s, that she'd hand the business over to him and Sharon "within a couple years." The wait turned out to be sixteen years. Eva just couldn't let go.

In 1975, when Eva was seventy-five years old and her husband, Frank, was eighty-two, Clark finally went to them with an ultimatum. "If I can't buy the place," he told his parents, "I'm going to have to move on and find a different job, something that pays more. I've waited and waited. I think I've waited long enough."

Clark's father was ready to sell. He'd had enough. But for Eva, the bridal shop was everything. Her reluctance to hand it over turned to bitterness. She complained that she was being pushed out of the business she had spent her life building. "They're kicking me out of the store," she told people.

But Frank knew it was time—past time—and urged Eva to accept it. He and Clark came up with what seemed like an appropriate price for the business—the figure was less than $100,000—and agreed that Clark could pay it off in installments. They shook hands and Eva, though unhappy, went along with the plan.

Within days, however, the agreement faced a new hurdle. When Clark's older brother learned of the deal, he thought the store had been undervalued. The less Eva and Frank received, the less they'd be able to leave as their inheritance. As often happens with family businesses, the friction that followed forever damaged relationships.

Eva and Frank reneged on their agreement with Clark and Sharon, telling them they'd have to pay more money. Clark felt betrayed, but accepted the new terms.

Within months, both Frank and Eva would be dead. In April 1975, Eva had a stroke and never recovered. In August, Frank choked to death on a piece of lettuce. And so it was left to Clark and Sharon to run Becker's without Eva's input—or interference. Some say Eva's spirit began inhabiting Becker's on the very day she died. But Clark and Sharon weren't spooked by that possibility. They accepted it. As Sharon explained to her kids, "Everyone is around us after they're gone. Grandma Eva is too." And Clark made sure to tell his children that despite the bad blood over the sale, he had great respect for his mother. "I'm proud of her," he'd say. "Her dedication and hard work made this business, and it's up to us to carry on from here."

Eva's passing was liberating for Clark and Sharon, but sad and frightening, too. They finally felt the freedom to re-create the store on their own terms, and for a new era, but they were on their own. They moved fast, increasing the inventory from about two hundred wedding dresses in 1975 to three thousand by 1982, the year the store also began accepting credit cards. And they worked incredibly hard—days, nights, weekends. They had to put in those hours, they said, to support all those kids. They kept the store open five nights a week until eight p.m., and their children pitched in too.

"You have a lot of kids, you ask them to help," says Sharon. "It's like the farmers, putting their kids on the tractor at an early age."

Sharon looks back today and has her own regrets about lost time with her children, and about school activities she missed. "Why didn't I take a day off?" she asks. "Why did I have to be down at the store six days a week?" Her life felt constantly hectic. Her responsibilities to get the brides' dresses altered in time for their weddings could feel overwhelming.

The children noticed, of course. "Do you have to come home every night and talk about the store?" they'd ask. But that's just the way it was. It was a family business, and the emphasis was on the business.

⌒

In the 1950s, department stores had about 85 percent of the wedding-gown business nationwide, but Becker's had stayed afloat through word of mouth in small Michigan towns. In the 1960s, thousands of mom-and-pop bridal shops began opening up as strip malls were built in every sub-urb in America. These boutiques flourished, but because Becker's had established itself so long ago, its customers remained loyal. The next big challenge would come in the 1990s, when the David's Bridal chain began growing, selling synthetic gowns starting at $99. As a result of this and other pressures, the number of bridal shops in the United States fell from a peak of 8,000 in 1990 to less than 5,000. Becker's held on.

Starting when Eva ran the store, some people in town assumed the Beckers were Fowler's version of the Rockefellers. There was a certain amount of jealousy and resentment. People didn't fully understand the pressures of a family business. They just saw all the brides roaming around town, buying expensive dresses, and they made assumptions that the Beckers had it made.

A lot of people in Fowler worked the assembly line at General Motors. Their lunch pail was pretty much their only investment in their jobs. They put in their eight hours, and when they got home, they were free. "I envied them," says Sharon. "We got home and we were still eating, drinking, and sleeping the business. We were putting ninety percent of what we earned back into the store. We were worried if there was enough money to pay the help and the bills."

For his part, Clark never liked the bridal business, never felt any great affection for brides, never felt much of a thrill selling dresses. "I should have left right out of high school and looked for other work," he says bluntly. "The store was a livelihood. That's all I got out of it." His passion became the miniature model train set he meticulously built, day by day, and which eventually took up most of the basement of his house. Using tweezers and razor blades, he built ninety-eight different structures, all at 1/87th scale. He used bridal netting for the windows, and the roofs were made from the cardboard divider sheets that came with each wedding dress. That model train set was his escape.

He placed a damsel in distress—a bride waving a veil—on one of the train tracks. "Maybe someone tied her here," he'd tell visitors. "Or maybe she's committing suicide." Somehow, he got a kick out of that possibility. And when a ceiling tile in the basement fell and destroyed his 1/87th model of the Becker's Bridal building, that somehow seemed apropos. He chose to never rebuild it. "If I had it to do again," he says, "I'd have built the biggest hobby shop in the country, not a huge bridal shop."

In his working years, Clark usually came home from Becker's at about eight thirty at night. Sharon often arrived later, since she'd stick around until the last bride was helped.

Shelley saw the strains the business put on her parents' marriage. They didn't have enough free time with each other. They were sometimes at odds about decisions that needed to be made at the store. And they handled the pressures of their jobs in different ways. Sharon always tried to keep her composure when dealing with customers. Clark could get to the point where he'd had enough.

Once Shelley watched as a bride and her mother screamed at Clark because the dress didn't fit right. The bride had obviously gained weight since the dress was altered, but she was blaming the Becker's seamstresses. Clark took the abuse for a while, then snapped back: "If God can't please everybody, I sure can't!" The bride glared at him and Clark walked off.

Even though the family didn't spend enough time together, and even though she longed for her parents' affection, Shelley knew she was loved by her parents. She knew this in the way she knew that Grandma Eva must have loved Clark. Through the generations, this was not a demonstrative family, especially by today's standards, but love was assumed. Clark sometimes came home from work bearing candy bars or popsicles for the kids. He didn't say "I love you"—he hadn't heard those words much in his own childhood, either—but at times he found his own ways to show it.

⟳

Because her parents were consumed with their responsibilities at the store, Shelley, as the eldest daughter, was called upon to be the at-home baby-sitter to her siblings. That became the role by which she defined herself. She doesn't remember thinking much about her own needs. The sharpest thought in her mind was this: "As long as my siblings are happy, as long as my parents are selling a lot of dresses at the store and making a living, then everything is OK."

When Shelley looks back and tries to understand the girl she was and the teenager she became, she wonders why she never allowed herself to dream. Hiding behind those bridal gowns, watching life at Becker's, it never occurred to her to ask her mom if she might be allowed to try on a wedding dress some evening after the store closed.

"I didn't think happiness was for me," she says. "Maybe it was because I felt I didn't deserve it. But more than that, I just didn't allow myself to go there."

Shelley spent a great deal of time babysitting her five younger siblings.

Her mother recognizes it now. "Shelley missed her childhood," Sharon says.

Or more precisely, she didn't have time—nor did she make time—to consider her own future. She gave no thought to whether she'd one day be the star of her own wedding, walking down the aisle as a Becker's bride. It occurred to her that she'd someday be a mother; her motherly instincts, and her babysitting experience, made that a more obvious thought. But a bride? She didn't consider that. "I think when you're so busy as a kid, and your mind is developing, you lose that dream time," she says. As a girl, she didn't have a lot of carefree hours to sit around playing with dolls, fantasizing about their lives and hers. She was a serious kid with serious responsibilities. Her parents were at work ten or twelve hours a day, and they needed her to help look after life at home.

People tell Shelley they're saddened to hear that she had something of a lost childhood, but she doesn't have many regrets. "It's OK, I understand," she says. "I accept that I was the caretaker, that my siblings needed me. That's how my head was geared. And I loved them, of course. So I wanted to look after them."

When Shelley was ten, her youngest sister, Jenny, was born. Later, Jenny's crib was sometimes kept in Shelley's bedroom so Shelley could keep an eye on her.

Shelley took this charge very seriously. "Come on, Jenny," she'd say. "Come sleep with me."

She did this not just because she had an urge to bond with her baby sister. The truth was, Shelley wanted to make sure Jenny was breathing all night long. She didn't want anything to happen to this precious little girl, especially on her watch. As long as she could feel her sister breathing beside her, things were OK. It was a mix of love, duty, uncertainty, and terror that led her to take Jenny out of her crib.

There's a photographic record of Shelley as a caregiver. In Becker family photo albums, she's always holding on to Jenny. In countless photos, she's a ten-year-old holding a baby or a twelve-year-old holding a two-year-old or a thirteen-year-old holding a three-year-old. "Shelley, you were just obsessed with me!" says Jenny, who is now thirty-five.

"In a way I was," Shelley tells her.

Shelley thinks her caregiver personality is a benefit now that she runs Becker's. She has a maternal urge to look after her employees and, just as important, to look after the needs of brides. It's almost as if she wants to protect them all from what may lie ahead.

Not long ago, she was treated for thyroid issues that are likely related to the stress in her life. "You are the oak tree, I can see that in you," her doctor told her.

"What do you mean by that?" Shelley asked.

"Well, an oak tree can be rotting from the inside and still be strong on the outside," the doctor said. "You'd never know by looking at the tree the damage that is inside it. You've got to take better care of yourself."

Shelley took to heart the doctor's words, but there were sixteen weddings that weekend, and much to do. She had no time to contemplate the oak tree she had become.

Megan, age two, in 1990

Chapter Eight

Megan

M egan Pardo has the bearings of a kindergarten teacher. She speaks with a smile and a pleasant lilt in her voice, but there's an authority there, too. You can tell she has a gift for explaining things patiently and carefully, that she pays close attention to how younger ears need to absorb what older people say.

A twenty-one-year-old senior at Illinois State University, engaged to an agricultural business major, she has come home to Grand Rapids on spring break and is now driving to Becker's. She's telling her mother how much she loves her current assignment student teaching in a kindergarten class. She says she has found her place in life: It's in front of a classroom rug, with cross-legged boys and girls spread out before her, helping them learn life's basic lessons. "This is what I'm meant to do," she says.

Her mother, Laura, a former schoolteacher, is now, at forty-eight, a professor of education at Hope College in Holland, Michigan. Laura remembers Megan as a girl, playing school with her dolls, vowing to follow in her footsteps as an educator. Megan took the Red Cross babysitting class when she was ten, the youngest age allowed. She worked in a day-care center at fourteen. Her senior year of high school, she was in a co-op program, working half days at a day-care center.

For Laura, whose job now is to teach future teachers how to teach, it's rewarding to see her daughter so enthusiastic about her current role in children's lives.

It's been a nice morning of mother-daughter bonding, and that continues after they arrive at Becker's and start picking through the dresses together. Megan is full of energy and enthusiasm, and Shelley gets a kick out of watching her try on dresses. Some brides go about their tasks with contagious smiles, and a real appreciation for the efforts of others: their mothers, the saleswomen. Even though Shelley has seen the process thousands of times, she still enjoys brides such as Megan.

Megan tells her saleswoman, Gwen, that she doesn't want a dress that's too showy; she hopes to find something without lace and beading. "Modest but classy," Megan says, passing around photos she has printed off of the Internet. She certainly doesn't want a heavy princesslike ball gown.

Soon enough, Megan has narrowed her choices to two favorites. The first is form-fitting—simple, sleek, and strapless, with a slight flare out at the hips. It has no train and there's a pretty bow on the back. It's just a bit too sexy for Megan.

The other dress she's drawn to is also simple, but more elegant—a lightweight gown with shoulder straps and an uncomplicated skirt with a small train. She's invited to wear it into the Magic Room, and her mother lets out a sigh when she arrives there.

"I love how it's laced up the back," Megan says, looking at her reflection at every possible angle in all the mirrors. "Now, if we can get this without the beading . . ."

"We can order it without the jewels," Shelley promises her.

"That's great," Megan says, then smiles. She turns to her mom. "I think I've found my dress."

Megan, born in 1988, is the Pardos' third and youngest child. Her brother, Chad, was born in 1986. Her older sister, Melissa, was born in 1984.

It's hard for Megan to even imagine what it would be like if her sister, Melissa, was also here at Becker's, helping her find a dress. She can't picture her sister, grown to adulthood, leaning against the mirrors in the Magic Room, weighing in on gowns.

To Laura and her husband Jack, a controls engineer, Melissa had been a much-loved first child, an easygoing baby with a nice smile. One day when Melissa was nine months old, Laura dropped her off, as usual, at a day-care facility operated out of a woman's home. Laura shared a few pleasantries with the babysitter, kissed her daughter good-bye, and went to work. Later that morning, Melissa's diaper needed to be changed and the sitter carried her to a table, put her down, and turned for just a second to grab the wipes. In that instant, Melissa stretched, rolled, and fell to the floor, landing at the worst possible angle, slamming the base of her spine. The injury turned out to be catastrophic.

Melissa remained in a coma for a week, and her doctors said pretty early on that there was no brain activity—and no hope. Eventually, Laura and Jack accepted this and made the gut-wrenching decision to remove her from life support.

They were twenty-three and twenty-four, suddenly childless again, and it wasn't easy to resist feeling as if the world had ended. But in his grief, Jack eventually had an epiphany. A soft-spoken man, more comfortable discussing engineering than his own emotions, he somehow found his voice. As he fielded all the sympathetic calls and condolences, as he thought about this terrible loss, he began to tell people the same thing again and again.

"The main thing I've learned," he'd say, "is that you bring children into this world, but you really don't know how long they'll be there. You really don't know how long you'll have them to love. Kids die every day. We don't think about how many times we see stories in the newspaper about people who've lost their children in accidents or because of illnesses. But all of those stories add up, while we're living our lives, not noticing. We just don't have our children forever. That's what I've learned."

As a result of Melissa's death, the babysitter, a woman in her thirties, lost her license to run the day-care facility. This saddened the Pardos. They knew it was a freak accident—it could have happened to any parent, any caregiver—and they forgave her quickly and completely. They've lost touch with her over the years, but they think about her often, knowing that she carries this loss with her, too.

"We've all turned away from our children to grab a diaper or a pacifier," says Jack. "The doctors told us Melissa's death was a one-in-a-million accident. She fell just three feet onto a carpeted floor. How many kids fall down a few stairs, or climb out of their cribs and fall? It happens every day, and the kids stand back up and are just fine. Our daughter landed on carpet, but she didn't stand up, and she wasn't fine. It just happened. I don't blame anyone."

A nine-month-old baby doesn't yet have a full personality, of course, so Laura and Jack don't have a great many memories of her. Near the end of her life, Melissa had begun sitting up, walking around furniture, holding on to things, giggling playfully. Two weeks before she died, Laura had brought her to watch Jack in a softball game. She forgot to bring Melissa's sun bonnet, and so the baby got a bad sunburn on her head. In the last photos they took of Melissa, she's smiling but sunburned.

Even though they were still grieving, or perhaps because of that, Laura and Jack decided they wanted to have another baby as quickly as possible. Their son was born just eleven months after Melissa's death. Megan followed two years later.

Jack and Laura would talk about Melissa to their surviving two children; they were committed to keeping her part of the family. A photo of Melissa hangs prominently in the house. While the other two kids got older, and new photos of them were displayed every year, Melissa remained forever a baby. Some people who visited the home, not knowing about the tragedy, just assumed the little girl in the photo was Megan.

The Pardos saw quickly that Megan had a different disposition from the more-easygoing Melissa. Megan turned out to be a strong-willed child, the sort of toddler who was assertive and argumentative. She never liked wearing a seat belt, and so her parents often had to stop the car, rebuckle her, and remind her of the importance of seat belts. Somewhere up the road, they'd see her in the rearview mirror, unbuckling herself again, and they'd have to pull over to the side of the road and start the process over again.

"She just has a mind of her own," Laura would tell people. "She's different than Melissa and Chad. It's hard to deal with her."

"Well, that will be a great trait when she's an adult," a friend once replied. "She'll be a leader. She'll have confidence. She'll think she can conquer anything."

Megan's middle name is Melissa, and she has always known that she carries that name in memory of her late sister. From an early age, she took it as a badge of honor. In first grade, there was another Megan in her class, and so she told her teacher and classmates to call her "Megan Melissa." That's the name she wrote on all her tests and homework. (Today, she uses it as her name on Facebook, and many of her friends and acquaintances don't know the origins of it.)

When Megan was in second grade, Laura left her job as a classroom teacher and began working for a textbook publisher, which required her to travel a lot. That's when Megan began crying almost every morning. She actually felt nauseated from the moment she woke up. "I don't want to go to school!" she'd say again and again, and it was hard to console her. Jack and Laura would tell her she had to go—they'd take her by the hand, walk her to the car, and drive her there—but inevitably, they'd get a call from her teacher. "Megan says she's sick. You've got to come get her. She's disrupting the class."

They eventually took her to a therapist who asked Megan to create a book of things that made her happy—her safety blanket, sucking her thumb for comfort—and the things that made her sad and worried. Megan was also given the outline of a person, and was asked to shade in different parts of the body. She was told to use a red crayon for the body parts that were sad or hurting, and a pink crayon for the rest of the body. Her stomach, her heart, her head—all were colored red.

Through this process, the therapist learned that Megan was fearful about losing her mother. "I had a sister and she died," Megan told the counselor, adding: "My mom goes away a lot." Megan didn't say it, but the therapist figured out what she was thinking: "Maybe my mom will die too, and she'll never come home to me."

Jack also was frequently out of town. He'd spend a week or two at a time working as an engineer, often at out-of-state warehouses, programming conveyor belts for companies such as Frito Lay. In that case, his job was to figure out how to get thousands of packages of potato chips into boxes, onto pallets, over to the loading dock, and into trucks. People thought he had a cool job, especially if they loved chips, but Megan missed her father and worried when he was gone, too.

Laura realized that she needed to spend more time with Megan, reassuring her, especially because Megan had trouble sleeping at night. "I'd lay in bed with her," Laura recalls, "and we'd sing songs like 'You Are My Sunshine.' We'd pray together. A mother and daughter can't lie together in bed like that, every night, and not bond."

By third grade, Megan's most strong-willed urges and her most vexing fears had begun to dissipate. She went to school happily and grew into a compassionate teen and a student leader. She sang in the choir and played softball.

Megan and her mom remained close. They'd bake together, and could talk about most everything, including sex. At one point, Laura stopped working for the textbook publisher and went to grad school. She and Megan sat each night at the kitchen table, doing homework together. "Some teens don't like having their mother around, especially when they're out in public," says Laura. "I remember being embarrassed by my mom when I was younger. But Megan wanted me with her, and so I'd chaperone school trips."

Over time, Jack and Laura saw that Megan had a good head on her shoulders. They didn't worry much about her. About the only thing that gave them pause was when she began learning to drive. She seemed naïve and a bit distracted. In Michigan, kids can get their permits at age fourteen and eight months. For some teens, including Megan, that could feel too early.

The first time she got in the driver's seat, she didn't even know there were two pedals. "Put it into drive," her father said.

"What does that mean?" she asked, and he explained, although not well enough.

They were in an empty school parking lot, and Jack had her pull into a parking space. "OK, let's back out," he told her. She put the car in drive, and flew over the curb, into the air, landing on the sidewalk.

She passed her driver's test and got her license at sixteen, but Laura worried that she didn't always focus on her surroundings as she drove. Early on, she hit a car at school. She also had a couple of speeding tickets. Then on her first day of class at Illinois State, she got in an accident and totaled her car, though no one was hurt.

All parents worry about their children driving, and the Pardos were no different. They were relieved that as Megan got older, she became more careful and alert at the wheel. Still, they kept reminding her about safe driving. "Even though we lost Melissa, I don't think that made us overprotective parents," says Jack. "But I've always told my children: We all make mistakes and some cost us more than others. You want to help your kids avoid mistakes, though of course, so much is beyond our control."

In the days after her visit to Becker's, Megan spent a lot of time on the phone with her fiancé, Shane, back in Illinois. Some calls lasted for hours. Her mom would hear her on the phone at one a.m. and tell her, "You've got to get some sleep. All these late nights are going to catch up with you!"

It was a prophetic warning.

Megan woke up on Sunday morning without a full night's rest. She went to church, kissed her parents good-bye, and then spent the next five hours driving herself back to college in Illinois. She stayed up late that night again, and woke up early the next day to teach. That Monday morning, March 29, 2010, she felt both exhilarated and exhausted from the excitement of her dress-shopping and wedding-planning excursions. She was in a good mood, looking forward to returning to her kindergartners.

On her way to the elementary school in Farmer's City, Illinois, feeling a bit groggy, she opened her window to let in fresh air to keep her awake. It didn't help. At about seven thirty a.m., she fell asleep at the wheel, maybe for a couple of seconds, and the car began drifting to the right, heading straight for an open field. She awoke with a jolt, and quickly tried to get back in her lane but overcompensated, and the car rolled completely over before landing on all four wheels on the opposite side of the road. She was just a mile from the elementary school.

An hour later, Laura Pardo got a call: Megan had been in a car accident. She was conscious, but her right hand was seriously mangled, with one of her fingers totally severed. She had serious lacerations on her forehead, nose, and elsewhere, and doctors were checking for internal injuries and brain damage.

Laura had already lost a daughter to an accident—a simple fall of just three feet. Laura couldn't protect nine-month-old Melissa as she fell those three feet. Now her other daughter had been in her own terrible accident three hundred miles away. She couldn't protect Megan, either.

She cried, she prayed, and too distraught to get behind the wheel of her car, she had her father drive her to Illinois.

That day, over at Becker's, Shelley was sending in the rush order for Megan's dress. She had no way of knowing that the wedding, slated for August, was now very much in jeopardy.

Chapter Nine

Life Preservers

*I*t is not lost on Shelley that so many Becker's brides come into the store trying to smile in the wake of personal setbacks and family tragedies. They have parents who are terminally ill or loved ones they've recently lost or they've been diagnosed with their own serious illnesses.

A wedding is a happy life-cycle event, yes, but the harsher life-cycle moments aren't kept at bay until after the wedding. Those moments keep coming, without warning, reminding brides that they can plan a wedding, but not how their lives will unfold.

Shelley is unable to shake her memories of the toughest stories she's witnessed over the years at Becker's. In her head, she holds on to images of certain brides, smiling in front of the old mirror by the front desk or hugging their mothers in the Magic Room. Those unlucky brides couldn't have fathomed what would happen next.

There was the ebullient bride-to-be who was hit by a car and killed while crossing the street to go to the post office. She was mailing thank-you notes to her bridal-shower guests.

There was the bride whose dad wasn't feeling well while they shopped at Becker's. That night, he ended up hospitalized. The bride came back the next day, found the perfect dress, and said, "I'd love to have my dad see this." She took a cell-phone photo of the dress and sent it to her father in his hospital room. He took a look at it on his phone, then called her to give his approval and to tell her she looked lovely in it. Right after he saw the dress, he died. She walked down the aisle without him, but appreciated that at least he'd seen her in the dress, if only on his cell phone, and had told her she was a beauty in his eyes.

Shelley sees plenty of giddy, happy brides, yes, but she also sees those who approach the dress search very soberly. When she detects sadness, she naturally wonders what's going on in a bride's life. Unless she senses they're willing to open up, however, she doesn't ask them "What's wrong?" She just tries to be as jovial as she can be, and hopes that will lift the bride's mood.

Once in a while, a bride will go into a dressing room, close the door, and Shelley hears muffled crying. She'll wait a little bit, then she'll knock on the door. "Honey, are you OK in there? Can I come in?"

And that's when she hears stories.

She has helped numerous brides with cancer find dresses that will cover their scars and the ports in their chests. She has found gowns for brides in wheelchairs, sliding dresses over their heads, apologizing that she can't get them up the stairs and into the Magic Room.

Shelley knows, from all her years at the store, that weddings are often optimistic islands surrounded by oceans of uncertainty, loneliness, and grief. For some women, a bridal gown can feel like a life preserver.

⁓

Given the changes these days in mother-daughter interactions, Shelley and her saleswomen find it refreshing when a bride shows great deference to her mother. One recent bride who stood out for them was Courtney Driskill, who drove in from Owosso, a town of 15,700 people forty-five minutes from Fowler. Courtney arrived without the usual entourage of bridesmaids. Her mother was her only companion. "There's no one else I'd want to share this moment with," she said.

A pretty twenty-nine-year-old with blond ringlets, Courtney has had serious health issues since her teens, when strep throat and mononucleosis often kept her out of school. It took until her early twenties for doctors to figure out why she was sick: rheumatic fever, an inflammatory disease that can affect the heart, joints, skin, and brain.

She spent most of her twenties in bed, sleeping up to twenty hours a day. She'd get up to eat and use the bathroom, and then she'd go back to sleep. It was hard for her parents to watch as the disease damaged her heart valves and her immune system.

To pay Courtney's insurance premiums of $660 a month, her mother got a job in the men's department at JCPenney. She started off earning $6.75 an hour. Given her mother's selflessness, Courtney found herself fighting off constant feelings of guilt. She'd be incredibly tired and sick, curled up on her parents' couch, and in her grogginess, she'd see her mother heading off to work on winter mornings. Ask Courtney to define the word "love," and she talks about her mother, helping men find ties and pants at JCPenney so she can make insurance payments.

When Courtney's health improved, and she roused herself from the couch to take on a few part-time jobs, she felt a bit like Rip Van Winkle. She returned to Owosso High School to coach the baton, dance, and pom-pom squads, and quickly saw troubling changes in the way many young women carried themselves—and in the secrets they kept from their parents.

She became a big-sister figure to a lot of the girls, and was taken aback by the ways in which sexuality is more blatant than when she was in school. "When I left high school twelve years ago, we were wearing baggy clothes and flannel shirts," she says. "Now girls are wearing stilettos to band camp. I feel for them. They want to be desirable and pretty, but they're confusing that with dressing like little trollops. It's alarming."

The school was filled with girls in short skirts and low-cut tops. A male teacher confided to Courtney that he's uncomfortable teaching his provocatively dressed female students. Some literally open their legs and expose their underwear to him while he's teaching. "He's afraid to look at them," Courtney says.

Courtney saw how girls, inundated with confusing messages all their lives, felt pressured to look "hot" at younger and younger ages. When those inappropriately dressed students were preteens, for instance, they were targets of advertising come-ons such as the one for Nair Pretty, a hair-removal product aimed at girls ages ten to fifteen. The mixed-message tagline: "I am a citizen of the world. I am a dreamer. I am fresh. I am so not going to have stubs sticking out of my legs."

Such messages can seem innocuous, but Courtney saw how it speeds up adolescence, and adds a toxic degree of pressure to girls' lives. Girls who fear that their worth depends on their ability to look sexy are often the ones who develop eating disorders or turn to cutting themselves—or do dangerous things sexually.

One girl Courtney coached allegedly got drunk at a party and had sex with five boys, one after the other. Courtney tried to convince her to go to Planned Parenthood for an exam, but the girl refused. "That's gross," she said. "I'm too young for that." Her mother learned of the rumors, but chose to accept the girl's denials. The promiscuity continued.

Courtney would encourage girls to confide in their parents. Some would. Others saw no upside in that; they said their mothers and fathers would be too judgmental, especially about sexual issues. Such comments mirror a 2009 study by researchers at Ohio State University. They found that while teenage girls share more with their parents about their dating lives than teenage boys do, when it comes to talking to Mom and Dad about sex, girls and boys are equally close-mouthed.

Spending time with girls who were confused and uncertain about themselves, Courtney naturally thought of her own teen years. She considered herself lucky that, most of the time, she felt comfortable turning to her mother to discuss sensitive issues—sexuality, drugs, whatever—even if she and her mom began by approaching topics indirectly. "We'd do it sideways," recalls her mother, Susan. "We'd talk about someone else who had made a bad choice or gotten into a tough situation. That made it easier for us to speak frankly about how we thought about our own decisions."

Courtney's mother also would talk to her preemptively. For instance, women in their family, going back a couple generations, struggled with serious premenstrual syndrome and the depression and crankiness that accompanies it. In her own life, Courtney has mostly avoided the worst side effects. "But I wanted her to realize there's a pattern to it," Susan says, "in case she found herself dealing with it too."

Over the years, Susan had watched as Courtney's health problems affected her romantic relationships. There wasn't much she could do to help, except to be supportive and a good listener. She tried to boost Courtney's self-esteem when she could, but she also thought it important to be realistic.

In her early twenties, Courtney had a serious boyfriend and thought she'd marry him. When her grandfather was on his deathbed, she brought this boyfriend to meet him, thinking it was important for the old man and the young man to make a connection. Her grandfather died a few hours later.

But rather than cementing their bonds, that deathbed encounter made the relationship too serious for Courtney's boyfriend. He broke up with her the next day. "He grew up on a farm, where his mother did everything for the family," Courtney says. "And there I was, sleeping a lot and having my good days and bad days. I wasn't the physical martyr his mother had been."

Looking back, Courtney says, she should have seen the breakup coming. Her mom certainly sensed the young man was backing away, and she offered Courtney a few light warnings. But Courtney ignored the signals. "When he left me, I was taken off guard," she says.

Her mom recalls how devastated Courtney was by the breakup, how she curled up on the couch, dead-tired as always and as sad as she'd ever been. "It looks like I'm going to be on this couch until I'm ninety years old!" Courtney said.

"I was heartbroken," Susan says. "I wanted to make it all go away."

But she gave Courtney her honest take—that a lot of men can't cope with dating or marrying someone who is ill. "Honey, you're smart, you're dynamic, you're intuitive, you're pretty. You're the kindest, coolest person I know. But you're also sick, and your health may hold you back. It may take you longer to find the right person."

"I wasn't sure it would all work out for her," Susan now says, "and I was sad and worried about that. But I also knew her challenges were making her stronger. I had hope."

Courtney ended up being very grateful that her illness scared some men away. That allowed her to eventually find John Schlaud, a Marine drill instructor who fell in love with all that was wonderful about her, and vowed to stand by her no matter how precarious her health might be.

John has a son and daughter from a previous marriage, and as Courtney's relationship with him blossomed, she talked to her mom about her feelings every step of the way. Was she up to the task of being a stepmother? Would it be fair to John if they married, given her health issues? What if her illness precluded her from having children of her own?

Mothers don't have all the answers, but sometimes they have maternal powers of observation, and they can sum things up in ways that comfort their daughters. "I see how much you love him, and how much he loves you," Courtney's mom told her. "You'll get through whatever lies ahead, and you'll get through it together."

⁓

During Courtney's visit to Becker's, Shelley and the saleswomen saw how lovingly and easily she interacted with her mother. But Courtney didn't tell them that she had a secret: Yes, she was planning a formal wedding. Yes, she wanted a beautiful dress. But she and John had already gotten married months before in South Carolina, where John was stationed.

The reason? She felt too guilty that her mom was working every day to pay for her insurance. "It's like a sin on my heart," she once told John, who then explained to her that if she became a military spouse, she could immediately be covered by his health plan. Getting married quickly became a no-brainer. Her parents agreed.

Still, that piece of paper wouldn't take away from the emotions Courtney knew she would feel when she eventually walked down the aisle with her mom and dad. "I spent a lot of years feeling so ill, sleeping on their couch day after day, while my mom showed her love by heading off to work," Courtney says. "After all that, my parents deserve to see me as a bride—and they definitely deserve an empty nest." Her parents had been there for her "in sickness and in health." Now she felt blessed to have fallen in love with a man who was willing to do the same.

Doctors told Courtney and John that they shouldn't consider having a baby together anytime soon—perhaps ever—because her body might not be able to withstand a pregnancy. Courtney is sad about that, but accepting. And she feels lucky that she is building meaningful bonds with John's two kids, especially six-year-old Samantha. Courtney has vowed to be a sounding board and a resource for her stepdaughter, helping her find her way to womanhood. (Already, Samantha has talked of wanting large breasts when she grows up, which left Courtney a bit speechless.)

When she is with Samantha in Owosso, Courtney likes to help her maintain her innocence, taking her to the parks where she herself played as a girl. Samantha rides her bike through the neighborhood where Courtney grew up, and Courtney has been shooting photos of her. "It's a subconscious passing along of the little things that marked my happiest childhood moments, of the things I did with my own mother," she says.

She thinks of what life might be like for Samantha when she enters high school. Will the culture be even more sexually charged and confusing for young girls then? Will she avoid the teen hazards—eating disorders, binge drinking, inappropriate celebrity role models, toxic friendships— and come out the other end with her self-esteem intact?

At Becker's, Courtney explained that after the wedding, she and John would be taking a "familymoon" to Orlando, Florida, with his two kids. They couldn't afford to go to Disney World, but they planned to visit Sea

World, which is free to active military and their families. Growing up in Michigan, the kids had never seen the ocean, so they vowed to also drive east until they hit the Atlantic. It all sounded so wholesome.

When Courtney eventually found the right dress and took it into the Magic Room, she thought, "Wow, this is such a soft room." It wasn't just the lighting. It was the way the room made everyone want to whisper. It was the way she and her mother looked at each other in those mirrors.

Her mother, so used to seeing Courtney lying prone on the couch, was understandably emotional as Courtney stood upright on the Magic Room pedestal.

"I didn't think I'd ever see this day," her mother said.

Outside the store, for a great many daughters and their mothers, the world was spinning with uncertainty—about their identities, their sexuality, and how they should interact with each other. But in here, for a secretly married woman and her proud mother, the mood was nothing short of joyous.

Courtney with her husband, John, and stepchildren Jacob and Samantha

Chapter Ten

A Becker's Bride

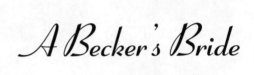

S helley first began working at Becker's in 1979, when she was fourteen years old. Her sister Bev, who was three years younger, took over the role as at-home babysitter, so Shelley could help out at the store.

Shelley didn't exactly ask herself, "Is this where I'll spend my life?" It was more a case of her assuming, "There isn't anything else. This will be my life." She'd had no real exposure to much beyond Fowler and the store. She can't remember if her parents ever said to her, "Someday, Shelley, you'll run the store." Maybe they said it. Or maybe they didn't need to. They knew and she knew.

Her parents didn't pay her a salary right away. For the first six months, they had her taking new gowns out of boxes and bagging dresses for pickups. But soon enough, they began paying her five dollars an hour, and she was on the floor, selling dresses.

She was understandably tentative at first, trying to act knowledgeable. But even though she was barely a teenager, she found the words inside

Shelley, trying on a wedding veil at age fourteen, when she began working at Becker's

herself, and began asking grown women, "So what kind of dress have you dreamed about all your life?"

The brides and their mothers would look at Shelley and smile. Who was this kid? But they'd tell her about their dream dresses, and they'd let her make suggestions.

"How do you think this looks?" a bride would ask.

"It's not exactly right for you," Shelley would say. "Come on over to this rack." And they figured this kid must know something, so they followed her.

The business was both frightening and exciting for Shelley. She saw the pressures her mother was under. She saw how brides could be terribly difficult. But she also observed a lot of lovely interactions between mothers and daughters. She came to appreciate the blind, familial love described best in the Moroccan proverb: "In the eyes of its mother, every beetle is a gazelle."

Shelley came to appreciate the camaraderie of the older saleswomen, including Eleanor, hired by Grandma Eva in 1935. Over the decades, these women had learned to calibrate the degree of patience each bride required. They'd found techniques to humor brides who believed they knew best, but didn't.

Many brides came in clutching a photo from a bridal magazine, insisting that *this* was the dress they were destined to wear. More often than not, a dress that looked so perfect on a thin model in a magazine wasn't close to the dress that looked best on them.

When Shelley was sixteen years old, in 1981, the soap opera *General Hospital* staged the TV wedding of the millennium, sending characters Luke and Laura down the aisle before thirty million viewers. Because Laura wore a champagne-pink gown, a hint of pink became the go-to color for countless Becker's brides. That was fine. But a lot of the brides also wanted to wear gargantuan, forehead-covering, doodad-dripping headpieces that echoed Laura's. Not all women look good in monstrous headpieces. Those with small faces and features get lost with them. Those with fat faces look fatter. At sixteen, Shelley learned how to tell brides, "No, that's not really you."

"But it's so perfect . . ."

"No, I'm sorry. It isn't. Not for you."

Shelley also learned to accept the futility inherent in waiting on certain customers. Because Becker's had such a large selection, brides would often drive from distant towns, fall in love with a dress, then leave without buying it.

"What happened?" Shelley would ask after such customers left.

"They're probably going to have their hometown store just order it," an older saleswoman would explain, "so they don't have to drive a hundred miles back here for second fittings." For Becker's saleswomen, the process could be demoralizing.

Shelley's mom, Sharon, was always worried about cash flow and making payroll. She sometimes took it hard when a bride departed empty-handed. "It was as if we failed," a saleswoman recalls.

Still, the store dealt in volume and racked up sales. Saturdays were usually crazy free-for-alls. Two or three brides would share each dressing room. Given how crowded it was, less-inhibited brides would disrobe right on the sales floor, out in the open.

It wasn't uncommon for a bride to come in without underwear on, so no lines would show. "Will you zip me up?" she'd ask. And that meant a saleswoman had to reach down her bare buttocks and start zipping. Some brides wore too much perfume. Others smelled of body odor. Saleswomen always made sure to wash their hands before lunch.

There were all sorts of techniques Shelley learned from the veterans on the sales floor. It was important to read the relationship between a bride and her mother. If there's tension, what's the root of it? Often, a bride would give her saleswoman a "help me" look, and it was easy to tell that she needed the freedom to think for herself, without her mom's sledgehammer bossiness. A saleswoman could help by directing questions almost exclusively to the bride. If a mother wasn't totally dense, she'd get the message.

On the other hand, a bride being disrespectful to her mother was harder to control. Even if a saleswoman could jolly the bride into being more courteous, there was no way to correct a lifetime of poor mother-daughter dynamics. In those cases, the goal was to make the sale and get the unappreciative bride and her beleaguered mother on their way.

Shelley saw that the older saleswomen had a sense of humor but remained as dignified as possible. As Sharon hired in local teens and twenty-somethings—including three girls who would go on to marry Shelley's brothers—the vibe in the store changed. The store might have been a hallowed institution, but the younger saleswomen were determined to entertain themselves there, and they found goofy ways to do so.

The place had mirrors everywhere, of course, and so the young saleswomen couldn't avoid looking at themselves all day long. Unless they had high self-esteem, they were always noticing their flaws, their acne, their less than movie-star-like profiles. The tools of their trade—tape measures and mirrors—led the young salesgirls to self-consciously assess one another. On a slow day, when no bride was nearby, they'd measure the length of one another's noses, fingers, or ears and compare stats.

When Shelley's mom was gone from the store for more than a few hours, the young salesgirls would sometimes try on dresses for one another and parade around. The jingle of the front door, signaling an arriving bride, would lead them scurrying to hide in a dressing room. Then they'd return, composed: "Can I help you?"

Once, a bride's mother did a double-take, asking the saleswoman: "Is there a reason you're wearing a veil?"

The saleswoman hadn't realized it was still on, but recovered well. "Hey, I'm single and I work in a bridal shop. I can't resist."

The Beckers worked hard, six days a week, but there was one workday a year, Good Friday, when they took a three-hour break. Each Friday before Easter, as noon approached, Shelley's mom would ask all the brides to get back into their street clothes because the store would be closed from noon to three p.m. Catholics consider those three hours to be holy; that was the time Jesus was on the cross before he died. Sharon made a grand embrace of Good Friday. She'd invite her whole extended family over to her house for salmon patties, and the youngest kids would get to decorate Easter eggs. It was a nice Becker's tradition, a respite from the unrelenting bridal trade. But by 3:05, all the saleswomen needed to be back at work. And there was often a line of brides waiting to get into the store as Sharon unlocked the front door.

Shelley often found herself looking around the store at the cluttered boxes, the less-than-elegant, warehouse-like ambiance, and she thought that if she ever ran the place, she'd make changes. Shelley always had a visual eye, and though she never offered suggestions to her parents, her urges to renovate someday were catalogued in her head.

She worked at Becker's every day after school from three thirty until it closed at eight p.m., and then all day Saturday, which meant in both junior high and high school, she had little time for her friends. While they were at the school dances on Friday nights, she was working at the store, waiting patiently for brides to step out of fitting rooms.

Again and again, Shelley saw how crucial it was to make sure every bride had the dress she selected, perfectly altered, in time for her ceremony. If Shelley screwed up somehow, brides might respond as if she had ruined their lives. Shelley figured out early that this was a serious business.

On September 30, 1981, when Shelley was a high school freshman, eight inches of rain fell in Fowler in a matter of hours, leaving Main Street completely flooded. The man who owned the gas station two blocks to the west drowned. At Becker's, water gushed uncontrollably through the front door.

Clark and Sharon had rushed out to get sandbags, but they couldn't hold back the water. "Grab all the sold dresses on the ground floor!" Sharon shouted to Shelley. "Get 'em upstairs. Go, go, go!"

The Beckers knew that the dresses already altered, or slated for weddings in the weeks ahead, had to be saved first. If they were ruined, the store would be dealing with mass bridal hysteria. It was the wedding-dress equivalent of "women and children first."

Shelley sprang into action, checking tags and carrying sold dresses, two at a time, over her head to higher ground. As the dresses were piled in heaps on the second floor, Shelley helped sort them, then ran down for more. Meanwhile, because there were news reports that Fowler was flooding, the phone at the store kept ringing with frantic brides asking if their gowns were submerged. "We're doing our best," Shelley heard her mom say again and again. Shelley knew that nothing less than their best would be acceptable.

The weeks leading up to the flood had been extremely busy at Becker's. More than 750 million people worldwide had watched Princess Diana's wedding two months earlier, and it seemed as if every Becker's bride was swooning over the princess's hugely poufy, hand-embroidered gown of 10,000 pearls. The brides loved seeing that twenty-five-foot, ivory-taffeta train stuffed into that not-big-enough carriage, and as a result, they also wanted endless trains and extra-poufed sleeves for their dream dresses. It was exhausting pulling all those poufy, long-trained gowns up the stairs and out of harm's way.

The store lost some inventory to the rising waters, but no bride waiting for her dress was disappointed. All the sold dresses were rescued. The Beckers brought in fans to dry the floors, and if any brides walked down the aisle smelling like flood water, their water-stained trains trailing behind them, no one came back and mentioned it.

⌒⌒

Shelley's young life carried her from sale to sale, bride to bride, and crisis to crisis. She did her homework on the run, when there was a lull at the store, or not at all. She never thought about going to college, never really considered getting out of Fowler, never dated much. During her senior year, she enrolled in a work-study co-op program at Fowler High so she could leave at noon each day and head down to Becker's.

When she thought about her life, she saw her purpose as helping out at the store and helping her younger siblings. But then it seemed her time had come.

One night, when Shelley was seventeen, she got out of Becker's early enough to attend a friend's party. Her friend had plotted to also invite an older guy named Gary Mueller so they could fix him up with her. And so Shelley found herself talking with this tall, handsome twenty-year-old who'd gone to school with her brother. Shelley and Gary had never spoken before, and she found him courteous but shy. She had to draw him out, but he was kind of funny in a low-key way if you listened closely.

In the weeks that followed, Gary fell for her fast, and Shelley remained taken by his quiet charm and good looks. He was a bit of a party boy—he often had a drink in his hand—but that described many of the young men in the area. And for Shelley, there was something exciting about that, too. When she was with him, she felt like she was escaping the confines and responsibilities of the bridal store.

For his part, Gary, then working in construction maintenance, didn't have the biggest of dreams. He was the youngest of six children, and the son of a General Motors line worker. His parents were older and had a Depression-era view of life, which left them very careful about spending and saving. Like many families in Fowler, they weren't very tactile or effusive in expressing their love.

Taking their cues from their families, Gary and Shelley weren't effusive about their feelings either. But once they started seriously dating, it seemed like an inevitable progression toward marriage. "I've found a guy," Shelley thought. "This must be it."

Gary had never been inside of Becker's Bridal when he was a boy, but after he started dating Shelley, he saw how the store dominated the Beckers' lives. He was impressed by the family's commitment to the place, and by Shelley's dedication to brides, her parents and her siblings. He sensed she'd make a good wife and mother.

One day in July 1984, Gary and Shelley were driving around Fowler and he pulled up onto the driveway of his parents' house. He seemed nervous, more bashful than usual. He pulled out a box of candy, and a box with a ring in it. He didn't really propose. "I want you to be my wife," he said. "What do you think?"

"Yeah," she said, "Sure." They kissed, they hugged, and Shelley was excited. She had friends who were engaged. Now she was too. Gary was twenty-one. Shelley was eighteen.

She tried on dresses after hours at Becker's, but didn't search in earnest until she joined her mom that fall on a buying trip to Chicago. Sharon remembered how Grandma Eva had picked her bridesmaids and steered her into a dress for her wedding. And so she gave Shelley time and space to look around and make her own decision. "Let's find something you'll love," she told Shelley.

At one point, a wholesaler showed Shelley a white satin dress that retailed for $3,000—quite a price at the time, and more expensive than any dress at Becker's. (Today such a dress would cost $10,000.) It had a wedding-ring collar, Renaissance sleeves, and a Cathedral train, and it was

Shelley and Gary, just married, in 1985

loaded with more sparkling beads and hand-sewn sequins than Shelley had ever seen in the store back in Fowler. "I love it," she said.

"Then it's yours," Sharon told her.

They paid the wholesale price—$1,400—and took it with them.

During Shelley's engagement, when she waited on brides at Becker's, she had a new affinity for them. She couldn't really describe it, except as "a secret feeling." Excitement mixed with trepidation and uncertainty.

The wedding day, September 7, 1985, turned out to be one of the hottest, most humid September days ever in the Midwest. The University of Nebraska football team hosted Florida State that day, and the temperature on the field reached 133 degrees. In Chicago, thousands of people left their stifling homes for relief along Lake Michigan. Meanwhile, Shelley and Gary sweated through their ceremony at the Catholic church in Fowler, then held a reception for 450 guests seven miles east in St. John's, in a parks-and-recreation building without air-conditioning. The temperature in the hall topped 100 degrees.

Shelley's hair sat flat on her head, and the wedding cake actually melted. The frosting kept slipping off the cake, coming to rest in blobs on the table. Every ten minutes, one of Shelley's aunts would pick up whatever clumps she could and plop them back on the cake, but she eventually saw it was useless and stopped. Meanwhile, two of Shelley's bridesmaids went MIA, having left the reception—twice—to go home and take showers. Several guests warned that they felt ready to pass out.

Shelley had walked down the aisle with mixed emotions. The thoughts in her head were: "I don't think I want to get married. I don't want to leave my brothers and sisters. They still need me." Her caregiver identity was hard to shake. She was especially focused on her kid sister, Jenny, then eleven years old. Shelley, who helped raise her from birth, felt guilty about moving out of the family home and leaving Jenny behind.

As for her feelings for Gary, well, she was young and he was young and there they were. He looked handsome and he was sweet to her, and he seemed to have fewer fears. Did she love him? In a way, of course. But she thinks back to the nineteen-year-old girl she was and knows she didn't fully understand love. How could she?

The reception was fine. A lot of dancing and drinking, some speeches no one really remembers. At midnight, Shelley and Gary started saying their good-byes before heading north to Michigan's Mackinac Island. The parks-and-rec building had hardly cooled down. Someone said the temperature outside was still ninety-nine degrees. The remaining guests were weary and wet from perspiration as Shelley kissed them and thanked them for coming. They seemed just miserable. All of them needed a shower.

When she approached her mother to say good-bye, Shelley heard something she couldn't recall ever hearing before. "I love you," her mother said, and hugged her.

Surely Sharon had said it to Shelley when she was a baby. Maybe she'd said it at other times when Shelley was growing up. But Shelley felt, in that moment, as if these were new words from her mother. Had Shelley been yearning to hear them? Hard to say. She would later analyze the moment and decide: "When you've never had something, you don't necessarily long for it. Maybe you don't know you need it." Her parents weren't expressive people. That didn't mean they didn't feel love.

Still, those words from her mom meant more to her than any other words exchanged that evening, including every "I love you" uttered by Gary.

"I love you," her mother had said, and the words lifted Shelley up.

"I love you, too, Mom," she responded, and hugged her mother tightly.

She left the hall with Gary, wearing her sweat-soaked wedding dress, and began her life as a married woman.

Chapter Eleven

Julie

S tanding on the pedestal in the Magic Room, Julie Wieber has a clear realization: This may be the most bittersweet moment of her life.

When she first came to Becker's in 1986, her mother and her future mother-in-law accompanied her. She was a twenty-one-year-old bride-to-be—bubbly, giggly, in love but naïve—chattering about her wedding plans and her hunky fiancé. She selected the very first dress she tried on. A few months later, she walked happily down the aisle with Jeff, an athletic and handsome young man she had known since childhood. They went on to have five children between 1987 and 1995—four daughters and a son.

Now, twenty-four years later and back at Becker's, her walk into the Magic Room is far more sobering because her life has taken an unexpected and unwanted turn.

A nurse at a hospital in Lansing, Julie spent her adult life assuming that she'd one day return to Becker's as a mother of the bride. Probably the mother of four brides. She never thought she'd be the bride standing on that pedestal again.

In certain ways, this 2010 Becker's appointment is a replay of her visit in 1986. She again has chosen the first wedding dress that she tried on, although this time it's ivory-colored and understated instead of white and full of flourishes. Her mother has again accompanied her, but this time, two of her daughters are here too.

As she stands here in her new dress, still beautiful at age forty-five, all the women in the Magic Room are crying—her mom, her daughters, the saleswomen. Shelley, leans against the east wall, also tearing up. (She and Julie are friends, as are their daughters.)

"I'd like to think that no one is crying unhappy tears," Julie says, "that you're all crying out of happiness because my life is coming back together."

"Of course," someone says, while everyone wipes their eyes.

At every step in this dress-buying process, Julie can't help but think back to the day in 1986 when she first came to Becker's. She closes her eyes for a second, remembering what it felt like to look at herself in the mirror as a twenty-one-year-old in a white wedding dress. She opens her eyes and here she is, middle-aged. That's part of the magic in these Magic Room mirrors. "When I came to Becker's the first time, I hadn't yet had all these life experiences," she later tells Shelley. "At age twenty-one, it was all about the dress. That's what we focused on. The dress. The wedding."

Back in 1986, she had decided to spend much of her savings—$900— to buy a fairly extravagant dress. She put $150 down, and planned to make payments of $100 a month. However, when she went to Becker's to make the first payment, she was told she didn't owe any more money. Her fiancé Jeff had already stopped by and paid off the dress. It was an early act of kindness by Jeff that would be followed by many more.

⌒

Julie was born in Fowler, and grew up hanging around Jeff, her brother's friend. Jeff, whose family owned the local lumber company, was a practical joker, the life of every party. People would say he was the most charismatic, friendliest guy they'd ever met, and he was known for his cheerful willingness to fix things for neighbors and friends. Dozens of people have stories about how Jeff stopped by and helped them fix their garage doors, or taught them how to fish, or checked the salt in their water softeners. Starting when he was a teen, he had this urge to offer people hands-on help. Many in Fowler described him the same way: He was a boy, and then a man, with a big heart.

Jeff was built like a linebacker, tall and handsome with baby-blue eyes, and as he aged, he began to look like Christopher Reeve, or a more rugged version of David

Julie and Jeff on their wedding day

Hasselhoff. From their first real date, when Julie was eighteen and Jeff was twenty-one, she felt this huge attraction. There's a photo from their wedding day, and Julie is gazing up at Jeff with a look that seems genuinely starry-eyed. For his part, Jeff liked to tell people that he loved Julie long before they ever dated—maybe all his life. At their wedding, a Bible verse was read: "Love never fails . . . love bears all things . . ."

Julie was devoted to Jeff in an old-fashioned way, committed to reaching for their dreams as a team. Her romantic role models were always her paternal grandparents—who died at ages ninety-nine and ninety-three, and were married for sixty-eight years—and her parents, married for fifty-eight years. Her mother, especially, is Julie's closest confidante. Since she was a girl, Julie says, her mother has been the wisest presence in her life.

Jeff worked as a tool-and-die maker for General Motors in Lansing. He and Julie worked opposite shifts—her nursing shift at the hospital usually ran from seven a.m. to five thirty p.m., and he'd work two p.m. to ten thirty p.m. at GM's Cadillac plant—and so their moments together were precious. They focused their free time on their kids' sports and activities. They played in a coed volleyball league together and escaped to their cottage on Houghton Lake, a couple hours north of Fowler.

Jeff liked wearing Hawaiian shirts, drinking beer, fishing, hunting, and entertaining those who came his way with a full arsenal of comic moves. He did a dead-on imitation of Mike Brady, the dad from *The Brady Bunch* and was equally famous for his impersonation of a rabid dog. He liked taking Julie to a certain nightclub where the dance-floor lighting made white clothing glow in the dark. He'd nonchalantly pull his pants down a bit to show off his glowing white underwear while he danced. Across the dance floor, people couldn't stop laughing, as a DJ kept instructing him over the loudspeaker: "You, with the pants down, pull 'em up!"

Jeff was proud of his ability to parcel out goofy nicknames to people, and he enjoyed watching little kids scratch their heads when he'd purposely mispronounce their names. At first, children would wonder why an adult would make such a mistake, and then they'd realize that Jeff's mispronunciations were terms of endearment.

Most everything about Jeff appealed to Julie, and that was part of the reason their marriage succeeded. Researchers now say that happy marriages are often fueled by "irrational optimism" and "self-delusion"—in which at least one spouse idealizes his or her partner. If a wife finds a husband to be smarter, funnier, and more handsome than he actually is, her positive perceptions are good for the marriage, according to an ongoing study by University of Buffalo researchers.

Realists' marriages can be more problematic, especially as years go by, and a partner's charms can seem monotonous or overrated, while his faults feel magnified and unfixable. People who continue to idealize their spouses, even irrationally, have what the researchers describe as "a level of immunity to the corrosive effects of time." Long marriages are more satisfying when at least one half of a couple resists removing the rose-colored glasses.

In Julie's case, whenever she talked glowingly about Jeff, she'd insist that she wasn't inflating his positive traits. And his daughters—Stefanie, Lauren, Camie, and Macy—agreed. They idolized him too. When Camie was in fourth grade, she won a local Father's Day essay-writing contest, beating out four hundred other children. "Any girl would love to have my dad in her life," Camie wrote. Among her reasons: "He worked two jobs so my mom could go to nursing school and get her degree." And: "You just have to see the oak benches and cabinets he makes, all from his heart and just for us!" Thanks to Camie's essay, Jeff was named "Father of the Year" and won a new suit and tickets for the family to attend a Lansing Lugnuts minor-league baseball game.

Over a beer, Jeff once told his brother, "You know, girls can be trying at times. So you've got to figure 'em out. That's the secret. In my case, I've got these four daughters, and I've come to realize that two of 'em are dogs and two of 'em are cats. The two that are dogs, I've got to give them a lot of attention. I've got to caress them. The two that are cats, they go their own way. They're happy to be left alone. So I've adjusted, see? When I'm with the dogs, I caress and I play. When I'm with the cats, I give them room. And either way, I just remember to love them."

Some fathers have trouble communicating with their daughters because, as researchers explain, males in conversation are hardwired to try to solve problems, while females usually want to first discuss their feelings. Jeff had a sense of how to talk to his girls when they had an issue. "Do you want me to help you find a solution," he'd say, "or do you want me to just listen to you?"

Jeff was certainly a man's man, and he raised the girls to be tough—to hunt and fish and know a thing or two about lumber—but he also recognized their femininity, their needs, the longings they felt.

Through most of the marriage, Jeff wasn't an especially demonstrative husband—he didn't always say "I love you"—but it was important to him that his daughters understood how much he loved Julie.

In November 2008, when Camie was fifteen, she went on a deer-hunting trip with Jeff, and they had a lot of light conversations about school, her friends, sports. He entertained her with impressions. But one night, in the middle of the woods, almost out of the blue, Jeff asked Camie a question: "Do you know how much I love your mother?"

Camie smiled at him. "Yes, I know you love her, Dad."

Jeff looked at Camie for a moment, and she sensed he wanted to say something important. The joker was being serious. "I don't think you and your sisters fully realize it," he told her. "I don't think you get just how much I really love your mother. And that's the love I want all of you to have, the kind of love I feel for your mom."

Julie and Jeff later in their marriage

Long ago, Jeff and Julie had attended a "marriage encounter" week-end with other couples. It made Jeff uncomfortable. Each couple had to tell the story of how they fell in love. When it was Jeff's turn, he couldn't bring himself to go too deep. "I am a friend of Julie's brother," he said. "One day he promised me five dollars every time I dated Julie. Then he offered me a twenty-five dollar bonus if I married her." Jeff later told Julie: "No one needs to know our love story. You know how much I love you."

"I do," Julie told him, "but it's always good to hear it."

After he reached his midforties, Jeff had a lot of back pain, but he'd grimace through it and not say much. His back problem gave him an even greater appreciation for Julie, who as a nurse was able to offer advice and loving, patient attention. Jeff had three operations on his back, but the pain persisted. Doctors were so focused on his back that when they perused his MRIs, they never noticed that he also had heart issues.

On February 6, 2009, Jeff was in the basement in the family home in Fowler, building sections of a fireplace that he could take up to the family cottage on the lake. Julie was always complaining that she was cold in the cottage, and Jeff thought adding a fireplace would be a nice surprise for her. He was down in the basement for a while, awfully quiet, and when his twenty-year-old son Lee called down to him, there was no answer. Lee headed down the stairs and found Jeff dead. He was forty-seven.

Pathologists later determined that Jeff—the guy everyone always described as big-hearted—had died from complications of an enlarged heart. "An enlarged heart," Julie repeated when given the news. "It doesn't surprise me."

More than 2,000 people showed up for Jeff's wakes and memorial service in Fowler, which was pretty incredible for a town of 1,100. As people reminisced about him, everyone had a story. At one of the wakes, the stories went on for almost two hours.

"Uncle Jeff taught me to drive," one nephew said, and paused for a punch line. "When I was eleven."

A middle-school math teacher in Fowler talked of how Jeff always volunteered to be chaperone on his daughters' field trips. "It was Jeff and all these mothers."

One of Jeff's pals spoke about what made Jeff a true friend: "A true friend is someone who stops over and brings you something you didn't realize you needed, and now can't do without. A true friend tells you how good you are at something and uses the word 'bastard' in the same sentence. Jeff Wieber is my true friend."

"Even if you met Jeff just once, you remembered him," said a doctor who worked with Julie at the hospital.

And Jeff's niece may have put it best. "Jeff wasn't just a character," she said. "He also had character."

Julie's best friend spoke about what she had long observed: "What struck me most about Jeff and Julie was the love they had for each other. They never had to say a word to me about it. I could just see it in their eyes when they looked at each other."

Shelley had left an underling in charge at Becker's so she could go to the wake. As she sat there, absorbing the eulogies, she realized that she knew no couple as close as Julie and Jeff. "How will Julie move forward?" Shelley asked herself. "She'll never be happy again." She wondered if Jeff was somehow present, listening to the speeches.

Jeff and Julie's daughter Lauren stood up and talked about the major snowstorm that hit Fowler three weeks before Jeff died. Even though his back hurt, Jeff got dressed in his heavy winter coat and headed outside to run the snowblower. Julie decided to join him with a shovel. When Jeff wasn't looking, Julie winged a snowball at him. He gave her the finger—but with a smile—and then tossed a few snowballs her way. Soon, they were like two kids, tumbling in the snow together.

Neither of them knew it, but their three youngest daughters were watching them from the living-room window. "We could just see it so clearly," Lauren said at the memorial service. "Our mom and our dad were each other's best friends."

Julie knew how true this was. Whenever the girls tried to play one parent against the other, Jeff told them straight. "Never try to come between me and your mom," he'd say. "Mom was in the picture way before you were. And when you're grown up and have your own life, she'll be all I have."

In the days after Jeff died, Julie couldn't sleep. She'd exhaust herself and then fall into bed, hoping her eyes would close and she'd have a respite from her sadness.

One night, lying in bed, she remembered a note Jeff had written to her after his parents died. It was just a simple message that he left on her bedside table, so she'd find it when she got home from work. He wanted her to know how grateful he was for the support she'd given him while he was grieving the loss of his parents. "Julie, I love you so much," he wrote, "and I appreciate everything you do."

And so shortly after he'd died, Julie rummaged through her night-stand, hoping she still had that note. When she found it, she held it in her hands for a while. Then she dug a little deeper into the drawer and came upon another note Jeff had written.

It was a note he left for her one morning before a hunting trip. Julie had always wanted to kiss him before he left—she was superstitious like that—and was angry that he had taken off without saying good-bye or kissing her. His note was simple: "Julie, I'm sorry you were upset about the way I left. You know you're my best girl and I love you."

"I had forgotten about that note," Julie later told Shelley, "but it was overwhelming to read it. I really felt I was meant to come upon it after Jeff died. I felt like he was speaking to me, like it was his apology for dying and leaving me behind."

After Jeff died, Julie and each of the five kids met separately with a grief counselor. There were wounded feelings and unresolved issues. The kids were on edge and sad, fighting with Julie and one another. It felt as if the family was falling apart.

Julie's mother, Helen—who had helped raise the kids while Julie was at nursing school—has always been close with all five of them. After Jeff died, the kids often turned to her for the solace that their mother couldn't provide. Helen was saddened to see the kids arguing day after day. They were all hurting, and blaming one another for their pain. "Sometimes it feels like I want to disown all of them," one of the girls admitted to Helen.

They'd find ways to bring each other down. One daughter would come home smiling about a good grade on a test, and she'd be told by her sister, "Who cares? Dad's not here to see it." It took a while for the kids to realize that, though they didn't have their dad, they still had one another.

Because of HIPPA laws, the counselor couldn't tell Julie much about what each of her children was saying in therapy. But the counselor did say this: "Your husband was an amazing man. Each of the five kids, individually, has told me the same thing. Each believed they were their father's favorite child. Jeff must have had a way of dealing with his children that made them feel very special."

In one session with the grief therapist, Julie admitted that she was struggling with great feelings of guilt—about not somehow saving Jeff, and about going on with her life and leaving him behind. "Can I point something out?" the therapist said. "You took marriage vows when you married Jeff, didn't you? What were those vows?"

"I vowed to be there for him in sickness and in health," Julie said.

"And do you remember the line 'till death do us part'?" the counselor asked.

He reminded Julie that neither she nor Jeff could predict who would die first, but in their vows, they were allowing the surviving spouse to move on. "I'm sure Jeff wouldn't have wanted your life to be over," the counselor said. "He'd say you lived up to your commitment to him, to your vows, and you were a great wife. And now that death has parted you, it's your choice what to do next. You can sit around feeling sorry for yourself forever, and ruin your life. Or you can resist feeling guilty, and move on."

The counselor spoke of Julie's responsibility to her four daughters and to her son. He told her: "The best thing you can do for your kids is be happy again."

Julie had no intention of getting serious with another man, especially so soon after Jeff's death. But her brother introduced her to a friend of his named Dean, a divorced man with four children of his own. Dean was a process engineer at the same Cadillac plant where Jeff had worked, though they were only acquaintances.

"He's similar to Jeff in a lot of ways," Julie would tell people. "He's funny and warm, with a huge heart. And he's easy. It takes no effort being with him. I used to describe Jeff as 'a hell of a nice guy.' That's how I describe Dean."

Very quickly—too quickly for some in Julie's family—Julie and Dean announced they would be getting married. At Becker's Bridal, her friend Shelley understood. "I've always found that if a widowed young woman had a good marriage, she'll remarry fast," she said.

Before they announced their engagement, Julie says, she and Dean were naïve. "We wanted all our kids on board," says Julie. "We had this dream that all the kids would be accepting, that they'd help us pick out the ring. It was an unrealistic dream."

They got engaged on a Friday night in March 2010, and woke up the next morning to tell the kids. Julie's oldest and youngest daughters, Stefanie and Macy, were the only ones home. When Julie shared the news, it was as if a bomb had been detonated. Macy was especially livid. She told Dean and Julie she hated them. "How can you do this to us?" she said repeatedly. "We don't want another man in our house—in Dad's house!"

Julie kept responding, "You have to trust me. Have I ever steered you wrong?"

Julie and Dean headed to Julie's mother's house to tell her of the engagement, but Macy had already texted her grandmother and other siblings with the news. It was like an angry, high-tech message chain was moving around Fowler as fast as people could type.

Middle daughter Camie tried to be accepting. "Mom, I'm happy that you're happy," she said, "but I'll need some time to absorb this." The others took it harder. For weeks, Macy spoke about her anger toward Julie to anyone who would listen.

Finally, Julie's mother, Helen, had had enough. "You know, you're talking about my daughter, my flesh and blood," she said. "I've watched her go through hell for fourteen months. And now, with Dean, she's happy again. As a mother, seeing that her grieving daughter is happy again, well, it's like an answer to my prayers. And Macy, I want to tell you something: You need to be careful about how you're talking about my daughter."

Julie's kids were surprisingly moved by their grandmother's tough message—by how sharply she defended Julie. That was a turning point. "My kids saw that I wasn't just their mother," says Julie. "I was my mother's daughter."

Julie tried hard to process the ways in which her daughters' grief was different from hers. "None of us can replace Jeff," she'd tell Shelley. "But I am able to fall in love again, to start a new chapter. For the girls, it's different. They'll never get another dad."

Sometimes fitfully, sometimes with true grace, the family began trying to reconcile all of this. And so Julie found herself, at age forty-five, back in the Magic Room at Becker's Bridal, with her mother and two of her daughters beside her, and her other two daughters at home, not yet ready to celebrate this new engagement.

Unlike in 1986, the wedding dress didn't signify young love or an arrival into adulthood. This time it was a tangible reminder that Julie was starting over. It was as if putting on the dress spoke about where she'd been in her life. And it was about going forward, and what it will mean to be married again.

One night, Julie told Dean, "I will always love Jeff. That's never going to change. But I know I can love you, too."

"That's more than enough for me," Dean told her.

Chapter Twelve

A Daughter's View of Marriage

A few months after Shelley's daughter, Alyssa, signed on to work at Becker's full-time in 2009, she began having what she calls "the white blindness nightmare." Now it comes several nights a week. The nightmare usually begins the same way. She is stuck in a thicket of wedding dresses, pressing up against her, and from beyond the whiteness (or the off-whiteness), people are chattering all at once. Some are telling her, in great detail, about what kind of dress they want. Others are complaining about ill-fitting gowns. In the dreams, Becker's is hosting a trunk show and the store is jammed with women. Barriers are in places, but Alyssa can't hold back the customers.

"They're breaking down the barriers!" she calls out to Shelley.

"Try to stop them," her mother responds.

"I can't!" Alyssa says. "There's no way to hold them back!"

Shelley isn't surprised by her daughter's dreams. She's been having her own "white blindness" nightmares all her life. Her dreams became especially disconcerting once her three kids were born.

In Shelley's dreams, she's at the store, helping customers, and she needs to break away. She has to get to one of her son's sporting events, or to a parent-teacher conference for Alyssa, or somewhere where her kids need her, but the store is just jammed with brides and mothers.

In the dreams, Shelley always feels trapped, but she never tells a bride she has to go. She never even walks over to the store's front door to attempt a getaway. She just knows that there's no way she can leave, and so she stays—missing moment after moment of motherhood.

"What kind of train are you considering?" she'll say to a bride, and then as she listens to the answer, smiling, there's a sinking feeling in her gut and she's thinking, "I've got to get out of here. I'm late. I've got to go!"

Maybe Shelley is recalling her own childhood, waiting for her mother to come home from the store. Maybe it's her own guilty feelings about all that she missed as a mother while running Becker's. Whatever the cause, it is the dream that keeps presenting itself. And, in another form, it is a dream that has found its way into Alyssa's head too.

"You look gorgeous in this dress," Shelley says to a bride, knowing that she belongs a few hundred yards across town, with her kids. But it might as well be a million miles away.

⟋⟋⟍

Shelley's 1985 marriage to Gary began on some high notes. They were a young, attractive couple, and people talked of how gorgeous they looked together. Gary was tall and dark, with a Tom Selleck mustache, and some said Shelley was the cutest girl in Fowler. For both of them, there was a natural thrill in the process of starting their adult lives. Just the concept of living together and making plans for dinner or the weekend, as husband and wife, could be exciting, especially for Shelley who for so long defined herself in just two ways: as her siblings' babysitter and as a saleswoman at the store.

For a while after they married, Shelley and Gary lived together across the street from the bridal shop, in a small upstairs apartment in the building where the store's seamstresses worked. Each morning, Shelley walked thirty steps over to Becker's Bridal, where she logged sixty-hour weeks working for her parents. Gary worked outside of town on construction jobs, and later took care of maintenance at a strip mall.

Gary's mother and father were much older than Shelley's parents. His dad, a World War II veteran born in 1911, worked the assembly line at a General Motors plant for most of his life. When Gary was born in 1963, his dad was fifty-two, and his mom, a homemaker, was forty-four. They were stoic people who clung to their Depression-era values. Given his frugal upbringing, Gary was very taken with the Becker family. True, like his parents, the Beckers weren't effusive about their feelings. But unlike his parents, they were ambitious risk-takers, and Gary admired that. The Beckers were self-employed businesspeople who understood the financial peril that could result from filling their store with thousands of wedding dresses. They did it anyway. Gary understood his father's desire to earn a steady paycheck working on the assembly line. But his dad was satisfied living a smaller life, while Gary's in-laws were building a modest dynasty.

"The Beckers made money and spent money," Gary now recalls. "Christmastime was crazy. You'd walk out of my in-laws' house with carloads of presents."

Early on, Shelley didn't give a great deal of thought to the question of whether she and Gary were ready to start a family. It was just the natural progression for young couples in Fowler: marriage and then, in a blink, children. Yes, Shelley saw that Gary still liked to go out drinking with friends, often to excess; he hadn't fully settled into responsible adulthood. But his heart seemed to be in the right place, and he had an obvious affection for Shelley. She figured he'd outgrow his immaturity.

Just twenty years old, Shelley felt prepared to be a mother, especially given a lifetime of looking after her siblings. And though she'd hardly been out of Fowler in her life, all of her experience at Becker's led her to carry herself with a certain confidence. Motherhood didn't scare her. And so even though neither she nor Gary were earning much money, and even though Shelley wasn't quite sure how deep her feelings were for him, she was soon pregnant.

Their first child, Alyssa, arrived in 1986, a month overdue. "That baby does not want to be born!" relatives had been telling Shelley, who ended up having a C-section.

Because Alyssa was so late in coming, she didn't seem like a newborn. She looked four or five months old, and she was totally wide-eyed and alert.

In the years that followed, Alyssa turned out to be precocious on many fronts. She walked, talked, and began reading very early. In kindergarten, while other kids brought in their dolls and their cats for show-and-tell, Alyssa brought in articles she was reading in the newspaper. Her teacher was concerned that Alyssa gave off such an aura of maturity, and seemed more driven than other kids in Fowler. The teacher asked Shelley, then twenty-six, if she was pushing her daughter along too fast.

"I don't think it's anything I'm doing," Shelley told the teacher. And in truth, Shelley was so busy at the store that she didn't have time to push Alyssa along academically. Besides, Shelley had never been much of a student herself. It just seemed as if Alyssa was naturally intelligent, soaking up everything on her own.

Alyssa attended kindergarten in the morning, and because her parents were both at work, she spent afternoons at a babysitter's house, which she didn't like much. For one thing, the sitter served peanut-butter-and-jelly sandwiches every day. It got monotonous. But mostly, Alyssa just missed being with her mother. And so she convinced Shelley to let her come to Becker's in the afternoons.

Alyssa and her father, Gary

Little Alyssa tried to be of help at the store. She'd crawl around on the floor, picking up stray beads, or she'd tell customers that a saleswoman would be right with them. To pass the time, Alyssa would leaf through the wedding invitations featured on a desk near the front of the store. She decided that the Disney-themed invites would be the ones she'd use when she grew up and got married. At least when she was very young, Alyssa was idealistic. A bride was a princess. A groom was a prince. And so Disney ought to handle the invitations.

Alyssa wasn't sure what to make of the brides, their wedding plans, and especially the uncertain feelings stirring inside of her about how men and women interact. Each day was an education, or a chance to play-act.

Once a young boy came into the store—he must have been the younger brother of one of the brides—and Alyssa walked back and forth in front of him with a pencil and a pad of paper, trying to look like an official saleswoman. The boy hardly noticed her, and she wasn't even clear in her own mind about what she was trying to do with this awkward attempt at flirting.

Like Shelley did when she was young, Alyssa would hide out behind the dresses, or in the closet underneath the main stairwell, where the slips were stored. It was her own little cave. She could nap or listen to the muffled sounds of the brides out on the showroom floor. She felt secure there.

Alyssa's grandparents, Clark and Sharon, were still running the store then, and once a year, on a Sunday afternoon, they'd put on a bridal show in a local auditorium. Daughters, daughters-in-law, and young saleswomen got paid fifty dollars to walk down the runway as brides. The Becker granddaughters, including Alyssa, got to be flower girls and junior bridesmaids. Grandsons were ring-bearers. Most of those in attendance never realized just how many Beckers were working that runway. Clark and Sharon would celebrate after the show by taking everyone to dinner at a restaurant in Lansing.

Shelley was very involved in planning these shows, just as she was becoming central to operations at the store. But through it all, she was still her parents' employee, which was not always easy for her. She had ideas for how Becker's could be better managed and promoted. She thought the sales floor had to be seriously spruced up. After all, the 1990s had arrived, and to compete, Becker's needed to look more like a chic salon than a small-town dry-goods store. But Shelley sensed her parents' resistance, and mostly kept her ideas to herself.

Alyssa didn't have a full understanding of the pressures her mother was under, but she did see that Shelley had a lot on her mind. In part because her mother was so busy with work, Alyssa became something of an attention-seeker when she was young. Like daughters everywhere, she longed to be noticed, to get her mother to look in her direction. Sometimes, she found calculated ways to do this.

She liked to hide out in different places, without telling anyone, and she got a charge out of knowing that people were looking for her. She enjoyed listening to what they had to say about her as they searched; almost like Tom Sawyer at his own funeral. Maybe she needed to hear people she loved showing concern for her.

In the summer of 1991, for instance, during a family gathering at her grandparents' lakeside cottage, five-year-old Alyssa slipped away from her parents, aunts, uncles, and cousins. She folded herself into a tiny closet where beach towels were stored, and waited to see what would happen.

When Shelley realized her daughter wasn't around, she started calling for her. "Alyssa? Alyssa?" And soon enough, Alyssa could hear fifteen of her relatives scurrying all over the house, chattering about her. "When did you last see her? Where was she?"

"Alyssa? ALYSSA?"

"Did anyone see her going into the lake?"

Alyssa could feel her loved ones' trepidation, the growing panic. Had she run off and gotten lost? Had she drowned? And yet she sat in her hiding place, saying nothing.

Even at age five, she was intuitive enough to know that she had ratcheted up the stakes. If she simply stepped out of the closet and identified herself, she'd be reprimanded for not responding to those calling her name. And so she decided she'd stay there, and when and if the closet door was opened, she'd pretend to be fast asleep.

After fifteen minutes of searching, someone did open the door to the towel closet, and shouted, "She's here. She's sleeping!" Shelley came running up and gave Alyssa a hug. "Honey, I'm so glad we've found you. We were so worried."

Alyssa rubbed her eyes, a little actress playing the role of a child just waking up, and hugged her mother back. She was relieved that she wasn't getting in trouble. Though she felt a bit guilty receiving that hug from her relieved mother, she also felt happy in Shelley's arms, happy to be front and center for that moment in her mother's thoughts.

At the time, and in the months that followed, Shelley didn't think much about Alyssa's motivations for her disappearing acts. But now she understands. Maybe smart little Alyssa was noticing things weren't always going well in their household, that her father was drinking too much, that her parents' marriage wasn't what it should have been.

"When a child is hiding, part of her is yearning to be found," Shelley now says. "By hiding, it was as if she was saying, 'Find me, talk to me, give me attention, notice me. I'm here.' At the time, I didn't see any of that. I just didn't see it."

Alyssa holds tightly to her warmest memories of her father and mother from the years when she and her two younger brothers were kids. On Saturday evenings, after Becker's closed, Gary and Shelley would often hold "Movie Theater Night" at their house. They'd buy a few bags of candy and rent a G or PG movie on VHS at Fowler's mom-and-pop video store. The kids would earn tickets for candy and the show by doing chores all week long: washing the dishes after dinner, keeping their rooms clean. "Those movie nights were kind of an adventure," Alyssa now says, "like we were going somewhere else, away from Fowler."

On weeknights, Shelley was often at the store, and Alyssa liked spending time with her dad, just sitting on the couch, watching kid-friendly TV shows such as *The Wonder Years.* Gary identified with the show because Kevin, the Fred Savage character, was from his generation. Alyssa was drawn to fact that it was a family show, but the family was far from perfect. She also liked the running commentary delivered by the adult Kevin off-screen. "I like being inside somebody's head," she told her dad.

They watched reruns of *Leave It to Beaver* and *Happy Days,* and one year Gary helped Alyssa put together a Fonzie costume for Halloween. Even if her dad was drinking, at least in those early years there was a softness about him, a fatherly concern and love that made it through the haze of alcohol.

When Alyssa was in first grade, she decided she wanted to lip-sync the Jerry Lee Lewis hit "Great Balls of Fire" with her friends at her school's talent show. After work one night, Gary surprised her by coming home with a cassette tape of the song. There was no record store near Fowler, and even down in Lansing, he had trouble finding the song. But he'd gone out of his way and tracked it down, and Alyssa loved him for that.

She practiced the song with her friends each day at recess, but before the auditions, the other girls chickened out, and Alyssa went by herself. Then she got scared too, and never performed in the show.

And yet Alyssa retains this warm memory of her father walking through the front door with that cassette tape, a wide smile on his face, eager to help her become a lip-sync star. It's funny, she thinks now, how little moments can come to define acts of love.

Gary worried about how hard Shelley was working. He saw the stress on her face, saw how that stress affected their relationship. "You're a slave to the store," he'd say. She'd shrug. That was her life.

Each night when Shelley came home, Gary needed to feel her out. Had it been a good or bad day? Was she overwhelmed by a nitpicking bride's mother, or was there a moment during the day that lifted her spirits, a bride whose story touched her?

Gary knew that Shelley was considering the possibility of someday taking over the store, and he knew she faced challenges working for her parents. Sometimes she'd confide in him about her dreams for the place, and for her life, and even for their lives together. Sometimes she'd shut down.

Alyssa, as a child, observed and absorbed the stresses in her mother's life. She knew it wasn't always easy for Shelley to work with her parents. She knew Shelley felt guilty when she wasn't at home. She never thought: "My mother loves her job." She thought: "Wow, my mother is working hard and it's not easy. I worry about her."

Shelley felt guilty about all the hours she was at the store, and so she sometimes overcompensated by taking on even more responsibilities on the home front. Alyssa's Girl Scouts troop needed a troop leader, and though there were plenty of girls whose mothers didn't work outside of the home, it was Shelley who stepped up to the task, serving for ten years. When the woman in charge of the entire territory of Girl Scouts troops resigned, Shelley took on that job too. It was partially the working mother's guilt, but she also relished the chance to escape from the store.

Alyssa's favorite Girl Scouts activity was Trade Day. The girls would bring items from home to trade with each other: candy, fruit, toys. Alyssa was the star trader on two fronts. First, she felt like she had a clear business

Alyssa and Shelley at a Girl Scouts outing

sense, just from hanging out at the store. On top of that, she also had the best stuff to trade, because her mother would let her take home pieces of inexpensive jewelry from Becker's that no one was buying.

Sometimes, Shelley would bring the troop down to Becker's for a tour or to try on veils and to look in the old mirror. "I wonder who I'll marry," she'd hear them saying as they looked in the old mirror. Alyssa, a store veteran, would show the girls all around, including a tour of her secret hiding place under the staircase.

For years, Shelley also hosted third- and fourth-grade classes at the store. Fowler was such a small town that the students could walk over, single file, from the local elementary school. Shelley talked to them about how the business was run, how the brides went about choosing dresses. Some brides enjoyed a pack of kids watching them conduct their dress searches. Others were a bit peeved that their big moment was being spoiled by curious third-graders.

Shelley hoped that she was inspiring all the girls who came through to notice that women could run businesses. But beyond that, she also hoped she was teaching them about growing up and falling in love, about finding a man and what a wedding dress represents—about starting a life. Offering rosy views of romance to wide-eyed third-grade field-trippers seemed like a simplistic no-brainer. Young girls needed the vision of happily ever after, didn't they?

It's ironic, really, that Shelley was selling the concept of love down at the store when there was so much uncertainty at home. And truth was, those years were overwhelming for Shelley on a lot of fronts. She was working hard at Becker's. She had an alcoholic husband, and there was a growing distance between them. And every moment she was not at work, she was committed to being there for her kids. It was like she was on a merry-go-round that wouldn't stop.

Alyssa saw this, day after day. She felt it. Her heart went out to her mother. And as she got to know her mother's caretaker soul, her selfless streak, she wanted to emulate it and celebrate it. Eventually, Alyssa found an outlet to showcase Shelley's unsung attributes. In sixth grade, she showed off her blossoming writing skills by winning a countywide essay contest on the subject "I Love My Mom Because . . ."

"I love my mom because she is like a lost-and-found box," Alyssa wrote. "When you lose your mittens, she brings them back. If you can't find your teddy bear, she can convince him to come home with a smile on his face, like the one my mom always has. If you lose your balance, she picks you up and gives you a hug. When you lose hope in yourself, a talk with her will make you feel like you can touch the sky. If you lose your friend, she will give you the strength to get her back.

"Unlike other lost-and-found boxes, my mother has love and a whole box full of it. She would never leave you in the dark without a flashlight. She would never forget to give you her heart of love."

All along, it wasn't just Shelley noticing that Gary had alcohol issues. Alyssa saw it too. She saw the tension between her parents. She saw that the more her father drank, the more her mother pulled away. Not infrequently, Shelley would get home from the store and Gary would be asleep on the couch, or passed out from drinking. She would wake him and berate him. She would nag. He'd be resentful. Or he'd promise to clean himself up, but he couldn't do it. Shelley sometimes wondered if he felt inadequate, having a strong working woman for a wife.

Most of all, Shelley worried about the children's safety. What if Alyssa or her brothers hurt themselves while Gary was watching them? Would he be sober enough to help them? What if he had to drive them to school or a friend's house? Would he be too drunk to get them there safely?

An incident would sometimes happen at home, while Shelley was at the store, and she'd never get wind of it. There were times when Gary got sick from drinking, and Alyssa would clean up after him. She was fastidious, making sure her mother wouldn't notice anything amiss. Like her mother before her, Alyssa was a caretaker, only she was looking after not just her two younger brothers, but at certain times her father, too.

Alyssa's heart went out to her father. As young as she was, she recognized that an alcoholic isn't really his true self when he's drinking. She longed for him to be sober, but loved him and tried to forgive him when he wasn't.

One evening, when Alyssa was in Girl Scouts, she attended a father-daughter dance with her dad, and entered the "cakewalk." Numbers were placed on the ground, music was played, and if a girl stopped on the right number, she'd receive a cake. Alyssa ended up winning a beautiful cake, and was very proud of herself. She was just beaming.

Gary had been drinking that night, however, and as they walked out of the dance, with him holding the cake, he dropped it, took a look at how it had plopped on the ground, and started laughing. Given his drunkenness, something about the way the cake fell seemed completely amusing to him. But he wasn't so drunk that he didn't see the look in Alyssa's eyes. "She was heartbroken," he now says.

He has apologized to her repeatedly in the years since. He has bought her several cakes. "There are dumb things I did," he says, "and when I think about them, I cringe. I know alcoholism is considered a disease, but that doesn't lessen my responsibilities. The look on Alyssa's face that day I dropped the cake, I won't ever forget that."

⌒

Her parents' strained relationship made things confusing when Alyssa went to Becker's to hang out with her mom and grandmother. It was hard for her to reconcile the images of smiling brides, heading into marriage, with her understanding of the marriage she observed in her own house. "To me, a marriage was a mom, a dad, and kids," she now says. "Marriage was a family. I didn't see it as a special love between two people. I have no memories of my parents in love, so I didn't know what love looked like."

Once, when Alyssa was eight, Shelley and Gary had been fighting, and afterward, Alyssa followed her mother into her bedroom and asked, "Did you ever love Dad?"

Shelley didn't fully answer. She acknowledged the struggles caused by Gary's drinking, and said she hoped he would get himself help. She reminded Alyssa that he was a good man in a lot of ways. But she couldn't bring herself to say that she had ever loved him. "My parents might have tried to teach me about love when I was young," Alyssa says. "But it wasn't by showing me the love between them."

By the time Alyssa was eleven, Shelley was sleeping with her on many nights. Shelley couldn't bring herself to share a bed with Gary. And yet each day, she'd dress herself up, head down to Becker's, and sell the idea of love to brides and their parents.

For his part, Gary knew that his drinking was creating a distance between him and Shelley that was becoming too wide to breach. "You're going to have to slow down or she's going to leave you," Shelley's brother told him one day.

"I know that," Gary responded. "I know I'm losing her."

Several times, Gary found the strength to quit, and he'd remain sober for a few months at a time. He always relapsed. As he sees it now: "Alcoholism is a disease that tells you that you don't have a disease."

He had been drinking a great deal of beer, hiding the bottles, and as he got older, he turned to hard liquor. He ended up in rehab five times, and several stays were required by law because of drunk-driving convictions. At one point, he spent sixty days in jail.

There were times when Shelley found herself trying to talk Gary out of suicide. She didn't think he'd actually do it. But she eventually stopped coddling him and got tough. "Who the hell do you think you are?" she said at one point. "If you want to knock yourself out of this world, that's one thing. But you're leaving behind three kids who love you. And that's just a selfish thing to do."

In 1999, when Alyssa was thirteen years old, Shelley told Gary she wanted a divorce, and they separated.

By that point, she felt she had no choice. Gary's alcoholism was a threat to the kids' safety. She had to take action. She tried to reason with Gary. "If there isn't an openly expressed love in the house, how unhealthy is that for the kids?" she asked.

Gary couldn't argue with her. He was upset, but he knew he couldn't blame her. "For a long time," he now says, "she was a caregiver and I was a care *taker*. At first she was very willing to help. But by the end, she was just disgusted. She was only looking out for the welfare of the kids. If I was watching the kids and drinking, would I be able to take care of them?" They both knew the answer to that question.

For the four years that followed, a good part of Alyssa resented Shelley for breaking up the family. She kept a journal, but couldn't always bring herself to write about her parents. But she wrote observations about Becker's Bridal, about what it took for her grandmother and her mother to run the place. When she was fifteen she wrote, "I suppose one day I'll be the one running the store. I'll be the boss. And when that happens, I'm going to have to be a bitch."

Shelley understood her children's sense of loss that Gary was out of the house. And so she always invited him over for holidays, always made sure he knew about the kids' school activities. He'd be there Christmas morning when presents were opened, and remained a constant presence in their lives. That wasn't enough for Alyssa, who felt her mother had taken her father away from her.

But Gary now looks back at the divorce with appreciation. The divorce likely saved him from dying in a car accident, or from cirrhosis of the liver. "Shelley gave me the tough love I needed," he says. "She helped me hit rock bottom, which started the whole process toward recovery. She did what she had to do.

"There's a good chance that I wouldn't have quit if she didn't leave me, that I'd have drunk myself to death. She helped save my life."

Shortly after Shelley told Gary she was leaving him, he was in court-ordered rehab and, as part of his therapy, wrote letters to Shelley and their kids. "I've never really told anyone my feelings," he wrote to Alyssa. "That's how I was brought up. I'm learning to express how I feel, and to tell you the truth, it's very hard." He wrote of his sorrow because he missed a school parade that Alyssa was in, "Everyone said how beautiful you looked and I thought to myself, 'She looks like that every day.'"

Gary missed Alyssa when she was on her school's homecoming court, but wrote her to say he heard she'd looked beautiful.

He wrote that he was praying for her to understand how his life had ended up in that rehab center. "The best I can do is to change myself for the better. I've been looking for a place like this ever since I admitted to myself that I am an alcoholic . . . This place has taught me that I am human and I'm allowed to make mistakes. I thank God for giving me another chance so I may correct my mistakes and the harm I inflicted on everyone.

"Alyssa, I can't explain how very proud I am to have you as my daughter. I just hope you know it. I miss you with an unconditional love forever."

He knew that Alyssa was angry with her mother about the divorce, and he knew Shelley had done what she needed to do. He ended his letter: "Give mom a hug for me. Tell her you love her on Christmas. Just do it, Alyssa. Thanks!"

As Gary worked to find his way to sobriety, as months and then years passed, he discovered something about love. "If you really love somebody, if it's really true love," he told Alyssa, "then sometimes you have to let it go. I knew your mother couldn't be happy with me, not the way I was. I knew that. And so I had to love her enough to want her to be happy without me. I say this without resentment, without any grudges. I still love her, and I want her to be happy without me. That's what I wish for her."

After a childhood of not really seeing or understanding the bonds between her mother and her father, Alyssa finally had a sense of things. Her father was describing a kind of love most of the brides at Becker's couldn't yet fathom.

Chapter Thirteen

Ashley

*H*ere on her first visit to Becker's, Ashley Brandenburg feels both at home and out of place. She grew up in rural Laingsburg, Michigan, a half hour southeast of Fowler, and her mother and most of her aunts were Becker's brides. When she was a girl, she had pulled herself into her mother's tiny, long-sleeved lacy dress, wondering when her time would come. And so being here at Becker's, picking out her dress, is the continuation of a family tradition.

And yet, Ashley also feels unlike everyone else in the store today, almost as if she's visiting a culture to which she no longer belongs. Now a PhD candidate in French literature at Cornell University, she is likely the only bride here who speaks four languages (English, French, Italian, and Spanish) and the only woman marrying a fellow Ivy Leaguer also studying for his doctorate. At twenty-seven, she also appears to be the oldest bride-to-be here today.

Some of the other brides are still in their late teens. "They're like babies!" she thinks. "How much of life could they have experienced? Why rush into marriage? Shouldn't they wait and explore the world at least a little bit?"

She keeps her thoughts to herself, though, as her mom and aunt help her narrow down her dress choices. She doesn't want to come off as an elitist—a highbrow academic looking down at the naïve, small-town girls she left behind. And who knows? Maybe these other brides' lives—even if they never leave Michigan—will be as fulfilling as the life Ashley and her fiancé are planning for themselves.

Ashley doesn't realize that the saleswoman helping a bride on the other side of the store—the owner's daughter, Alyssa—empathizes with her conflicted feelings. When Alyssa sees customers such as Ashley, former local girls who've moved away to find big jobs or get advanced degrees, she finds herself thinking about the days she studied fashion in Paris and New York. "I miss that part of my life," she later explains, "and I'm torn about it." After discovering just the basics of Ashley's story, she's a bit envious. "A major struggle in my life is asking myself questions: Is this what I'm supposed to be doing with my life, working at Becker's here in Fowler, focused on the idea of getting married one of these days and having children? Or am I supposed to be doing something else, somewhere else, something bigger, in some big city?"

Ashley is cognizant, of course, of her own observations and feelings as she shops alongside other brides at Becker's. But she doesn't know how the brides and their attending saleswomen are taking note of her—how she carries herself and the small talk she makes with her mom. Is she coming off as some academic outsider, or does she seem like she's just another local small-town bride?

"This looks a little like the dress you wore to your own wedding," Ashley says to her mother, Sue, as she holds up the gown she will eventually wear into the Magic Room. "It's sort of the same overlay of lace."

Sue tells a saleswoman that she got her dress in 1971 at Becker's, when the dressing rooms were separated by curtains. "I still have it," she says. "It was a sample dress, and was very tight on me. I realized I'd have to really go on a diet before the wedding to fit into it."

Ashley knows well the story of how her mother ended up being able to fit into that dress. But neither she nor her mom offers details about that here in the store. Instead, they head up the stairs to the Magic Room, past all the young brides, to see what Ashley looks like in the dress that echoes that too-tight gown from 1971.

~~~

Ashley's mom was twenty-two years old when she came to Becker's. And Sue turned out to be one of those brides who saw firsthand how tenuous the hold can be on happy bridal moments, given the randomness of life.

In early June 1971, a few weeks after Sue bought her bridal gown, her sister was driving her to the post office to mail out her wedding invitations, and they came to a rise in the road. In a car coming the other way, a dog had just vomited in the backseat, and the driver had turned to comfort the sick animal. In that instant, the driver veered into the oncoming lane of traffic and slammed into the car driven by Sue's sister.

Unlike her sister, Sue wasn't wearing her seat belt, and her head slammed through the windshield. She blacked out and woke up to see the whole scene in a yellow hue, since her eyes were so full of blood. Her face required 1,000 stitches and extensive plastic surgery. Though her jaw wasn't broken, the stitches were so tight on her face that she could barely open her mouth. For three weeks, unable to eat any solid foods, she subsisted on milk, milkshakes, and soup run through a blender and consumed through a straw.

"I won't look at myself," she told her family in the early days of her recovery. "I just can't do it." When she finally found the courage to hold up a mirror, fifteen days after the accident, she cried. "Two black eyes and a face stitched like a baseball" was how she described herself. Her wedding was two weeks away.

There are moments of that experience that would become meaningful memories for Sue, and that served as inspiration to Ashley growing up.

At the time of the accident, Sue's future husband, Rick, hadn't yet given her an engagement ring. He brought it to the hospital and presented it to her there, telling her he loved her before the 1,000 stitches and he loved her just as much afterward.

"If I can look somewhat normal, I'll go through with the wedding," she said. Ten days before the big day, her stitches were removed. By then, given how little she could eat through those straws, she'd lost fifteen pounds. And so she fit perfectly into that once-tight dress from Becker's. "I knew you'd get into that dress somehow," her mother joked.

Wearing a great deal of pancake makeup, Sue made it down the aisle smiling. "I always thought she looked great in her wedding photos, despite the makeup," Ashley says. "She was just beautiful, in this early seventies way, with her long, platinum blond hair."

Sue recovered well from the accident, but it helped make her

a woman who would one day want her two children to experience everything—literature, art, music, travel— because they'd never know what might await them over thenext rise in the road.

Ashley's parents, Sue and Rick, on their wedding day in 1971

At first, Sue and Rick weren't sure they wanted to have children, and they waited seven years before they did. She was a social worker, and he was a rising professor in the School of Packaging at Michigan State. Over time, he became an expert in "shock and vibration" issues concerning packages that are shipped by air, rail, or truck.

Their son J.P. was born in 1979 and Ashley arrived in 1983.

Like many children of a professor, they grew up in a house that celebrated the cerebral. Ashley, especially, embraced every opportunity to think. "You'd be great at doing scholarly things," her father told her. "You have that in you."

Ashley always described him to people as "an all-around science guy" whose scholarship and education covered several disciplines. He even taught about astrophysics and astronomy. She'd brag to people about his work on rocket engines, and liked when he spoke exuberantly about subjects he'd researched, such as the basic physics of packaging. He had written a textbook on vibration issues that was widely used by those in the field. When a package is dropped, the contents undergo a rapid deceleration. Appropriate packaging can control the deceleration and protect what's inside.

Her dad offered fascinating explanations of how vibration, especially by rail, can destroy products. The circuit boards in early computers were often damaged by the time they got to their destinations. Packaging was eventually developed to limit vibrations before they reached inside the computers. Few people have any sense that advances in box-making helped fuel the computer revolution.

Rick was able to offer Ashley other real-life examples to contemplate. "Let me tell you about ketchup," he'd say, and then he did. Over the years, a lot of ketchup would be shipped by rail in large containers. But by the time the ketchup containers got to their destination, vibrating rail cars had turned them into vats of unpleasant liquid, with a yellow sap on top and a tomato stew on the bottom. By limiting vibrations, package engineers were heroes of the fast-food revolution. "Think of that," her dad would say, "when you put ketchup on your french fries."

Ashley admired her father's academic life, and early on, thought she might want the same for herself. She's an example of how daughters today, when compared to women who came of age in previous generations, are far more likely to work in the same fields as their fathers, according to a North Carolina State University study. That's partially because of the increase of women in the workforce and partially because fathers and daughters are closer today than in the past.

Ashley was a focused, hard-charging student, which made her stand out in a small town like Laingsburg, where many students were the children of farmers or blue-collar workers. Because her mother wanted her children to embrace every moment and every opportunity to learn, Ashley took lessons in piano, violin, trumpet, and trombone. She studied dance for twelve years. Her mother enrolled her each summer in academic programs and art classes. And Ashley was constantly reading books.

Other kids called her a "brainiac," and she had a tough time socially during middle school. "I was tall, eccentric, with braces—twice—and I embraced my inner nerd too much," is how she explains it now, "and so I got picked on by ignorant kids." She and her best friend at the time both wore big glasses and strange clothes. They couldn't resist telling kids when they got a wrong answer. Ashley even found herself correcting her teachers.

One day when Ashley was in middle school, the principal called Sue. "Ashley is in my office, and she's in tears. You need to come get her."

"What happened?" Sue asked, but the principal gave few details.

"She's OK," he said. "Just come pick her up and I'll explain."

What happened, it turned out, was the collapse of the Soviet Union.

It was 1997, and Ashley's teacher had told the class that "Russia is a communist country." By then, of course, given the Soviet breakup, that was no longer the case. Ashley argued it. The teacher insisted. Ashley burst into tears. The teacher remained insistent. Her mother came and continued the discussion, helping the teacher improve his understanding of the issue.

Throughout her school years, Ashley couldn't help but assert herself. She was an unabashed academic show-off, winning sixth-grade student of the year and turning in the fanciest science and social studies projects. She was in a program for gifted students and spent a year putting together a presentation about physicians. "You ought to be a pediatrician," her mother said. Later, given her ability to argue a case, her mother thought she'd make a great lawyer. But Ashley waved her off. She was good at a lot of things. And she wasn't afraid to articulate her confidence. "In high school," she says, "I was the only person raising my hand and saying anything worthwhile. In college, there were a lot of people with a lot to say, and I loved that. Part of me just needed to get out of Laingsburg."

After he made his name in packaging dynamics, Ashley's dad went on to even greater acclaim as associate dean of Michigan State's School of Agriculture and Natural Resources. But as busy as he was on campus, he remained very involved in the kids' lives, as did Sue. They were willing to do whatever it took to help Ashley succeed and stand out. One year they helped her mold this incredible diorama of Ellis Island for a school project. "The other kids' dioramas were just a bunch of sticks," she came home and told them. Another year, for a project on ancient Egypt, her dad used his fanciest engineering rulers to help her build an ultra-precise, exactly-to-scale model of a pyramid.

Ashley knew she was different from her classmates, and that her mom and dad were likely the most academically focused parents in their small conservative town. But she didn't always think of the socioeconomic issues at play. Her family was able to go on trips across the United States every summer. They found their way to Maine, Alabama, Alaska, and Colorado, usually to visit land-grant universities where her dad met with other academic deans. They once did a stint in France so her father could collaborate with educators at a French university. Many of her classmates, meanwhile, spent summers working the family farms and had never been out of the state of Michigan. Their parents didn't have the time or the inclination to build showy dioramas that far exceeded the teachers' expectations.

Ashley's parents weren't the most tactile in town when it came to showing her affection. They were quiet about their emotions and didn't say "I love you" much. But as Ashley saw it, they showed their love by the way they encouraged her academic pursuits, and by giving her every opportunity they could.

In high school, Ashley took French for two years—not from a live teacher, but from a video feed, which is all her school could afford. The school offered no upper-level French courses, so she enrolled in a Michigan State program for high-achieving high-schoolers. There, she took college-level French, driving twenty-eight miles each day round-trip from Laingsburg.

At the end of her high school career, she graduated first out of a class of eighty-four students. She didn't consider it an especially great accomplishment. She said it wasn't hard to get all A's at her high school. "To do any less would have been to do nothing," she says.

She spent her undergraduate years at the honors college at Michigan State—as the daughter of a professor, tuition was half price—and graduated early, in December 2004. She ended up spending a year in France, teaching English, before beginning a five-year French literature program at Cornell. Her dream was to teach French literature at the college level.

Around this time, her mother, Sue, had been diagnosed with Parkinson's, a degenerative disease that can be caused by a blow to the head. Though her doctors couldn't say for sure, the onset of her illness could have been related to her crash through the windshield in that 1971 car accident before her wedding.

For Ashley, this was yet another reminder of her father's sense of science: He often spoke of the repercussions of one unanticipated act.

In those early years, her mother had very few physical symptoms, but emotionally, she took the news very hard. She was diagnosed with depression and anxiety issues, which led to hospitalization for a nervous breakdown. She helped herself recover by re-embracing the message driven home by her 1971 accident; that life is tenuous, and you need to appreciate every moment of it. Sue didn't know when and how Parkinson's would take pieces of her life away from her. While she was able, she promised Ashley she'd savor all she could.

During college, Ashley had met a man from France who was two years older and had come to Michigan State for a master's in marketing. Manu was charming and handsome, with an accent that made him sound like the quintessential romantic Frenchman. Ashley, so often a serious young woman, and not especially sentimental, found herself very drawn to him—or perhaps the idea of him. He was certainly more exotic than any boy or man she'd come across in Laingsburg.

When she graduated from college, the school's Department of French Classics and Italian awarded Ashley a $4,000 scholarship and told her she could use the money for any pursuit she'd like. She decided to visit France for two months—Manu had already returned there—and so her relationship with him deepened. The next year, 2005, she got that job as an elementary school English teacher in Challans, France, a rural community near Nantes.

In some ways, this was the adventure Ashley had always dreamed about during her childhood in Laingsburg. But it was more difficult than she expected. For one thing, especially given her mother's health issues, it was hard for her to be away from home.

Manu lived in Paris, four hours away, and she saw him every weekend. She felt very lonely in Challans—the town was isolated, her mother was far away, and she was the only American working at the school—and so her time with Manu felt like a lifeline for her. At least at first.

In his own way, he was supportive and engaging, but Ashley began to notice something. "I realized I was still lonely when I was with him," she says.

Manu just wasn't as mature as Ashley, and he was very much a mama's boy. In European countries, that's not uncommon. Young people rely on their parents longer, and live at home far longer than Americans do. In Italy, for instance, the percentage of men ages thirty to thirty-four living with their parents now tops 36 percent, up from 14 percent in 1990. (For women in that age group, 18 percent live at home.) High unemployment and rising living costs are a factor. But the declining marriage rate may be the biggest cause. Adult children in Europe don't usually leave home unless they're married, and fewer and fewer feel any rush to marry. The number of marriages in Italy has fallen from 500,000 a year in the early 1970s to about 260,000 today. Meanwhile, the average Frenchman today doesn't marry until age thirty-one, a jump from an average age of twenty-three in 1980.

There's almost no stigma in Europe for a man living with his mother well into adulthood. In fact, when surveyed, more than half of Europeans approve of the idea. A guy can live with mom and date the field. Many see that as the good life.

By contrast, the percentage of Americans ages thirty to thirty-four living with parents is now 5 percent for women and 9 percent for men. More than their European contemporaries, young adults in the United States are more apt to move away for college, to move in together with friends before marriage, to cohabitate with lovers—and to wonder about why an adult man would want to still be living with his mother.

Given all of these differences, Ashley struggled with culture shock. She prided herself on being from the Midwest, where people tend to be more self-reliant and self-determined. And here was Manu telling her that if they ever got married, he'd never join her in Michigan for Christmas because he needed to spend every Christmas with his mother. She had to have her appendix out while she was in France, and Manu was not as attentive as she would have liked, which was a signal to her about how attentive he was likely to be as a husband. The two words in her head: "not very."

Also, monogamy is not as important in France as it is in the United States. "If you're not used to that," Ashley says, "it can be shocking." Manu's mother never divorced her husband and had a very open relationship with another man who was also married. Ashley had a difficult time with that. "Maybe she considered herself a feminist, but to me she was an adulterer," Ashley says.

Manu saw no problem with his mother's choices, and that naturally gave Ashley pause. If she married him, how would he view his vows to her up the road? She knew his culture. She knew his mind-set about his mother. Deep down, she knew the sort of husband he'd end up being.

Ashley and Manu remained together after she enrolled in the PhD program at Cornell. They visited each other and talked of marriage, but Ashley recognized that part of the reason he wanted to marry her was because it would be more convenient for them; he could live in the United States without restrictions. "I don't want to get married just because it will simplify things," she told her mother.

So much about the relationship began to feel forced to her. "The truth was, we just weren't that compatible," she now says. "I wanted him to be someone he really wasn't—someone who would put me first. And he wanted me to be someone different from who I was. Maybe he needed somebody more independent. I was more in love with the fact that he was a French person than I was in love with him. It took me a while to realize that."

When she told Manu she wanted to break up, he thought she was giving up too easily. He talked of their chemistry, the future they could have in both countries. But she knew. The relationship was taking way too much energy. And so she came to a conclusion. "I realized I didn't want him in my life at all. We needed to break things off completely."

She was alone again, and she was comfortable with that. But eventually, she made a decision. At Cornell, students tend to hang out with others in their immediate fields, and so there's not a great deal of socializing between disciplines. Her fellow students in the foreign language PhD programs were all gay or taken, and she just wasn't meeting anyone else.

She thought about her parents, who had met on a blind date. Her brother, who went on to become a geophysicist, met his wife via an Internet dating service. She figured online dating is the twenty-first century version of blind-dating. And so she signed up for a one-month subscription to eHarmony.com.

That's how she met Drew, a curly haired, bearded graduate student in materials engineering at Cornell, who grew up in the academic community of Princeton, New Jersey. He was science-minded and practical, like her father, and that attracted her to him. He was serious about his studies, like Ashley was. He came from a family that valued education; his father was a dentist and his mom worked in higher education. "I've always been attracted to intelligent women," he told her early on, which of course appealed to her too.

To Ashley, Drew was awfully cute. "You have such a beautiful face and smile," she told him early on. Her mother later told Drew that he looked just like a cherub. Ashley was embarrassed by that observation, but Drew decided to take it as a compliment.

Ashley was born Catholic but raised without much religion—her scientist father is an atheist—so the fact that Drew was Jewish was not a deal-breaker for her. He said he wanted his children raised Jewish; Ashley thought about this possibility, and decided she'd be OK with that.

Drew was more romantic than Ashley, sending her flowers on the monthly anniversaries of their first date. Not fully shaking her inner nerd, Ashley found the flowers annoying after a while. "There's only one anniversary," she told him, "and that's a wedding anniversary."

She fell for him gradually. "I don't believe in love at first sight," she said. "I'm too pragmatic." But eventually, she just knew.

Ashley and Drew

When Drew decided to propose to her in October 2009, he plotted to make it very special. "I want to take her out to dinner, and then to a place that has some meaning," Drew told his friends. He decided they'd go to the site of their first kiss, at Cascadilla Gorge near the Cornell campus. It's a gorgeous spot with breathtaking waterfalls.

By the time they got there, however, it was after sunset, a drug deal was taking place, and the part of the park where they first kissed was closed. He and Ashley stopped far short of their special spot, but she already knew what was about to happen.

Drew began to get down on one knee, and Ashley stopped him. "Oh no, don't do that, not here," she said. There were a few people around, and she'd always been averse to public displays of affection. She appreciated his chivalry, but she also thought this was silly and a bit embarrassing. "Come on, Drew, get up!"

For Drew, this was problematic. As he later told the story: "I was half-way down—stuck in this funny position, with one leg forward and bent, but my knee not yet fully down. And because she told me to stop, that's where I was when I handed her the ring and asked her to marry me—not yet down on one knee, not yet fully standing. It was awkward."

"Of course I'll marry you," Ashley had told him. "Now stand up, OK?"

They hugged and kissed, but there were no tears.

It was a few weeks later that Ashley's mom told her she looked forward to visiting Becker's with her. "It's a store that has a special place in a lot of people's hearts," Sue said.

Since she was a little girl, Ashley was always determined to be more cosmopolitan. But as her mother spoke about Becker's, Ashley didn't think of saying that she'd rather find a gown in Paris or even New York. She realized that she was very pleased to honor her mother's roots.

Her road to marriage had taken her from small-town Michigan all the way through France, to the edge of a gorge in Ithaca, New York, and now back to Michigan, where the Magic Room awaited her.

Chapter Fourteen

Danielle

anielle DeVoe has returned to Becker's for a second fitting, and Shelley remembers the twenty-five-year-old social worker because she was pretty and vivacious, but also because she was there without her mother. When a bride doesn't make at least one visit with her mom, it always means there's a story—whether there was an argument the morning of the dress search or a long-term estrangement . . . or something. Some mothers live far away but still make it in to look at the dress at least once. Or the brides are taking a lot of photos, so they can e-mail them to their out-of-town moms for feedback.

In Danielle's case, she has again brought her grandmother, Cynda.

The relationship between Danielle and her grandmother has come to resemble a mother-daughter relationship, with the deepest loving feelings intermixed with all the attendant demands and annoyances.

Though Cynda and Danielle are in agreement about the wedding gown, which Cynda is buying, there are other nagging issues—with "nagging" being the operative word.

Danielle would like her four bridesmaids to wear long satin dresses and pearls. "I'm a huge fan of Jackie Kennedy," she says. "If it was up to me, I'd wear pearls and sunglasses every day." Cynda wants the brides-maids to wear diamonds.

And Danielle and her grandmother have been at odds over the wedding cake. Cynda has been arguing that a special wedding needs a special cake, and she's willing to pay $700 of her own money for a three-tiered showpiece. Danielle appreciates her grandmother's generosity—the wedding dress alone is costing Cynda $1,000—but Danielle thinks it's frivolous to overspend on a cake. She's perfectly happy buying a less-extravagant cake for $180. And since she's the bride, shouldn't her opinions win out?

Why is Cynda pushing for this cake? In the days before arriving at Becker's, Danielle had been talking through this question with her fiancé, Brian. "My grandmother is nitpicking," Danielle said. "She wishes my mom could help with the wedding, and so she ends up focusing on the little things. That's the way it has always been between me and her. Always. We nitpick on the stupid stuff instead of dealing with the main issue."

In the Magic Room, however, any differences melt away, at least for the moment. It's always this way between brides and their loved ones. That's part of the magic of the space. It's a bit of an echo chamber, so people find themselves lowering their voices. But more than that, when a bride steps onto that pedestal, she loses the inclination to argue, or to dwell on past differences. And those who love her, well, they just love her more.

Shelley arrives in the Magic Room with her usual smile and gets down on her knees, working on Danielle's hem. The off-white satin dress is strap-less with a crystal bodice, and Danielle looks breathtaking in it. Cynda leans against the mirror in the corner, holding back a swell of complex emotions, including, again, her memories of that home-from-the-hospital dress she bought Danielle twenty-five years earlier.

"I really love this wedding dress," Danielle says, "Thanks again, Grandma, for buying it."

"I love you," Cynda tells her.

The Magic Room

Cynda gives Danielle a lot of credit. Her granddaughter has turned into a poised young woman, overcoming the toughest of circumstances. Cynda often thinks back to how close Danielle was to her mother, Kris, and how they buoyed and entertained each other. Cynda marvels at her daughter, Kris, too: Kris and her husband had met as teens, and their relationship was marked by both great passion and a troubling volatility. Kris was pregnant at her small, subdued wedding in 1985, and she was just nineteen when Danielle was born. Given that Danielle's father, an iron-worker, turned out to be regularly irresponsible and absent, with substance-abuse issues, Kris had no choice but to find the courage to divorce him after two years, and to raise Danielle by herself.

After Kris got a degree in early childhood education, it was Cynda who gave her the seed money to open her preschool, and Kris turned her mother's monetary investment into an investment in children's lives. It was lovely to see.

This was the perfect occupation for Kris. When she was young, she had been crazy about dolls long after her friends outgrew them. Even when she was ten years old, she still kept a baby crib in her bedroom and took turns giving her two dozen dolls a chance to sleep in it. "I'm going to have eleven or twelve children when I grow up," she'd tell her cousin Holly.

"I believed her," Holly now says. "She was a fanatic about those dolls of hers. Every one of them had a name and a story. When she started running the day-care center, and I watched how great she was with kids, I remembered those dolls of hers, and all the children she wanted to have. It all made sense."

After spending full days with the twenty-five preschoolers under her charge, Kris came home each night and tried hard to make Danielle's life feel as special as possible. This was partly because Kris had this pure connection with children, and partly because it saddened her to see how much Danielle longed for her father's attention. Kris felt a responsibility to compensate for that.

Kris also seemed to have an awareness that she'd never have another

Danielle and her mother in 1996, when Danielle was eleven years old

child. The childhood dream of raising a dozen children of her own had passed when her marriage collapsed. "I've got one beautiful, wonderful girl," she'd say. "I'm happy and I just want Danielle to be happy."

She found countless quirky ways to do that. After Danielle's nightly baths, Kris wouldn't just give her a snack. She'd give her four different kinds of fruit on skewer sticks. Kris wanted Danielle to always know that she was the priority, and if that meant the house wasn't always neat or the dinner dishes weren't done right away, that was OK. Stuff like that was secondary. She understood that there was a messy essence to child-hood, and she indulged it. She'd tell Cynda, "If Danielle cooks and makes a mess, too bad, that's how you learn. If she's painting and it gets all over, too bad. Paint is supposed to get all over the place. We'll clean it up later."

Kris had warm memories of going with her own father every Saturday morning to a doughnut shop. It was their little getaway ritual. "Danielle doesn't have a father to take her for doughnuts," Kris told Cynda. "But I'll always be there to take her everywhere."

When Danielle was five years old, Kris, Cynda, and Cynda's mother rented a motor home and mapped out a four-generation road trip to Disney World. They stayed in motels along the way, and all three of the older women—a mother, a grandmother, and a great-grandmother—doted on little Danielle. As an only child, Danielle spent a lot of her life with adults, and that gave her a kind of maturity, and an appreciation of adult conversations. She fit right in with her older traveling companions.

Kris and Danielle often drove up to northern Michigan together for the weekend, and Kris had activities planned from the moment Danielle's eyes opened. Kris loved to fish. It was her calming refuge, and she was happiest when Danielle came along, even if they were just sitting silently, waiting, waiting, for their fishing rods to jiggle.

In 1993, when Danielle was eight, Kris met a divorced man named Ted and fell in love. Ted was a garage-door installer with two kids, and he became the first positive father figure in Danielle's life; he was reliable, loving, and playful, with an easy nature.

The first time Danielle visited Ted at his house, she noticed that the big tile floor in his kitchen looked like a checkerboard, with large black and white squares. "I have these giant checkerboard pieces," she told him. "We should play checkers." She went home and got them—her checkerboard pieces were the size of dinner plates—and from then on, she and Ted loved to sit on his kitchen floor, playing checkers.

Even though Danielle was thrilled to have Ted in her life, he saw how much she also wanted to maintain a relationship with her natural father, and how he disappointed her. It was hard for Ted, and for others who loved Danielle, to shake their image of Danielle as a sad little girl in her winter coat, her suitcase packed, as she waited in vain for her father to take her for the weekend as promised.

Ted tried to be the substitute dad in any way he could. Once he and Kris began dating, they'd spend most weekends at a cottage up north. Ted would drive there in his truck with his two dogs along for company, and Kris would drive her car alongside of him, with Danielle in the passenger seat. Kris and Danielle always brought along their favorite cassette tapes—Dwight Yoakam, Prince, Alanis Morissette—and every time Ted looked over at them, they'd be bopping up and down to their music, laughing all the way, their heads almost hitting the roof as they sang. Ted knew he was seeing something special; not every mother and daughter enjoyed each other's company that much.

Ted had fallen in love with Kris, and he quickly loved Danielle, too. "She's just so mature," he'd tell people. "It's almost like she isn't a child." Kris and Ted talked about marriage, but didn't see an immediate need. They kept putting it off.

Kris could be a disciplinarian, with her preschoolers and with Danielle, but she also had an intuitive sense about when to be firm and when to be lenient. She demanded good grades because she wasn't always a conscientious student when she was young. Kris had been the kind of teenager who didn't think about studying hard or going to a top college; she was more interested in plotting a night out with her friends at the next Journey or Foreigner concert.

Once she was a mother, however, she had different priorities. "She didn't want Danielle to party her way through high school, like we did," says her cousin Holly. "She knew education mattered." Danielle had to grow up and be able to support herself. Kris was vehement about that. Kris had learned from her own life: You can't put yourself in a position where you're fully dependent on a man.

Kris also became a stickler for facing responsibility. She told Danielle: "If you start something, you need to finish it. You want to join the band? Great. But once we buy the instrument, you need to play it. In the band."

Kris insisted on respect, too. Sometimes Danielle would march into her bedroom, angry about something, and she'd slam the door. That wouldn't fly with Kris, and Danielle knew it. So minutes later, Danielle would open the door a crack, call out "sorry," and then close the door more gently. She has memories of seeing her mom out on the couch, trying to hold back a smile, as the apology was issued. It's as if Kris was thinking, "I know Danielle's a good kid. I love her."

As Danielle entered her teen years, she and Kris didn't always get along. Sometimes things could get heated, but looking back, it was all pretty normal. (Every two and a half days, the average mother and her teenaged daughter have an argument that lasts fifteen minutes, according to researchers at Cambridge University. Adolescent boys are less argumentative. They have tiffs with their moms in six-minute bursts every four days.) In any case, Kris believed in never going to bed angry, and she didn't like to part with Danielle unless a disagreement was straightened out.

One morning when Danielle was in ninth grade, she missed the bus for the third day that week. Kris was unhappy about it; she'd have to drive Danielle to school yet again, and that would make her late for work. She and Danielle had a fight about this, and on the drive to school, Kris was lecturing. "You're fourteen years old now," she said. "You need to be more responsible. I can't be late to work every day because you're not getting up in time to make the bus. It's not fair to me. And it's irresponsible of you."

Danielle listened quietly, ready for the ride to end, but as usual, as they pulled into the school parking lot, Kris softened. "I'm sorry to come down hard on you," she said, "but you have to get up on time. That's the bottom line. Anyway, you know I love you."

Danielle got out of the car, and before she closed the door, her mother called out to her, "I'll pick you up after swim practice." And again: "I love you."

Danielle closed the car door, gave her mom a slight wave and sheepishly thanked her for the ride. "I love you, too," she mumbled, then turned to head into the school.

That was the last time she ever saw her mother.

Kris went to work at the preschool that day—December 9, 1999—and at lunchtime, stepped outside and collapsed. She was pronounced dead at the scene. She was thirty-three years old, and had been a healthy, active young woman who exercised and watched her diet. Cynda thinks her daughter died of a heart issue—Kris had mentioned what she thought was heartburn the previous week—but an autopsy was unable to determine a cause of death.

When Cynda got the call that her daughter was dead, she sped to the preschool, where staffers were frantic and emotional. Some even said they'd heard gunshots. (That turned out not to be true.) The staffers quickly tried to shield the children from seeing what was going on in front of the school. The kids were kept inside, and paper was put over the windows. Calls were put out to parents to come pick up their children, and they were directed to take them out the back door.

Cynda stayed at the school for a half hour or so, in a horrible daze, and then found she had an agonizing decision to make: Should she remain with Kris's body, or get Danielle out of school and let her know what happened? "I decided that my daughter would have wanted me with Danielle," she says.

Danielle was inconsolable after Cynda broke the news. There's no other way to describe the sadness of a fourteen-year-old girl who had just learned of her mother's unexpected death. But even in those first terrible hours, Danielle was able to recognize that her life would now be divided into "before" and "after." To deal with her changed world, to cope with all that awaited her, Danielle knew that she'd need to find a great maturity within her.

For three days before her mother's memorial service, there was visitation at the funeral home, and Danielle observed the adult ritual of mourning from a front-row seat. Most of it was not comforting to her.

Cynda had always bought Kris a poinsettia every Christmas. She had resolved to do that shortly after Kris got divorced: "She doesn't have a husband to buy her a poinsettia, so I'm going to do it." More than a few people who knew Kris knew about this, and the funeral home was filled with poinsettias they'd sent.

But these were the sort of touches that adults would find meaningful. It was tougher for Danielle.

She sat at the funeral home, eight hours a day for three days, watching the same scene unfold again and again, as hundreds of visitors came through: They all signed their names in the guest book. Then they walked over to Cynda to offer their regrets. Then they stopped by the casket to pay their respects to Kris. And then they'd see Danielle, and they'd just lose it. They'd approach her, many of them tearfully, and say, "Honey, we're so, so sorry." Of course, they were sorry. Danielle knew that. But it was hard for her to endure hour after hour of their long faces, their urges to take her hands, the way they hovered over her, and then whispered to each other as they left her, "Oh God, what will happen to Danielle?"

"It's getting on my nerves," Danielle said at one point to Ted's son Kris.

"Let's get out of here," he said. "I'm taking you to McDonald's."

When they got to McDonald's, Ted's son tried to amuse Danielle by dipping his french fries in his milk shake and waving them around. After days of crying, Danielle found a reason to laugh. All these years later, she remains grateful for his impromptu McDonald's performance, helping her smile at a terrible time.

The funeral was on a Sunday, and when Danielle woke up that morning, her first thought was "I can't go to Mom's funeral without a haircut." It's odd, the things that come into your head at the worst moments of your life.

"Are you really sure you need a haircut?" Cynda asked, a bit incredulously. "I mean, there's so much to do today . . ."

But Danielle insisted. Kris had been very particular about Danielle's hair, always making sure that she looked presentable. Maybe that's what was motivating Danielle to demand that she get a haircut.

Cynda had a friend who cut hair, and so Danielle went to her that morning. The adults seemed to understand. Danielle was focusing on little things to distract herself.

Danielle had asked to speak at Kris's funeral, and on that cold December day, people were awed by the poise of this fourteen-year-old girl. She stood at the front of the chapel, speaking directly to Kris in the present tense.

"Mom, you are still so young," she began, reading from a sheet of paper. "I wish I could just hold you for a moment, touch your hair, smell your perfume, feel your heartbeat in my ear. I will miss you so much. A day will not go by that I won't think of you . . ." The place was still. Though it was heartbreaking to watch, the other mourners knew they were witnessing an act of bravery.

"It's going to be hard, Mom," Danielle continued. "I know in my heart you will give me the strength. You'll be there to pick me up and push me forward. I will be OK. I have many people who care about me, Mom. They will take great care of me, just like you have done."

She took a breath, fought back tears, and looked up at all the adults at the service. There were those who loved her, those who would make great efforts to be there for her, but all of them combined could not equal her mother.

Danielle looked back down at her notes. "I will make many rivers when I think about you, Mom. All the good times we had; the secrets we shared. The short thirty-three years you were with us, you were so giving. That was you, always helping others." Her voice cracked as she continued. "I'll take care of everything I can, Mom. I will try to make you proud of me. I will miss you and I love you with all my heart."

After Kris's death, everything felt surreal. Kris had just sent out forty Christmas cards, and most of her friends and loved ones received them the day she died. She had also ordered a Christmas present for Danielle, a $50 light-blue coat with fur trim that Danielle had been eyeing. It had arrived in the mail a few days earlier.

"I'm so excited. The coat came in," Kris told her mother in a phone call. "Should I give it to Danielle now or wait for Christmas?"

"Might as well give it now," Cynda told her. "It's cold and she could use it."

And so a couple nights before she died, Kris had given the coat to Danielle, with a big hug, as an early Christmas present. Danielle just loved the coat, but couldn't bring herself to wear it to the funeral. (The coat remains at Cynda's house today, on a sturdy hanger, wrapped in plastic.)

The weeks after the funeral were devastating on several fronts.

Danielle moved in with Cynda, but her father quickly went to court to win custody of her, and that exacerbated Danielle's grief. She didn't want to live with him. She said that plainly. She felt it deeply. But he wouldn't back down and because she was a year too young to contest it the decision would have to come from the courts.

Danielle resented her father, and not just because he had so often disappointed her. She also couldn't shake her memories of how he had treated her mother. He had been verbally abusive to Kris during and after their marriage, and when he drank, things got even worse. Danielle knew that her father loved her in his own inept way, but she couldn't bring herself to live with him now that her mother was dead.

Cynda feared Danielle's father might show up unannounced and take Danielle away, and so they plotted for that possibility. Danielle slept with her cell phone and promised her grandmother that if her father came and took her with him, she'd run away from his house by climbing out a back window. Then she'd call Cynda to come get her.

In court, Danielle's father made defamatory accusations about Cynda: that she was an alcoholic, that she had put Danielle on the pill. The charges were horrifying and untrue, and it was hard to shield Danielle from what was going on. But then, after eight months of court battles—including testimony from Danielle that she desperately wanted to stay with her grandmother—her father suddenly agreed to give up his right to custody. Cynda's lawyer said his strategy was to wear down Danielle's father, and in the end, it worked. When Cynda got over her anger, she came to respect him for surrendering, and for accepting what was obviously best for Danielle.

"I've forgiven him for what he did to my mom," Danielle would tell people, "And I've forgiven him for not being there for me for all those years." But she no longer wanted him to be part of her life—and she would hold to that decision into adulthood.

⌐◦

Danielle and Cynda—having lost a mother and a daughter—were emotionally fragile for a long time, yet both resisted showing their sadness because they didn't want to bring each other down. They now know that it wasn't healthy, but that's how they handled things. "She cried alone," Cynda says, "and I cried alone."

Danielle has the same recollection, with slightly different wording: "She was sad and I was sad. I'd go to my room and Grandma would go to her room. That's how it has always been."

Like other teenage girls whose mothers died suddenly, Danielle found herself replaying her last day with her mother—missing the school bus, being reprimanded by Kris in the car, the final "I love you." The preteen and teen years are when girls start pushing their mothers away, and mothers struggle to deal with their girls' sense of autonomy, their surly teen tantrums, even their sharpest declarations: "Leave me alone!" or "I hate you!"

Danielle and Kris didn't have major issues, but they had their moments. It's natural for teenage girls whose mothers have died to feel as if they weren't as loving as they should have been, or that they let their mothers down. There's a layer of guilt which can exacerbate the grief. Danielle had to deal with this, too.

Cynda found reasons every day to be proud of Danielle. She had been an A and B student, but after Kris died, her ability to concentrate suffered, as did her grades. She got C's for a while, but eventually rebounded and found welcome diversions in extracurricular activities.

There was a saying etched in large letters on the family-room wall of Cynda's house: "Home is where love resides, memories are created, friends always belong, and laughter never ends." It was a sweet sentiment, of course, but it also reminded Cynda and Danielle of a love now absent, of memories too sad to indulge, of friends who looked at them both with pity, and of days when there was no laughter.

Cynda sold the day-care center as soon as she could, and focused on parenting Danielle. She felt a responsibility to chronicle every moment of Danielle's life because she thought Kris would have wanted that. And so Cynda diligently kept scrapbooks with everything she could find to boost Danielle's self-esteem: report cards, honor-roll certificates, newspaper clippings about Danielle's swimming successes and her selection to be in a Junior Miss pageant and on her school's homecoming court.

Cynda gathered all the photos Kris had taken of Danielle over fourteen years and put them in scrapbooks too, then added photos of her own, taken when Danielle was fifteen and beyond. The scrapbooks were a nice record of Danielle's life, but they too became an obvious reminder that Kris was gone. In the early scrapbooks, Kris is in photo after photo with Danielle. And then, abruptly, Kris was gone from the photos.

Some relatives thought Cynda was too indulgent with Danielle. She didn't force her to do chores or to clean her room. Her impulse was to let things pass, to resist making demands. After all, look at what this girl had been through. "Cynda coddled her," says Kris's cousin Holly. "It was hard for her to say to Danielle, 'You have to do this because I said so.' I worried that Danielle might turn into a big baby—or that she'd become a party girl. But that's not how it went. Danielle kept herself on the straight and narrow."

There were times when well-meaning people would tell Cynda, "All girls need to feel a mother's love. Eventually, Danielle will probably start calling you Mom." Cynda rejected the idea. "She had a wonderful mother who loved her," she'd say. "She doesn't need another mother."

When Danielle graduated from high school in 2003, Cynda had photos of her at various ages blown up into life-size posters on thick cardboard. She placed them on sticks leading up the driveway on the day of her graduation party.

Cynda saw Danielle crying on the day she graduated, but neither of them talked about the obvious reason for the tears: that Kris wasn't there to see this moment. Kris had taken many of these blown-up photos, and Cynda knew the posters triggered memories, good and bad. But Cynda had to do something, and so she settled on celebrating Danielle with a this-is-your-life display, hoping that might lift her granddaughter's spirits on a day of tangled emotions.

Danielle went to Eastern Michigan University, majored in psychology, and became a social worker. The job suited her. She empathized with families in crisis. Her heart went out to children who didn't have both parents, or had endured sexual or physical abuse. She thought of how connected she had been to children from the time she was young and her mom ran the preschool.

Sometimes, she'd drive past the preschool and she'd see the latest crop of toddlers playing out back. If she was passing in the early afternoon, the shades would be drawn, and she'd think to herself, "Oh, it must be naptime." And of course, she'd think of naptime when her mother oversaw everything. She never thought to knock on the door and introduce herself. "It would be too weird to walk in there now, as a stranger," she'd tell people who asked why she never went back.

From time to time, she'd run into some of her mother's former preschoolers, now teenagers. She even babysat a few of them. The kids remembered the day in 1999 that Kris died, but they didn't bring it up, and neither did Danielle.

As she threw herself into her career as a social worker, Danielle was less focused on her love life. But then, on St. Patrick's Day 2007, her friends dragged her out for a drink, and at a local bar, she met a thirty-four-year-old police officer named Brian Wenzel. She knew his uncle and aunt, who were there that night and made the introduction.

Brian thought Danielle was too beautiful to be interested in him, but then they talked for a little while and he asked her to dance. She accepted, they danced, the song came to an end, and Brian smiled at her. "Would you like to dance again?"

"No," she said.

And he assumed that was that. "Well, thanks for the dance," he said.

Even though he figured Danielle wasn't very taken with him, Brian got her phone number from his aunt and nervously called her a couple days later.

"Hi, this is Brian. We met on St. Patrick's Day," he said.

"I remember."

"Well, I thought maybe we could go out on a date," Brian said.

"That would be fine," Danielle answered.

As soon as she agreed to see him again, Brian desperately wanted to get off the phone. "When I'm nervous, I babble," he later explained. "I knew if I stayed on the phone with her even ten more seconds, I'd just start babbling uncontrollably."

And so he told Danielle: "I've got to go. I'll call you with details. Good-bye." The phone call was over in forty-five seconds.

On their first date, Brian got over his nervousness and very quickly there were many things that bonded them. They talked about their families, their dreams, and the similarities in their jobs. Danielle was especially drawn to the fact that Brian, hailing from a family of cops, had a beat that encompassed an entire school district of 4,000 students. He's the school district's police "resource officer," and Danielle was touched whenever he talked about the issues that damage children and families. She saw his compassion, and at the same time, felt that his heart was reaching out to her over the losses in her own childhood: an absentee father, a mother who died young.

Brian talked with Danielle about the challenges young girls face today. He observes so many girls getting by without parental supervision, without enough love in their lives, with too much of a focus on sex. He has helped high school girls break up with their abusive boyfriends, and has seen the struggles of pregnant teens.

"It's tough for kids now," he told Danielle one evening. He had just watched four TV comedies in a row: *How I Met Your Mother, Two and a Half Men, Rules of Engagement,* and *Mike & Molly.* "Every show was filled with sexual jokes," he said. "Every show had sex as the plot. And that just made me kind of sad. When I was younger, the sitcoms weren't all about sex. We had a chance to just be children. We were watching *Full House* and *Family Matters.*"

After Brian and Danielle got engaged—he proposed to her at their favorite restaurant, the Melting Pot—she wanted to think through what connected them. She wrote down her thoughts:

"Every day, Brian and I deal with families in crisis. We see so many hard things—a lot of heartache—and that redirects us to appreciate the little things in life, and to never take each other for granted. I've had to try

Brian and Danielle

to help children who are hungry every day, who don't have a home. For his part, Brian sees a lot of bad things—and bad people, too—and he also feels it makes him grateful for his life, and the love between us.

"I tell Brian every day that my favorite thing is to come home to him. From a world of chaos, I come home to someone who is so level-headed and loving, supportive and stable. I'm very lucky."

Not long after Danielle got engaged, the New York Life Foundation funded a study of adults who were young when their parents died. One in nine Americans lost a parent before they were twenty years old. And a sobering 57 percent of them said they'd trade a year of their lives for one more day with their late parent. When Danielle heard about the research, it felt very familiar to her. She counted herself in that 57 percent.

Clare Booth Luce, the writer, once said that "the loss of one's mother is the end of one's childhood." The 2010 study showed just how true that is. It found that bereavement rooted in childhood often leaves emotional scars for decades, and that our society doesn't fully understand the ramifications or offer appropriate resources. Educators, doctors, and the clergy get little or no training to help them recognize the signs of loneliness, isolation, and depression in grieving children—and in adults who lost parents in childhood. The early loss of a parent can make some people more resilient, responsible, and independent, the research shows. But there are risks. Kids who get through by being stoic and behaving like adults can pay an enormous price: They miss out on their childhoods.

When polled, most doctors say they would prefer to die of cancer rather than a heart attack. The reason? Because with cancer, you get to say good-bye. Danielle understands that feeling too. She has met people whose parents died after long illnesses. She doesn't exactly envy them, but she recognizes that they had what she didn't have: that chance to truly say good-bye.

For many who lost parents young, two birthdays are highly anticipated—and bittersweet. When Danielle turns twenty-nine, she will have spent more time without her mother than she spent with her. When she turns thirty-four, she will have lived longer than her mother lived. (Danielle has seen a cardiologist who assured her that she doesn't have the heart disease that likely killed Kris.)

Danielle has told Cynda that it is a strange and melancholy feeling to know that her mother will stay forever young in her eyes. She has watched the wrinkles spread across Cynda's face. Looking in mirrors for the rest of her life, Danielle will watch herself age too. But Kris will never be older than thirty-three.

All these realizations seemed to be heightened since the engagement. Danielle admitted she was finding it difficult not having her mother around as she planned her wedding. A wedding is often the most emotional mother-daughter event of a young woman's lifetime. It's said that no one in a young woman's life can love her like her mother does. And so for those without mothers, every activity—especially finding a dress—serves as a reminder that their mothers are gone.

Salespeople in the wedding industry are used to mothers being the decision-makers, check-writers, and hand-holders. They would ask Danielle, "So, has your mother weighed in on this yet?" She'd take a breath and explain.

When she stepped into the Magic Room for her second fitting, Danielle had brought along a four-person entourage—her best friend, her cousin Holly, her "sister" Meghan (Ted's daughter), and of course, her grandmother, Cynda. They oohed and ahhed with all their might, and they showed her their love. But they knew that even if Danielle came with a hundred supporters, they couldn't equal the one person she yearned to have there.

Danielle tried to find perspective. "Yes, I wished my mom could be with me, to see me in that dress," she later explained. "But I have moments like that every day. It's just that since I've been engaged, there are more of them. I've wanted to call her and say, 'Hey, you want to look at the invitations? Can you come with me to the caterer?'"

Of course, it's understandable that she'd feel her mother's absence most acutely when trying on her wedding dress. Shelley and her saleswomen seemed like well-meaning people, but they earn their living by telling brides they look beautiful. Sometimes a girl needs her mother to give her an honest assessment. Or she needs her mother to say "You look just breathtaking . . . more beautiful than I've ever seen you!" Kris would have said that to Danielle.

She found solace when she reminded herself that Kris packed a lot of memories, and a lot of love, into the fourteen years she had with Danielle. Few mothers with triple the time with their daughters could find a way to give the gift of so many meaningful experiences.

Danielle also appreciated the fatherly love shown to her by her mother's boyfriend, Ted. Even after he found another woman and married her, he remained a real presence in Danielle's life. He invited her on regular daddy-daughter outings, even into adulthood; they'd go fishing or pick blueberries or just talk. Danielle had asked if he would join her grandfather in walking her down the aisle, and he tearfully accepted.

"I'd be honored," he said, and as he hugged her, Danielle thought her mom would be pleased to know that when the time came, she'd have Ted's arm to hold on to.

⌒

For weeks, Cynda was aware that she was annoying Danielle by arguing for a more extravagant cake, and giving unsolicited advice on other wedding issues. "I'd love to be more involved," Cynda later explained. "I'm not being included as much as I'd like. Maybe this is my way of trying to hold on to her. But I need to get over that, don't I?"

It also occurred to Cynda that Danielle was distancing herself because when they were together, Danielle couldn't help but feel visceral reminders of her mother. To her credit, on the day of the second fitting at Becker's, Danielle recognized that it wasn't just her emotions that were running high. She knew this wasn't an easy day for her grandmother, either.

There was one moment when confusion over simple semantics reminded Danielle of the issues that haunted her grandmother. After Danielle made her way out of the Magic Room, she told Cynda that she'd need to buy a "mother-of-the-bride" dress to wear down the aisle.

"Please don't call it that," Cynda told her.

Danielle smiled. "Grandma," she said, "that's how they refer to the dress. That's what it's called."

Cynda gave that a thought. "Well, all right then," she said. "That's what I'll wear. A mother-of-the-bride dress."

Later that day, Cynda asked Danielle if she'd spend one night at her house before she got married. "I will, Grandma," Danielle answered.

Cynda's emotions swelled, and she figured she'd just say it. "You know, honey, I used to be able to put you on my lap and hug you and love you. I miss that."

"Grandma, it'll be great to come spend the night again before the wedding," Danielle told her.

Both Cynda and Danielle knew: At this pre-wedding sleepover, neither of them would discuss their shared feelings of loss. They wouldn't talk about missing Kris. They'd stay away from their opinions regarding the expensive wedding cake versus the cheap one. They'd just be together, quietly holding on to their memories. And each other.

.
.

Chapter Fifteen

Erika

*E*rika Hansen is back in the Magic Room for her first fitting, and Shelley is glad to see her.

After Erika left the store on the day she bought her dress, the saleswomen at Becker's couldn't help but talk about her vow of purity. Like her sisters before her, Erika had promised to save her first kiss for the man who would become her husband. Not many brides today walk into Becker's with that kind of story.

To some on Becker's sales force, this sounded completely romantic and inspirational. The Hansen girls are making a personal stand in the face of a casual-sex society that long ago abandoned the concept of modesty, or of a slow and respectful courtship. Others at Becker's argued that the Hansens are overcompensating. No premarital sex? That's one thing. No kissing? That's extreme.

For her part, Shelley is open-minded. She's taken by the way Erika carries herself. There's just this unruffled sereneness about her. Even here, standing on the pedestal in the Magic Room, speaking so softly and respectfully, Erika projects an air of certainty. Where did that come from?

She looks lovely, too, having carefully curled her hair this morning exactly the way she hopes to wear it at the wedding.

At first, Shelley just talks with Erika about the dress. "How does it feel on you?" she asks, as Erika's mom, Lynn, takes photos on her cell phone.

"It feels beautiful, but it's loose up here," Erika says, pointing at the bodice. She has lost fifteen pounds since she was last at Becker's, and has seen a doctor about intestinal issues.

Shelley holds the fabric at the bustline in her hand. "I'll take in an inch at the top," she decides. Most brides weigh less at their first fitting, and then lose even more weight before their second fitting. They're running around, they're dieting, they're too nervous to eat. Shelley has to take all of this into account as she calculates alterations. Every day, she has to measure not just the dress, but her sense of a bride's stress level and eating habits. If a bride is losing weight, how thin will she get? If she's gaining, how many pounds will she add on? If she's pregnant, what's she going to look like on her wedding day?

Sometimes there are simple remedies. When weight-losing brides complain that their dresses feel like they're falling off of them, Becker's saleswomen make a simple recommendation: "Häagen-Dazs."

After circling Erika a couple of times, Shelley sees that the satin lining is too long by just over an inch. She gets down on the floor, her knees tucked under the overhanging lip of the pedestal. Scissors in hand, she begins hemming the bottom of Erika's gown. "Hold real still," she says, "because this is the first dress I've ever cut."

It's one of Shelley's favorite lines, and it sometimes elicits a gasp from a bride or her mother—if they're paying attention. "Well, we'll need to have somebody else do the cutting!" a bride's mother will say, and Shelley has to tell them she was kidding. "It actually feels as if I've been kneeling here, hemming dresses, for centuries," she'll say.

Erika and her mom know Shelley is joking. As Shelley cuts, Lynn offers her own funny question: "What if Erika grows an inch taller before the wedding?"

"Only the child brides grow like that," Shelley says, and everyone laughs.

While Shelley works, Erika can't stop smiling at herself in the mirror.

Her gown, like almost every gown at Becker's, was made in China. It usually takes four to six months for the finished dress to arrive, because the Chinese manufacturer always waits until it receives five hundred orders, from around the world, for a particular gown. Only then do its employees start making that style. Erika's dress passed through the hands of six Chinese workers. "A dress is built like a house," Shelley explains to her, "and each person has a role in the construction. There's the fabric person, the lace person, the 'beader,' the crystal person, the hemmer—and then the inspector."

For Chinese bridal-gown workers, sending dresses to America reminds them that there's a crisis in their country when it comes to brides and grooms. Because girls are less desired in Asian culture, many parents now use ultrasound scanning to determine a child's sex, after which they selectively abort female fetuses. Some practice infanticide. As a result, there are an estimated 100 million more males than females in Asia today. Demographers from organizations such as the American Enterprise Institute say tens of millions of potential brides have been lost to "gendercide," and tens of millions of men will never see a wedding day. China's one-child policy helps fuel the problem, but there are other factors too: the continuing cultural preference for male heirs, the trend toward smaller families as China modernizes, and the easy accessibility of ultrasound technology for as little as twelve dollars a session. Chinese factory workers don't have a lot of time to ponder their culture's marriage crisis. But as they spend their days sending lavish dresses to the United States, it's easy for them to conclude that American daughters are more plentiful, celebrated, and valued.

Shelley, of course, doesn't share with Erika any geopolitical asides related to the origins of her dress. Instead, she keeps things light, asking Erika what type of veil she's considering. Erika is leaning toward a "waterfall veil" that would cascade down the side of her face. Until a couple decades ago, 90 percent of Becker's brides wore veils covering their faces. But nowadays, almost all brides wear open veils that allow their guests (and videographers) to see the expressions on their faces as they walk down the aisle.

Shelley asks Erika what kind of bustle she'd like, and Erika chooses the French bustle, which requires numbered ribbons that tie together. "Is it complicated?" Erika asks.

"Not really," Shelley says, "Once I'm finished, I'll enroll your mom in bustling school for five minutes. Then she can help your bridesmaids do it at the wedding."

Erika stands patiently on the pedestal—it's been about a half hour now—as Shelley continues fidgeting with the dress. After a while, Shelley decides she'll need to do a traditional bustle because there aren't enough sturdy points on the fabric to hang a French bustle. "The skirts hang differently on each dress, and brides' torsos are different too," she explains. "So I have to get it right. Thanks for being patient."

"I'm in no rush," Erika tells her. "I love standing here. The longer you take, the more time I have in the dress."

Patience is a virtue not all brides display, but Erika has had practice. After all, she patiently waited a lifetime for that first kiss.

⁓

When Erika was in second grade, in 1994, she naturally looked up to her oldest sister, Leanne, who was a fifth-grader. That was the year when Leanne read a Christian young adult novel in the Sierra Jensen series titled *With This Ring*. In the book, written by Robin Jones Gunn, the teenage main character, Sierra, told her father that she had written down her personal creed.

"It says that my body is a gift and that God gets to decide who to give the gift to, not me," Sierra explains. "And the best presents are the ones that are all wrapped up, not the ones that have been opened and rewrapped and now the paper is torn or the bow is squished. I believe God's best plan is for me to be like a wrapped present. Then, when I get married, my husband will know that I'm a special gift just for him."

A young couple in the book had pledged not to kiss each other until their wedding day. When they were rehearsing in the chapel the afternoon before the ceremony, the pastor came to the "you may kiss the bride" moment, and the groom-to-be just looked into the bride-to-be's eyes. As one of the characters later described it: "He was an inch away from her face. It was about the most romantic, totally make-you-melt scene in the world. Then I heard him whisper to her, 'Tomorrow my love. Tomorrow.'" (On the day of the wedding, when the kiss finally happened, the couple's friends held up cardboard cards, all with the number 10 on them, rating the kiss as if it were the Olympics.)

For young Christian readers such as Leanne, this story felt thrilling. "I wonder what it would be like to save my kisses," she said to her sisters. "The more I think about it, the more I want to do it." Leanne started telling everybody about her vow—teachers, family friends, other kids. She thought this would hold her more accountable, because she'd be embarrassed if she broke her pledge.

Soon enough, Erika decided to make the same promise, as did her two other sisters. It would not be easy for them.

When Erika reached her teen years, her peers often gave her a hard time. Girlfriends debated the issue with her: How could she know a man was right for her if she didn't know if he was right for her physically? Her answer: It's too selfish to focus on measuring how a future husband might please her physically. The marriage bonds have to be about so much more than that. If the love and sense of duty to each other is there, the physical relationship will follow—and be even stronger. She was sure of that.

When adults asked her, she'd maturely explain herself: "Some people say your purity isn't worth saving anymore, that the whole message of being physical is different today. But I see it as a blessing for a husband and wife. You have a physical aspect to share that you haven't shared with anyone before."

Erika admits that the teen years were often lonely for her and her sisters. Their mother's heart sometimes ached for them. "If you were a Hansen girl, a lot of the boys stayed clear," says Lynn. "Some people mocked them."

Their father, Vic, told them he admired their decisions "even though your mom and I did our share of kissing before we got married." The girls' embrace of purity fit with the things he was trying to teach them, about both faith in God and a plan for life.

And actually, the Hansen girls are not as rare as they might seem. Robin Gunn has sold three million copies of her forty young-adult books. She estimates that more than a half-million young women today have been influenced by their churches, parents, and Christian authors such as her "to direct their futures toward purity, rather than going along with what they see on TV." Of course, they're a clear minority. Just 16 percent of young couples actually end up putting off sex until after marriage, and more than a third of high school kids today already have had intercourse, research shows. Still, new data from the National Center for Health Statistics suggests that a growing segment of young people are willing to admit to a yearning for more traditional values. The US government's 2011 report shows that among people ages fifteen to twenty-four, 29 percent of women and 27 percent of men say they've never had a sexual encounter. That's up from 22 percent for both sexes in a 2005 survey. The percentage of women ages twenty to twenty-four who say they've never had sexual contact with another person has risen to 12 percent from 8 percent. (The media dubbed the results as "a trend toward postponement," with headlines announcing "Virginity's making a comeback.")

Gunn knows that most young people have not embraced the Christian philosophy espoused in her books, but she's gratified when she hears from those who have. "I hear daily from girls who say, 'I want to hold out for a hero.' It's almost like the alternative lifestyle today is purity. Girls are saying, 'We've seen it all. We've watched our parents. How can we be different?'"

Gunn dismisses the notion that our daughters need to make certain that they're sexually compatible with a man before marrying him. "It's beautiful if you can enter a marriage at the level of inexperience and innocence that gives you the space to grow up together," she says. A 2010 study of 2,035 married couples, reported in the *Journal of Family Psychology*, found that those who delay sex until marriage often have stronger marriages and better sex lives, in part because early in their relationships, they focused on communicating rather than having sex.

Critics say the modesty movement with daddy-daughter "purity balls," gives girls the message that they are property traded from their fathers to their husbands, and that their bodies and their sexuality need to be guarded and monitored by men. They also argue that programs touting abstinence don't work. While teen pregnancy rates are down, researchers say the credit is mostly due to safe-sex education and better use of contraceptives. Some argue that girls who take purity vows and then break them are more apt to engage in risky behaviors, because they haven't been educated about contraceptives.

Vic and Lynn Hansen are aware of all the arguments. And in their efforts to give their four daughters a more sheltered upbringing than they had, they did have some pushback over the years.

When Erika and her sisters were younger, they weren't allowed to watch certain popular television shows, including *Friends*, which Vic didn't like because, as he put it, "That show has a tone of approval about premarital sex. The message is, It's OK to sleep with multiple partners and it's all funny."

Lynn told the girls: "Yes, the show is fun to watch. But I'm struggling with exposing you to something I don't believe is appropriate."

The girls fought back. A vow of purity—that they could handle. But going to school, where all their friends were talking about *Friends*, and having to admit they weren't allowed to watch it—that was unacceptable to the girls. They challenged their parents, saying they were being overprotective. "We're smart enough to judge things ourselves, to make our own observations of what's right and wrong," argued Leanne.

And so the girls were allowed to watch *Friends* and a few other shows their parents didn't like. Mostly, however, the dominant culture was kept at bay.

Erika 169

Fathers like Vic Hansen, who only have daughters, often feel blessed. But they also can feel conflicted. Gallup polls have repeatedly shown that about 45 percent of men would prefer having a son if they had only one child, compared with 19 percent who'd prefer a daughter—a ratio little changed since 1941.

Once a daughter arrives, her parents are 6 percent more likely to get divorced than if she were a boy, according to a study of "boy bias" by researchers at the University of California at Los Angeles and the University of Rochester. Parents with three daughters are about 10 percent more likely to get divorced than parents of three sons. Meanwhile, divorced mothers of daughters remarry at higher rates than divorced mothers of sons. And the researchers even found that when unmarried couples have an ultrasound to determine the sex of their child, men are more likely to marry their partners after learning the child will be male.

Dads with sons are more likely to stick around in part because they feel a greater need to serve as male role models, and they're usually more comfortable around boys, the researchers say. In their hearts, a lot of men know themselves: They want a child in their image, a pal to share their love of sports, or a testosterone-fueled partner to join them someday in business. They want someone to carry on their family name. They want sons.

For his part, Vic Hansen never felt this way. From the start, he embraced his role as a father of girls, and his daughters confided in him easily. In fact, Erika now sees her dad every day because she works in customer service at Display Pack, Vic's packaging company in Grand Rapids, a second-generation family business with four hundred employees. (Display Pack makes the small plastic and cardboard boxes that computer ink-cartridges and cell phones come in. Vic's dad started the business in a one-stall garage. "If you ever need a machete to open plastic packaging," Vic jokes, "it's our fault. But the companies we supply worry about shoplifting, and they want us to make their products difficult to open.")

Vic is consumed by the business at times, but as a father, he has always believed that it's vital to carve out individual time for his daughters. And so when each of the girls turned sixteen, he took them on a one-on-one father/daughter trip. Erika's trip was to Hawaii, and while they were there, Vic set aside time for some very direct conversations. He asked Erika about her goals and dreams. He talked to her from his heart, speaking about the risks of dressing provocatively, and about the urges teenage boys have.

Erika and her dad talked about how our culture has changed, how a lot of men these days are no longer the pursuers in relationships. Too many young women are throwing themselves at men; their role models are trashy characters on TV shows such as *Jersey Shore*. "That's not the way it should be," Vic told Erika. "I ask you and your sisters to be a little mysterious. Make it so boys want to learn more about you."

He warned Erika about the limitations of courtship by computer. Young people today are too often alone in their bedrooms, texting and trading Facebook chatter. As Vic sees it, real love is discovered face-to-face, and so he urged Erika to spend time with a boy, talking. "When you're sitting behind a computer, there's a veil of security," he said. "Face-to-face, there's more vulnerability. If a guy is only pursuing you electronically, and doesn't want face time with you, ask yourself if this is really a full relationship."

On Erika's sixteenth birthday trip, Victor pulled out a passage from Psalm 45, which touches on matters of love and marriage. "When it's time for you to pick a partner," Vic said to Erika, "what qualities do you think are nonnegotiable?"

He encouraged her to write down ten character traits she sought in a husband, asking that she look beyond tall, dark, and handsome. (Among the qualities her sisters came up with on their birthday trips: "joyful," "loves what's right, hates wrong," "thinks before he speaks," and "set apart.") Erika gave her dad's request a good deal of thought, and her list included "virtuous in character," "blessed by God," "truthful," "humble," and "displays awesome deeds." She ended with "most excellent," which made her dad smile. "That's a terrific list," he told her. "When you date, you can use it as a filter."

Victor had a rule. If a boy wanted to date one of his daughters, he needed to first come to the house to introduce himself. More than a few boys saw that as a deal-breaker. It wasn't just the lack of kissing that kept boys away: It was having to meet Mr. Hansen.

That turned out to be a great filter too. "The guys who weren't willing to wait for that kiss, the guys who weren't willing to come talk to me—they didn't pursue our girls," Vic says. "But the ones willing to take a risk, to come and introduce themselves to me—I found that they were much more self-sufficient and confident men. And I think that has led us to have terrific sons-in-law."

The Hansen women: Kayla, mother Lynn, Leanne, Erika, and Aleece

Lynn Hansen is very proud of her daughters, of their decisions over the years, and the way they chose the men they'd marry. But the truth is, along the way, there were great worries. Would the girls grow up to be so sheltered that they'd be terribly naïve and vulnerable to others? She'd ask Vic: "Have we been overprotective to the point where we've done them a disservice?" (The Hansen girls are certainly outliers. In a 2011 survey by OneHope, a Christian youth outreach group, 96 percent of 5,100 teens polled said premarital kissing is acceptable.)

And Lynn wondered: How have the girls been affected by the scars she has carried with her through her life?

Born in 1960, Lynn grew up in Muskegon, Michigan, in a family she describes as "the Brady Bunch without the happy faces." There were nine children total. Before her parents married, her dad already had four sons and her mom had two daughters and a son. They then had two children together: Lynn and her brother.

It is hard to even contemplate the degree of untreated dysfunction in that home. For starters, there was easy access to hard-core pornography. "It was in almost every room," Lynn recalls. As a girl, she'd come upon these images, nonchalantly tucked in a magazine rack or in a drawer. "My mother was aware we were finding this stuff. If we were caught looking at it, we'd be reprimanded and shamed."

"But you look at it," Lynn once said to her mother.

The answer her mother gave her was a variation of "do as I say, not as I do."

At times, Lynn's mother was physically abusive. Her dad did even more harm. When Lynn was three years old, in 1963, her father was charged with sexually abusing Lynn's older sisters. It was a different era, and after Lynn's mom asked that the charges be dropped, the authorities barely slapped his wrists. He was told to go to three counseling sessions. His abuses continued, and eventually, Lynn was also a victim. Her father's abuses lasted from when she was a toddler until she was a preteen.

"He made it seem as if this was his way of showing love," says Lynn. "He never touched us any other time. And so it messed with our ability to understand a father's affection."

As a girl, Lynn would watch *The Brady Bunch* and think, "That's the way it's supposed to be. That's what a mom should be like. That's what a dad should be like." She became obsessed with the show, and with Mrs. Brady.

Actress Florence Henderson, who played Carol Brady, often heard from young girls in troubled families who yearned to be a part of a bunch like the Bradys. In the late 1960s, she'd receive letters from girls asking her to please come and get them. One Iowa girl even included directions to the street corner where she'd be waiting with her suitcase.

Yes, the show was idealized and syrupy, but to young girls like Lynn it felt like a balm, a window into what a loving family could be. Lynn never wrote to Henderson, asking to be rescued, but she understood the urges of those who did. "Given the chaos in my family, my heart was so hungry for good parenting," she says. She'd sit in her room, writing stories about girls in functional, loving families—her own Brady-like storylines.

Though there was no faith to speak of in her house growing up, there was a Baptist church down the street. From the time she was five years old, Lynn would go there by herself. She found solace there.

A few times, Lynn would actually say, "I don't feel loved in this family." Her father answered: "I put a roof over your head, clothes on your back, food in your belly. If that's not love, I don't know what is." One time when she was older, Lynn asked her mother why her father abused his daughters. "He did those things because he hadn't been loved as a child," her mother answered.

Given her upbringing, and the unfortunate choices her parents made, it would be almost impossible for Lynn not to have residual issues.

Early in her marriage, she'd have nightmares and she'd wake up, scrambling across Vic, "as if she was trying to get away from something," he recalls. At age thirty, she spent six weeks in the hospital being treated for depression. Vic understood Lynn's childhood traumas had cast a cloud over their marriage, but he didn't know how to enter that part of her life. At times Lynn resented him and felt urges to abandon the marriage. She was a yeller, and the more she yelled, the more passive he got. Some mornings, she'd wake up, look at Vic, and think, "What have I done? Why did I marry him?"

But through it all, Vic dug in. "We're never getting divorced," he'd say. He was raised in a Christian family, and he suggested they attend a faith-based marriage conference called Intimate Allies. It was an eye-opening weekend for Lynn.

At one point, the discussion leader told the couples in attendance: "Look at the person next to you. That's the person God has given you to accompany you through life. He's not your enemy. He's your ally."

"When he said that, it was a huge epiphany for me," Lynn says. She and Vic began to rebuild their relationship, to see each other as teammates.

Lynn's upbringing shaped her as a mother, too, of course. When she had her own children, Lynn found herself angrier at her mother than she was at her father. How could her mother leave her girls so unprotected?

Lynn vowed to fiercely protect her daughters. When they were young, she wouldn't leave them alone with her parents, or let them sit on their grandfather's lap. Sometimes, Lynn would be running errands, she'd call home to check in, and one of the girls would say that Lynn's parents had stopped by unannounced. She'd speed home, in a panic, as if she was rushing to rescue her girls from a fire. "Stay on the phone with me," she'd tell Erika, hoping to monitor the goings-on in the house until she made it back.

Lynn's urge to protect the girls extended to every area of their lives. She was nervous if they went to play at a friend's house. She encouraged her girls to hang out with each other at home, rather than risking the evils that might be lurking in some other family's home. The Hansen sisters got very close, but their friendships with classmates and other girls were limited. "I was so afraid of the outside world," Lynn says, "but I could control what went on in my home."

Once, she wouldn't let her daughter Leanne join other girls at a sleepover party. "We're not a normal family!" Leanne blurted out to Lynn.

Lynn had an answer: "Because we're Christians, God called us to live abnormally, to live in the world and not of the world." It was an answer, yes, but not fully satisfying to a girl who wanted to be with her friends for a sleepover.

Eventually, when the Hansen girls reached their teens, Lynn told them about the abuses in her childhood. Though she didn't go into the awful details, they listened intently, trying to read between the lines. All of them cried. At one point, Erika got angry at Lynn and said, "It can't be true!" But in time, the girls accepted their mother's journey, and responded compassionately.

They maintained a relationship with their grandparents, though cautiously. "Your past can make you bitter or better," Lynn told them. "I'm trying to use my past to make my life, and your lives, better." (When Lynn's father was in his seventies, after learning he had cancer, he tried, in his own limited way, to apologize to her. By then, because of her faith, she had already forgiven him. Both of her parents have since died.)

Looking back, Erika marvels at the power of forgiveness. Did she love her grandparents? "Very much so," she now says. Despite everything. She recognizes how their own troubled childhoods led to the great deficiencies in their parenting decisions. And she is grateful for her good memories with them, and for the ways in which they were able to be loving as grandparents.

For her part, Lynn knows that her childhood experiences have played a role in her daughters' lives and decisions—including their choices regarding purity. She grew up in a house of chaos; she ended up raising her girls in a house with many rules, with reminders that every action has consequences, good or bad.

She knows that because the girls lived sheltered lives, they might encounter situations where they're not prepared, or they'll feel overwhelmed. That worries Lynn.

Her daughters tell her not to worry.

Now that they've become adults, they've started to sift through the ways in which their mother's life affected their lives. Lynn makes good points about the influences from the secular world, they say. Erika used to like the popular Maroon 5 song "This Love." Then she looked closely at the lyrics. "I was ashamed," she says, and it saddens her that the song is played all over the radio. While the song's chorus speaks of a love that takes control of the singer, other verses focus blatantly on sexual pleasure, and how a man's fingers can enter a woman's body.

Such lyrics make Erika think of how she'll raise her own daughters someday, and the parts of the culture she'll try to protect them from. "My mother gave me a beautiful childhood," she says. "I believe the lessons of her own childhood helped her do that."

Erika was admittedly nervous about getting married. When she was younger, her family called her "the runaway girlfriend" because she had a fear of commitment. "She's OK this time," Victor told people after she got engaged. "I know she's nervous and scared, but she won't be the runaway bride. That's because Reuben is the real deal."

As Erika put it, "I can get over my fears because Reuben is the man I've been waiting for."

Reuben—who is twenty-three years old, twelve days older than Erika—met her at a Halloween party in 2005. He was back in Michigan for a visit after Marine boot camp. "A friend asked me to go to a party at this girl's house," he says simply, "and the girl turned out to be Erika." It was a low-key evening. They watched *The Princess Bride* and played a card game.

Reuben had a girlfriend at the time, but he and Erika became friends, and kept in touch while he was overseas. Given his Christian upbringing, he also had vowed to wait for marriage before sex. "In the Marines, everyone talked about sex all the time," he says. "I said 'I'm practicing abstinence. I'm waiting until I marry.' Most guys around me wanted to see me give that up. When we were in the States for training, they'd try to get me drunk and introduce me to girls. They saw it as a challenge to get me to have sex."

Some of his fellow Marines admired him, but still gave him a hard time. A few said they wished they had waited to have sex too. They talked of breaking girls' hearts, or their own regrets about promiscuity.

Reuben's girlfriend broke up with him while he was in Iraq, and he found himself corresponding with Erika. The bond between them grew through e-mail and Facebook.

Reuben didn't want Erika to know the degree of danger he was facing during his deployments in both Iraq and Afghanistan, but the truth was, his unit of "scout snipers" had too many frightening experiences. His best friend in his unit lost a leg to a bomb while on patrol. Several other friends lost both legs. Another man in his unit lost a foot.

At the time that Erika was getting serious with Reuben, her sister, Kayla, was already planning her wedding. And Kayla's fiancé, Gavin, was also stationed in Iraq. On June 19, 2007, Kayla was in a meeting for her job as a customer-service rep at her dad's company, and she couldn't concentrate. She just had a feeling Gavin was in danger. And so she began praying, whispering to herself the names of each man in Gavin's unit.

Two hours later, she got the news. A suicide bomber had driven a garbage truck full of explosives to the barricades outside where Gavin's unit was sleeping. The driver blew up himself and his truck, leaving a crater thirty feet wide and shattering windows in homes a mile away. The blast broke Gavin's jaw, and left him with a brain injury, permanent muscle damage to his leg, and shrapnel wounds all over his body. He'd end up hospitalized for three months, but still made it down the aisle in October, wearing his dress blues, to give Kayla a long-awaited kiss at the altar. Because of the broken jaw, his bite would remain off center, which means he may contend with headaches for the rest of his life. And yet Gavin says he feels blessed. "I have buddies who are a lot worse off than me. At the hospital, I was just glad to have all my fingers and toes. Most of the other guys were missing at least a limb. So it's hard to feel sorry for yourself."

Just days after Gavin was injured, Erika had her own premonition that Reuben was in danger. It was just this wave of worry, and so she prayed for his safety. That was the day that another suicide bomber driving a dump truck full of explosives sped toward the house where Reuben and his unit were staying. A Marine posted on the roof saw the truck approaching and shot the driver. Luckily, the truck blew up thirty feet outside the house, sparing the lives of those inside. Reuben was uninjured, but twenty-one men in his unit received Purple Hearts for collapsed lungs, shrapnel wounds, and concussions.

Erika and Reuben later figured out the time differences, and realized that, at just about the time she said her prayers, that suicide bomber was driving toward Reuben's unit. "God was watching out for us," Reuben says, "and Erika's prayers helped."

Now that his tour of duty is up and he's been honorably discharged from the Marines as a sergeant, Reuben is in college, studying for degrees in mechanical and biomedical engineering. Having seen so many fellow Marines lose their legs, his career aspirations are personal and ambitious. "I'd like to design a better prosthesis," he says. He's already at work, collaborating on a design that could lead to a new artificial leg for a friend.

Given all he's been through, it wasn't hard to wait until he got engaged to get his first kiss from Erika. "It hasn't been bad at all," he'd tell people. "In fact, it's been a good opportunity to get to know each other. Instead of making out for an hour on the couch, we've been talking and learning things on a personal level."

Sure, he admits his mind wanders. "If you're a guy attracted to a woman, there's going to be sexual tension," he'd say. "But I try to keep my focus on what's right, and my faith helps me reduce the tension. Knowing Erika has similar values helps too."

Reuben expected his wedding night to be more special as a result. "The Bible says that when a man leaves his parents and is joined by his wife, they become one flesh. Having not done that with any other woman, it will make my bonds with Erika that much stronger. I really believe that."

Reuben will be Vic's second son-in-law who is a former Marine. "I've seen a change in both of these young men," Vic says. "Something changes a guy when he has been in battle. He comes home and his friends want to play video games or have fun. But my daughters picked men who came back and said, 'I need to man up. I need to be mature.' They became a lot more serious about family, marriage, commitment."

Just as Erika and her sisters are unlike most young brides who come

Erika and Reuben

to Becker's, Vic believes that the men they've chosen are out of the ordinary too. A part of him is proselytizing, but he feels this deeply. For those who enter marriage embracing faith, patience, and respect, he says, the odds of a happy ending just have to be higher.

During her second fitting at Becker's, while gushing over her dress, Erika doesn't mention any of the deeper issues that have carried her to this point. But later, on reflection, she's able to articulate her feelings.

She realizes that many of the people she has loved in her life have been wounded in certain ways. Her mother was wounded by an abusive childhood. Her grandparents were wounded by their own upbringings. Her fiancé and brother-in-law were wounded by all they saw and endured in Iraq.

"We all have wounds," she says. "And I know that some people's wounds can cause them to spiral downward, and they never come back. And yet, it's amazing to see all of those who do come back. I believe our wounds can draw us nearer to God."

She believes that her mother, especially, is now stronger, and a more giving parent, because of the pain in her childhood. "Knowing she went through so much and can handle so much, I feel like she's better able to walk me through my own problems," Erika says. "Her struggles have made her wiser. My sisters even call her Lady Wisdom. I see her laughing and enjoying life. I think about the beautiful childhood she gave me and my sisters. And if she can be the woman she is, despite everything, then I know I can make something special of my life too."

Chapter Sixteen

When Shelley Stepped Away

*T*he town of Fowler never did decide to hang bridal-gown banners from its lampposts. Still, when brides-to-be drive into this tiny community, looking around, they're sometimes reminded of their weddings—and their futures as married women.

Over at Fowler High School, the mascot is an eagle, not a bride. But there's a large sign by the football field: YOU HAVE ONE CHANCE! It's meant to inspire athletes and students, but brides can't help but apply the words to their own decisions about the men they're marrying. Do they really have just one chance to get it right? Or, as their divorced parents might tell them, is life about second chances?

Much of Fowler is drab and tired, but it also has special spots. There's a playground with tiny play horses pulling a kid-size carriage. It looks like something a pint-size Cinderella would ride to the ball, or that a little girl might fantasize about stepping into on her wedding day. The playground makes brides smile when they pass it.

In the pre-Internet 1980s, about 10,000 Becker's customers would drive through Fowler each year. In-store visits are down from those highs, to about 7,000 annually, but local businesses remain appreciative of the traffic. The brides order sandwiches at the local Subway. They fill up at the corner gas station. And Shelley sometimes sends them over to the auto body shop around the block. Why? Because brides and mothers can get so focused on the dress search that they lock their keys in their cars. "If you can get 'em back into their cars," Shelley tells the body-shop manager, "I'll get 'em down the aisle."

Besides the former bank building that houses Becker's, the town's most imposing structure is the Most Holy Trinity Catholic Church, dating to 1881. When Becker's customers drive by the large stone church on a Saturday, they often see bridal parties milling outside. It's nice to come upon that scene on the way into the store.

The Becker's building, meanwhile, is crammed not just with dresses, but with history. The basement, where brides never go, is dominated by those concrete slabs designed to hold up the bank vault that is now the Magic Room. Scattered in the basement are naked mannequins from the old days. They're lying there, looking dead, eyes open. Nearby are curious items left behind by Grandma Eva, including her large needle-and-bobbins kit, a complicated tin contraption dating to 1929.

Several shelves contain meticulous records dating back decades, including stacks of calendars on which each day's sales were recorded with slash marks. If you leaf through these calendars, counting slash marks, you'll find obvious trends. Valentine's Day is always slow because brides are focused on romantic dinners with fiancés, not buying dresses. The Martin Luther King holiday, on the other hand, is busy, and not just because customers have the day off. Women get engaged at Christmas, and have done a lot of looking around by the third week of January. On MLK Day, they're ready to buy.

Pull out the calendar for 2001, flip to September 11, and the slash marks tell a story. Shelley recalls she was signing a slip for the UPS man, who was delivering boxes of dresses when the World Trade Center's second tower collapsed. It was a somber day to sell bridal gowns. And yet, as the slash marks indicate, four brides actually bought their dresses at

*Some Becker's saleswomen say that at night
the store is guarded by the ghost of Grandma Eva.*

Becker's that day. Shelley had to enthusiastically congratulate each of them. Only three dresses were sold on September 12. That was the day desperate people were tacking posters of their missing loved ones around Manhattan, and the images were all over television. On one poster, LOOKING FOR BEST FRIEND was scrawled below a photo of a lovely young woman wearing her wedding dress. It was hard for Becker's brides to shake off the sadness of such images. And yet by Saturday, September 15, life went on and sales were picking up: sixteen dresses were sold that day.

Shelley's gown from her 1985 wedding is in the basement too, on a hanger; she doesn't know what to do with it. On another rack are twenty dresses that were never picked up because of broken engagements. Shelley won't ever take them upstairs to sell. "It would be bad karma for the new brides who'd buy them," she says. "I think it's unfair to sell someone a dress with a sad backstory. It's better to let them rot down here."

Some Becker's saleswomen say the ghost of Grandma Eva is down here in the basement (when she's not upstairs, haunting the attic). And they suspect there may be other ghosts, too: long-ago brides or former saleswomen or maybe that farmer who hanged himself during the Depression after losing all his money when this building was a bank. Sometimes, saleswomen say, given all the banging and creaking at Becker's, it feels like a ghost convention.

Shelley doesn't think of ghosts when she's down here. To her, given the stacks of old receipts and slash-marked calendars, the abandoned dresses from yesteryear, the silent mannequins—it's a place of memory. When she's in the basement, she remembers what the store was like before she owned it. She contemplates the reticent, compliant girl she was when she started, and the assertive woman she slowly became. She thinks of being a granddaughter and then a daughter to the women who ran this store, and what it took to step out of their shadows.

By June 1999, Shelley had already told Gary that she wanted a divorce. His alcoholism had injured the marriage beyond repair, and because he had trouble holding jobs, the burden of supporting the family had fallen on Shelley. None of it was easy.

Shelley would go to work, smiling at brides as always, but inside of her, things were churning. She had arrived at the store at age fourteen, earning five dollars an hour. Now here she was, a thirty-four-year-old woman running much of the business—the bookkeeping, overseeing the sales force, handling alterations, buying from wholesalers. And yet she was still her parents' hourly employee, making eight dollars an hour. She had no health insurance for herself or her kids.

She had been asking her mother about her compensation for a long time, without much luck. If her parents, Sharon and Clark, had a good year at the store, they'd give her a bonus of between $1,000 and $4,000 at Christmastime. But some years there were no bonuses at all. Shelley struggled to stay ahead of her debts.

When Alyssa was born via a C-section, there was no insurance to cover the $11,000 in medical bills. Shelley's parents helped by paying the anesthesiologist's fee, and the rest fell to Shelley and Gary. It took them five years to pay off that bill alone.

"I need to be earning more," Shelley would say to her mother.

"We can't afford it," Sharon answered. "I'm already paying you a dollar an hour more than everyone else."

"How about health insurance?" Shelley asked.

"I'm sorry," Sharon said. "We can't do it. Things are tight right now. The budget won't allow it."

Shelley would always return to the sales floor with a smile—brides never knew that she was upset—but she was increasingly unhappy with her situation. And it wasn't just the money. Shelley had ideas for modernizing the store, for bringing in more-upscale dresses, for streamlining operations and creating a commission system for employees. Her parents' response was usually the same: "That's not how we do it."

And so, having already changed her world by separating from her husband, Shelley decided that maybe it was time to reevaluate her work life, too. "You're so stinkin' cute," the woman who ran the snack shop a few doors down from Becker's would say to her. "You don't belong in a small town. You belong in a city!"

A city? That was too formidable a step. But Shelley felt she had to do something.

She confided in her friends Jeff and Julie (Jeff's fatal heart attack was still a decade away) and they helped her get her bearings. It's common wisdom among family-business consultants that younger family members should first spend time working elsewhere. It can give them confidence, experience, and a sense of how other businesses work. Shelley never did that when she was younger. "It might be best if you leave the store and find your own path," Julie advised her. "Someday you can return, but for now, why not see what life is like in the outside world?"

At the time, Julie, a nurse, was working for a cardiovascular surgeon who was looking to hire a receptionist and billing clerk. Shelley interviewed with the doctor, impressed him, and soon had a job offer. The pay was ten dollars an hour and included benefits. She decided to take it.

When Shelley Stepped Away 185

She never told her parents about the interview. She just came to work on a Thursday, and after the store emptied out, she asked her mother if she had a minute to talk. "I've accepted a job," Shelley said. "I'll be working for a doctor. I start Monday."

Her mother was stunned. "You're going to do what?"

Shelley explained the job again. "A doctor's office?" Sharon said. "What does that have to do with wedding dresses? What does that have to do with what you know how to do?"

"I want to try something different," Shelley told her. "I'm sorry, Mom. But it's time for me to go." Shelley knew she hadn't given enough notice. She knew her mother saw this as abandonment. But she'd always done what others had expected of her. If this was an overdue rebellion, so be it.

Her mother was upset and angry. She was also a bit panicked at the idea that Shelley was leaving her. She had to ask: "What can I do to change your mind?"

"It's too late, Mom," Shelley said. "I've accepted the job."

Shelley worked two more days at the store—Friday and Saturday— and she and her mother hardly exchanged words unless it pertained to a bride. Saturday was especially busy, and when Shelley left the building that evening, exhausted, there were no warm hugs from her mom or her coworkers. Just a few quick good-byes. No one knew what to make of her leaving.

A good part of Shelley was sad that night. She thought, "Why has it come to this?" But in her heart, she knew she'd likely return someday. And even if she didn't, this was a move she had to make. She loved her parents, but the time had come.

After all those years in the bridal business, Shelley liked her new job, and the challenge of learning medical technology. She liked her boss. But she also felt out of sorts. Calling insurance companies to ask questions about claims, talking to faceless voices, well, it just wasn't as rewarding as talking face-to-face to an excited bride. Her new job was responsibility without emotion, service without personal connections. Much of her time was spent alone in the office while the doctor was off doing surgery.

The doctor was pleased with her work, which proved to Shelley that she could be good at something besides selling bridal gowns. But as the weeks went on, she felt pangs. She thought about the brides she'd helped before she quit, and about how she wouldn't be there to see their reactions when their dresses arrived. Who would do their fittings?

A bridal-gown wholesaler tracked her down at the doctor's office. "What the hell are you doing?" he asked. "Don't you know that you belong at Becker's? The store could fall apart without you." Shelley assured him that Becker's would survive, but his admonition remained in her head.

Meanwhile, the near-estrangement with her mother lasted a couple of months, and then her mother started calling her at the doctor's office. "I'm having chest pains," she'd say. "Can you ask the doctor if he has any advice?"

Shelley saw the call as her mother's way of breaking the ice. But her mother was serious, too. "The business is going to kill me," she said at one point. Since Shelley's departure, the stresses at the store were eroding her health.

Finally, one afternoon in November 1999, five months after Shelley had left Becker's, her parents came to her house. They weren't there to talk about Shelley's need to spread her wings, or about her new job. They came with a question. "What will it take to get you back?" Sharon asked. "The store isn't working without you."

It was a huge admission, a genuine plea, but also, a parental compliment of sorts.

Shelley felt stunned. "What do you mean? What exactly are you asking?"

"We need you," her mother said.

Shelley, who had spent her life being compliant, now felt emboldened. She was a thirty-four-year-old woman on the verge of a divorce, and she felt that the time for tiptoeing in any area of her life was over. That included her relationship with her parents. Now she was going to say it as she saw it.

She took a long breath, and then spoke. "The store is in my blood, there's no denying that," she said. "But I can't raise three kids on eight dollars an hour. And I need health benefits."

"We understand," her dad said. "We'll do whatever it'll take. You set your price."

"And it's not just about money," Shelley told him. "I know this business can't go forward and thrive if we don't change the dynamics of how it's run. And I don't think you both can be part of the changes that need to be made. If I'm going to leave this new job, if you're serious about entrusting me with everything, for the long haul, then I want a fresh start." She paused. "Mom, I can't run this business if you're there."

Her mother's eyes widened. "What do you mean?" Sharon asked. She was only fifty-seven years old. It felt too early to retire. Was this how Grandma Eva felt at the end of her reign . . . pushed out?

"Look, I have a vision for the store," Shelley said, "but if you're in the building, Mom, I'll be walking on eggshells, wondering what you're thinking. Or I'll know, from the expression on your face, when you don't approve. I've got to be on my own here."

Shelley's dad understood. "Whatever it takes, we trust you," he said. And to her great credit, Sharon would come to agree too. If this is what would save Becker's, she'd step aside. "It's hard for a daughter to show tough love to her mother," Shelley now says. "But I had to do it."

Shelley's parents agreed to pay her thirteen dollars an hour, to give her health benefits through the business, to increase bonuses to as much as $10,000 a year—and to let her run the operation without their interference.

Naturally, Shelley felt guilty leaving her medical job after just five months, and the doctor was not pleased. Shelley had gone through training, she was getting up to speed, and now she was leaving? "I'm disappointed in you," the doctor snapped. A few days later, though, he calmed down. He took Shelley into his office and gave her fatherly advice. "Family businesses can be tough," he said. "You can end up being a scapegoat for a lot of things. You can get sucked up in a lot of old issues." Shelley told him how little she had been earning. He was taken aback.

"If you're going to return to Becker's," he said, "then you need to do it right. You need to buy the store outright. That's my advice."

Shelley kept his words in her head, and seven years later, in 2006, she made her parents an offer for the store. By then, she was forty-one years old and had logged more than a quarter-century on the sales floor at Becker's. It was time. And her parents agreed.

Helped by a lawyer and an accountant, they came up with a purchase price in the low six figures. Shelley would take responsibility for the payroll, and Sharon and Clark would extend her credit at a low interest rate.

The day of the closing was understandably bittersweet for Shelley and her parents. For Sharon and Clark, it was a relief and a loss at the same time. They were grateful that Becker's was staying in the family, and they had great faith in Shelley. Indeed, Sharon had come to admire many of the things Shelley instituted after she returned to the store—renovating the sales floor, bringing in more upscale lines of dresses, putting saleswomen on commission. But Sharon also realized she would be forever on the sidelines now.

The customers coming through the door knew nothing of the Becker family drama, or that a torch had been formally passed. The day after the paperwork was signed, Shelley came to work just as she always had since she was in her teens. She complimented brides and commiserated with their mothers, just as she had the day before. Only now the stakes were raised. The dresses, the veils, the racks, the walls—everything belonged to her. And all the challenges of running the place were in her lap too.

As for Sharon: She agreed to continue doing seamstress work for Becker's, at her home and at her leisure, which would keep her connected to the business. Shelley was grateful for her help and appreciated that Sharon still could be there to offer advice.

In a way, the mother-daughter relationship had come full circle. Shelley would now be paying her mother an hourly wage.

Shelley ended up slowly taking $250,000 out of the store's sales to remodel Becker's. It was an ambitious, risky undertaking, but it felt necessary. The place needed to be updated. The most crucial renovation, of course, was the Magic Room.

The project was a joint creation with Seth Kruger, a Minnesota-based sales rep for the wholesaler Allure Bridals. In the years after Shelley got divorced, she had dated Seth, who'd come through Fowler for trunk shows. Seth was a tall, self-assured, nattily dressed bridal business veteran, and as he developed feelings for Shelley, he threw himself into helping her brainstorm ways to give the old bank vault a measure of magic.

In his early fifties then, Seth carried himself as a straight-shooter and a proud romantic. He'd tell people: "I believe in love, and I think marriage should last forever. And I say that even though I've been married three times." He explained that he conducted his life by focusing on three words: "love," "kindness," and "forgiveness."

Shelley was drawn to Seth's charisma and cockiness, but she also found herself rolling her eyes, too, when she was around him. His patter was a bit much sometimes. Still, she saw how brides and mothers were drawn to him.

Seth would be purposely tactile with brides. At trunk shows, he'd ask them, "Would you mind if I touch you?" It was a question that sounded both respectful and intrusive all at once, and few brides said no. He'd then touch them very lightly, jiggering the dress on their frames or smoothing out the beading.

Because he traveled to bridal shops nationwide for Allure, Seth developed a clear sense of regional differences. He said Southern brides are often more respectful. They're always saying "Yes, ma'am." Their mothers are easier too. They help hang up the bridal gowns their daughters have rejected, rather than just piling them in the arms of saleswomen. Midwest brides are sometimes less agreeable; maybe the cold weather makes them moodier.

No matter what, though, Seth always loved brides. And he grew to love Becker's, too. He found it remarkable how the family kept the place going for seven decades.

When Shelley asked his advice about the Magic Room, he said mirrors would be crucial. "You want mirrors everywhere, taking every bride into infinity," he said. "You want them to think about how many different people they are, how many personalities they have, as they see themselves everywhere they look."

Shelley and Seth agreed that the history of the room as a bank vault gave it a kind of power. If a bride loves a dress she wears into the Magic Room, that's where she decides to buy it. "Remember," Seth said, "it's still very much 'the money room.'"

A lot of time was spent picking the carpet color, which ended up being a cross between emerald and teal. They decided the paneling on the walls would be the Sherwin-Williams color "mannered gold." Everything else in Becker's is a variation of white—the dresses, the veils, the banisters—so they thought it would be striking if brides entered the Magic Room and come upon all those mirrors framed by rich gold paneling.

For years, there had been racks of dresses in the vault. But Seth and Shelley emptied it out of everything except a pedestal adorned with two large letters, BB, for Becker's Bridal. The pedestal is circular, "like a wedding ring, like life," Shelley decided. "The beginning is the end is the beginning."

At first, when soft track lighting was installed in the room, it felt too dark. And so Shelley made plans to add more lighting. But then bride after bride stepped into the room and onto that pedestal, and they just swooned. "You look flawless," more than one mother said to her daughter. That soft lighting turned out to be exactly right. It didn't overwhelm the dresses, yet somehow picked up the sparkle in each gown's beading. It was flattering to the bride's facial features without showcasing blemishes. And it created an absolute mood of serenity. Families who'd been arguing out on the main floor spoke softly and lovingly to each other in here. It was magic.

Shelley called the electrician and told him not to come.

As the Magic Room came together, and the bonds between Shelley and Seth got stronger, he thought of making Fowler his base of operations. He discussed marrying Shelley. But as a traveling man, he struggled with commitment. ("Because we were so connected, I overlooked things," Shelley now says. "I'm a nurturer, and I nurtured him and accepted him as he was, when I should have demanded more from him.")

In the end, Seth realized he couldn't live in a tiny town, and he couldn't be the man Shelley needed him to be. They remained friends, but any chance at a lasting romance passed. Shelley is grateful, though: Their partnership yielded the Magic Room.

Lately, when Shelley is alone in the store, she will sometimes stand in the Magic Room by herself, proud of what she created. Just as each bride had a journey that led her to stand on that pedestal, Shelley has journeyed here too. The road she took is chronicled in all those slash-marked calendars in the basement, in the agreement she signed when she bought the business from her parents, and in the now-middle-aged image she sees of herself, carried into infinity, here in the Magic Room's mirrors.

She can't help but smile. Maybe it's the soft lighting. Or maybe it's the magic. But she's mostly satisfied with how she looks and who she is. She's still standing, and so is Becker's Bridal.

Chapter Seventeen

A Family's Love Story

*I*t's a Sunday morning in September, and Becker's is jammed with women for the store's annual "Blowout Sample Sale." Sample dresses have been drastically reduced—$1,100 gowns are as low as $300—but Becker's won't be doing any alterations.

"It's grab and go," Shelley explains to customers. "Everything is 'as-is.'"

For Shelley, the sale will free up floor space for new arrivals, and make some cash to pay bills. For a segment of brides, "as-is" is a chance to stay within their wedding budgets. They're willing to take a chance on missing buttons or lost beading.

When the store opened, sixteen brides and their entourages were lined up outside. A few hours later, forty more brides have shown up. Each dressing room is being shared by three brides, and the Magic Room line is six brides deep. Alyssa and their all-hands-on-deck sales team are trying to prevent confrontations, but it's a free-for-all.

One bride's mother approaches a saleswoman, steaming. "That mother over there just came into our dressing room and took a dress my daughter was about to try on," the mother says. "She grabbed it out of my hands and walked off with it."

"Where's the dress?" the saleswoman asks.

"Over there!" says the mother. The other mother's daughter actually has the dress on and is admiring herself in the old mirror near the counter.

"Well, we can't rip it off the girl's body," the saleswomen says, correctly.

As Alyssa walks toward the mother who grabbed the dress, hoping to negotiate a solution, she hears the daughter say, "Actually, I don't like the back of this."

"Let's hold on to it, just in case," her mother says. When asked whether she took the dress from another customer, the mother feigns surprise. "I didn't steal anything," she says. "Those other people were about to put the dress back on the rack."

Eventually, the thieves relinquish the dress—they decide it's not "the one"—and the first bride tries it on. She doesn't like it either. That's how it goes sometimes, especially lately.

Alyssa is convinced that too many customers in recent years are trying to re-create that episode of *Friends* in which Monica goes to a "Running of the Brides" sale in Brooklyn and fights other shoppers for her dream dress. At one point on the sitcom, her friend Rachel says, "These bargain shoppers are crazy!"

They're not really crazy. It's just that some wedding-gown shoppers today figure fighting for a dress is part of the bridal hunt.

Alyssa finds Shelley in the back office. "It's anarchy out there," she says. In the morning, they had used ribbons to separate the sale dresses from the full-priced dresses, because on a wild day like today, there's no time to help brides peruse the regular stock.

"They're breaking down the ribbons!" Alyssa says.

"Try to keep them back," Shelley tells her. "Ask nicely."

"Yeah, sure, Barbie, that'll work," says Alyssa.

It's her "white blindness" nightmare come to life.

Later in the afternoon, when things settle down, fifty-two-year-old Carol Otto arrives. She has four daughters, ages twenty to twenty-nine, three of whom are with her today. Carol was a Becker's bride in 1978. Her two older daughters bought their gowns here in 2003 and 2005. Now her third daughter, Missy, twenty-four, is engaged and ready for the Becker's experience.

The Ottos know they're supposed to look only at the sale merchandise. But, like other bridal scofflaws, they can't resist peeking beyond the ribbons. They're especially taken with a $1,600, trumpet-fit dress that is off-

Carol and Paul Otto, 1979

limits on a mannequin. Carol asks Alyssa, "Can my daughter try that on?"

Alyssa gets Shelley's permission to undress the mannequin, but they both know the "bridal mannequin principle": A bride who loves a dress on a mannequin will rarely love it on herself. Dresses just look better on mannequins than on hangers. That's why most mannequins aren't naked for long. (The mannequins may seem eternally stone-faced, but saleswomen detect a slight smile when they get their gowns back.)

Missy Otto turns out to be the exception to the mannequin principle. Wearing the mannequin's dress, she's thrilled. She loves the way the bow sits, and how soft the lace feels on her body. And so she heads up to the Magic Room for a formal look.

A Family's Love Story 195

Seeing her on the pedestal, Missy's twenty-year-old sister, Rochelle, starts to cry; it's common for a kid sister to be the first to get teary in the Magic Room. Soon, middle sister Heather is wiping away tears. Then their mother, Carol, feels overwhelmed too, and steps away, ducking into a nearby dressing room to have a moment by herself.

Turns out, it is the same dressing room Carol used when she came to Becker's as a bride-to-be in 1978. And as she stands in here, a memory comes clearly into her head, an unexpected reminder of her mother, who passed away fourteen years ago.

The memory is this: On that summer day in 1978, she and her mom had finally found a dress that fit well, looked good and, at $165, was affordable for her dad, a supervisor in a prison kitchen. Both Carol and her mother felt their emotions rise as they looked in the dressing-room mirror. "This is it," Carol said. "This is my dress."

And that's when Carol's mother reached up and slowly moved Carol's veil away from her cheek, and with a catch in her voice, said, "You're just a beautiful bride."

Standing in this same dressing room in 2010, it's almost as if Carol can again feel her mother touching her face, gently and lovingly. She can almost see her mom standing against the mirror, facing her, smiling proudly. The vividness of her recollection surprises Carol. "Wow, that memory was locked inside of me for thirty-two years," she thinks.

Now she needs a moment to compose herself before she rejoins her daughters. She's wishing, of course, that her mother was alive to be with all of them today. And she also wishes her mother had been around these last fourteen years to give her guidance. How might she have counseled Carol as her girls made their way to adulthood? How would her mother have consoled all of them now, as the family faces new struggles?

Carol stands inside that dressing room, thinking of everything, as her daughters call to her from the Magic Room, asking her to come back for another look at Missy.

————⸓

Great Grandma Peggy in the 1940s

Carol's mother, Lois, had been a very giving and attentive parent, even though she never knew what it felt like to be loved by a mother.

Carol's grandparents—Lois's parents—married at age seventeen, and after Lois was born in 1929, they quickly divorced. Lois's mother, Peggy, looked after her for a few months, but then one day decided she'd had enough of motherhood. She left Lois alone in her crib, walked out of her apartment in Michigan, and headed for Chicago, never to return. Given this abandonment, a court declared Peggy an unfit mother, and an aunt and uncle were left to raise baby Lois. Lois's father disappeared too. When he wasn't in jail, he was allegedly a truck-driver for Al Capone.

For a long time, Lois never knew what became of her mother. But in those silent years, Peggy's story would take some surprising twists.

In the 1930s, Peggy blossomed into a glamorous young woman. She spent time as a fashion model, then got a sales job in an elite Chicago dress shop, where she'd work for five decades. She never had any more children. Beyond a few Christmas cards signed "Peggy," she had almost no contact with her daughter Lois, who always struggled to understand why she had been rejected and abandoned.

But then, in 1989, when Peggy was seventy-eight, she called Lois one night at three a.m. She apologized for leaving her, and for evading all the duties of motherhood.

Lois listened and then spoke. "I forgive you," she said. The words came so easily that she surprised herself. They reconciled, and Lois agreed to visit her mother in Chicago. It was a remarkable reunion: an old woman trying to make amends to the sixty-year-old daughter she'd turned her back on.

In 1993, Peggy began showing signs of dementia, and Lois, the daughter she never cared for, and Carol, the granddaughter she never knew, brought her back to Michigan to look after her. At first, they set her up in her own apartment. Then they got her a room at an assisted-living facility. And then, in 1997, after Lois died of heart failure at age sixty-eight, Carol fulfilled her mother's wish by continuing to care for Peggy.

For Carol's daughters, having this long-absentee great-grandmother dropped into their lives was curious and instructive. They learned a good deal about forgiveness, and about the regrets and secrets that can accompany adults through their lifetimes.

Great-Grandma Peggy had arrived in Michigan with a batch of letters from a man who at one point was the love of her life. She was eager to talk about him. She said she had first met him in Sarasota, Florida, in 1954, where he had come for business. His business was baseball. His name was Ted Williams.

Williams, the Boston Red Sox slugger, had separated from his wife weeks earlier, and went on his first date with Peggy on March 5, 1954, during spring training. He would continue writing to her, and visiting her in Chicago when his team came to town. The relationship lasted into the fall of 1958. Three years later, Williams married another woman, his second of three wives.

The Otto girls were fascinated to learn that their unconventional and flawed great-grandmother had an ongoing affair with the legendary ballplayer. Peggy wasn't just a groupie who had a fling with him. She wanted the girls to know this. As an old woman, her most prized possession was a hundred-page, overstuffed scrapbook that she created in the 1950s to track Williams's exploits. She chronicled his injuries, his on-the-field triumphs and his off-the-field dates with her. She kept his letters to her, written on the stationery of various hotels. One night, just before a road trip to play the Chicago White Sox, Williams wrote to Peggy promising that when he arrived in town "I'll grab you close and not let you get away." Williams signed another note "T.03773." Did it refer to his batting average—he remains the last player in major league history to bat over .400 in a season—or did it represent an intimate code between them? Peggy never said.

Carol's second daughter, Heather, ended up writing her grad-school thesis about her great-grandmother's relationship with Williams. She described meeting Peggy when she was seven years old and explained how she wanted to spend time with this old woman "to learn who she was and what she had done with her life if it was not mothering children. . . . I came to appreciate the value Ted Williams's letters held for this lonely, heartbroken woman my great-grandmother eventually became." As for Peggy's place in her family, Heather decided: "Her motivations for her actions are beyond my imagination. But I recognize the courage it took to apologize decades later."

Peggy died of Alzheimer's disease in 2000.

Given this backstory, it's understandable that Carol would be so moved by the memory of her mother's touch in that dressing room at Becker's. Lois had never had the experience of shopping for a wedding dress with her own mother. She never felt her mother's loving hand against her cheek. And yet she instinctively knew to offer her hand to her own daughter. It made that gesture incredibly meaningful for Carol—both in 1978 and in her memory of the moment, in 2010.

Looking back, Carol is glad she was there for her grandmother in her final years. Peggy had not acted properly in her life. She made selfish decisions that reverberated through other people's lives for decades. "And yet she was family, and she needed to be taken care of, and so we forgave her," Carol says. "People make mistakes, but their families take them back. It was a good lesson for my daughters."

The Otto Girls when they were young, posing as Charlie's Angels

Over the years, raising four daughters, Carol Otto developed a set of philosophies. She'd tell them: "I'm going to stick with you girls, no matter what. I'll be on your side, but I'll be in your face, too." And she was.

When her daughters bickered, Carol wouldn't send them to separate corners. She'd make them stand, face-to-face, their noses touching. In a minute or two, they'd be laughing, almost like teammates, and everything was better.

Long before the girls got their wedding gowns, they'd been taught to see the magic in receiving a new dress. Carol and her husband, Paul, an insurance executive, liked to make special presentations for special occasions. For Christmas and Easter, the four girls would line up, close their eyes, and when they opened their eyes, their parents would be holding their new dresses, and the girls would ooh and ahh. Each also received a new dress on her sixteenth birthday.

Jennifer, the eldest daughter, born in 1981, was idolized by her sisters. "She could do no wrong in my eyes," says Heather, who is two years younger. "I wanted to be like her. She thought Jordan from New Kids on the Block was the cutest, so I said I did too, even though I secretly liked Donnie best. She took art classes and drew amazing cartoons, so I used my birthday money to purchase a sketchpad."

When Jennifer misbehaved, she was grounded from going to her friends' houses. She wasn't allowed to venture farther than the Ottos' front porch. Heather loved when Jennifer was grounded and couldn't see her friends because that meant she had her older sister all to herself. They could sit on that porch—a simple cement platform that was hot during the day but cool against the skin at night—talking and playing for hours.

Heather's hero worship got a jolt, however, when she was fourteen and Jennifer was almost sixteen. Heather came home from cheerleading practice one day and was met by her mother who was obviously distraught; she said she needed to talk to Jennifer. Heather was told to go to a neighbor's house until her mother came for her. It all seemed very strange to Heather. She'd never been asked to leave her own home before.

Later that night, she learned what happened. Their parents had discovered that Jennifer was having sex with her boyfriend. Heather, who hadn't yet even been kissed, was overwhelmed by the news.

"Was it just once?" she asked her sister when they were alone in their shared bedroom. Jennifer shook her head.

"More than ten times?" Heather asked, her eyes widening.

"We've been having sex for a while," Jennifer said. "Yes, more than ten times."

Later, while studying for a master's in English, Heather wrote about that night as a defining moment of her childhood. What made her ask if Jennifer had sex ten times?

"It was as if ten was a magic number that would save my sister from humiliation and judgment," Heather wrote. "My parents had made it clear to us that sex was an expression of love between husband and wife. I was not prepared to hear that my sister had disobeyed my parents by having premarital sex before she had turned sixteen."

Heather couldn't contain how furious she was with Jennifer. "I didn't feel like I knew her anymore. Even though she knew all of my secrets, I apparently knew none of hers. I couldn't stand the thought of looking at her every day in our shared bedroom."

The next morning, she asked her parents to switch the room arrangements. She wanted to move in with Missy. Her mother, Carol, didn't take immediate action, so Heather began the transfer on her own. Soon enough, all her belongings—her clothing, her porcelain dolls—were in the other room.

Heather would later write: "The change in my relationship with Jennifer was drastic. My love for her had been so natural before. I didn't have to try to love her; I just did. Now, I didn't know how to love her. All I saw were her faults. Wasn't an older sister supposed to set an example? How was I to love Jen?"

Jennifer would enter adulthood uneasily. She moved away to college, did her share of partying, and one night when she was nineteen she accepted a dinner invitation from a man who later date-raped her. "I told him no," Jennifer said, tearfully, again and again, after she returned home and called a family meeting to talk about it.

It was a terrible shock for her three younger sisters, and it was cathartic for Heather to later write about that night:

"There was nothing we could say or do to prevent Jen's hurt. It had already happened. I felt helpless. My mom had known of her experience and was sitting in a chair by my father, sobbing . . . Jennifer did not reveal her own vulnerability that often, but that night, she was exposed. I started to hate boys for larger reasons than simply acting immature in class and not asking me to high school dances."

Two years later, in the spring of 2002, Jennifer told Heather she was having unprotected sex with an older man she had begun dating.

"Are you on birth control?" Heather asked her.

"No."

"Are you using condoms?"

"Not usually. Sometimes."

"You're going to get pregnant, Jen. Is that what you want?"

Obviously, twenty-one-year-old Jennifer wasn't thinking clearly. She had known this man for just a month. There was passion between them, yes, but she ignored warning signs.

"Don't go on the pill," the man had told her. "It'll make you fat."

He didn't want to use protection himself, so they tried the rhythm method.

Soon enough, Jennifer was pregnant. That's when she learned that this man already had three children out of wedlock. It all felt so overwhelming and anguishing. Jennifer had been a typical, hard-working college student who liked to have fun and didn't always make smart decisions. Some young women survive their bad decisions without incident. Jennifer assumed, wrongly, that she would too.

It took her a couple weeks to find the courage to approach Carol with the news. And before she even got the words out, Carol looked in her eyes and knew; it was a mother's intuition. Jennifer crumbled into tears.

Later, Jennifer told her father, who soberly discussed her options. She had been studying graphic design, and was three semesters from graduation. It was decided that she'd get a job to support the baby and continue in school. Her parents would help her by moving into a home with more bedrooms, so there would be room for the baby. And her parents and sisters assured her: the love in their family was unconditional and would carry her through.

Jennifer's boyfriend tried to convince her to stay away from her family and to have an abortion, but from the beginning she knew she couldn't do that. And she had no interest in giving the baby up for adoption. "I knew how hurt my grandmother was when her mother abandoned her," Jen says. "Great-Grandma Peggy was in my head. I didn't want to repeat what she had done."

Jennifer and this man spoke briefly about marriage, but in her heart she knew better. When she told her paternal grandfather that she was considering marriage, he put it perfectly: "You've already made one mistake. Don't make a second one."

Jennifer's pregnancy was hard on the whole family. Heather, who had already distanced herself from her older sister, remained distraught. Missy developed bulimia, which her mother thought was related to the stress and depression in the household.

Meanwhile, Jennifer's relationship with this man deteriorated. He'd call at all hours: "I hate you!" Then: "I love you." He eventually got so abusive, verbally and physically, that she got a restraining order. When Jennifer was five months pregnant, he was jailed for seven days. The last time she ever saw him was in a courtroom.

Jennifer finished college while pregnant, spending long days studying while also working as a saleswoman for a flatware company in a local mall. Then, one day in December, a man walked into the store where she worked. He wanted to buy kitchen utensils as a Christmas present for a childhood friend. "My friend needs stuff for his apartment," he said.

Jennifer, then seven months pregnant, was affable and helpful, and the customer started telling her about his friend. "Matthew is such a great guy," the man said. "He's a doctor in his first year of residency, and he works really hard. He's twenty-six. He's single. Believe me, he deserves all good things. A knife set isn't enough!"

"Sounds like he needs a good woman," Jennifer replied, just conversationally.

"Of course he does!" the man said, and then looked at Jennifer more closely. "You know, you seem great. You're beautiful. Are you single?"

Self-conscious about being pregnant and unmarried, Jennifer had bought a twenty-dollar gold band at Target to wear on her ring finger. But she took a breath and answered the man directly. "Look, I'm seven months pregnant," she said as she followed the man's eyes to her belly, partially hidden behind the counter. "But yes, I'm single."

There was silence. Then the man smiled. "Well, you'd be perfect for my friend."

"I remind you I'm about to have a baby," Jennifer said.

"I see that," the man responded. "But everything happens for a reason. I think I was meant to meet you today."

He left the store and Jennifer was left contemplating his final words to her. Ten minutes later, the man returned with his fiancée, who'd been shopping elsewhere in the mall. "This is Jennifer," he said to his fiancée. "I think she'd be perfect for Matthew." The couple gave Matthew's phone number to Jennifer on a little piece of paper.

When she got home and told her family what happened, they advised her to be cautious. It all sounded odd. But Jennifer was so uncertain about her life. She felt as if she was wearing a scarlet letter, and that she'd end up alone forever. And so something within her told her to follow through. She called Matthew and left him a message.

First, she explained how she had met his friend at the store. "He probably told you about my situation," she said. "I'll completely understand if you don't return my call. . . ."

Matthew was surprised to learn that his friend had handed out his number, and so he asked for an explanation. The friend first talked about how beautiful and engaging Jennifer was. Then he said: "There's just one small thing."

"And what's that?" Matthew asked.

"She's seven months pregnant."

"What are you doing?" Matthew responded incredulously. "You're really trying to fix me up with pregnant women?"

Matthew didn't return Jennifer's call for ten days. But then he decided, what the heck, he'd call this mystery woman. They ended up speaking on the phone for two hours. About everything. The long phone conversations continued for a month, but they both felt it seemed too weird to meet. Jennifer was about to have a baby. Matthew was leaving Michigan soon for a residency at the Mayo Clinic in Minnesota. How could it work?

Finally, on Matthew's twenty-seventh birthday—February 1, 2003—they agreed to meet for lunch at a restaurant in the mall where Jennifer worked. As she remembers it, she was immediately taken with his blue eyes. He thought she was beautiful and charming—and out of his league.

Yes, she was pregnant; she looked huge. But that seemed secondary somehow to the chemistry between them.

Given that she was eating for two, Jennifer was ravenous that day; she had pork chops, mashed potatoes, dessert. Matthew watched her eat with a half-smile on his face.

It was understandably a strange first date, and yet their attraction to each other was undeniable. "This is crazy," Matthew said at one point.

"Completely crazy," Jennifer answered.

Matthew later approached his parents. "I've met a girl," he said, "and she's eight months pregnant." They listened, and then his mother spoke: "If Jennifer is worthy enough for you to mention her to us, then she means something to you."

Matthew had been prepared for his parents to show a degree of angst. He would have understood. But he was touched by how nonjudgmental they were. They had faith in him. He had their blessing to follow his heart.

On their second date, when Jennifer was just short of nine months pregnant, she and Matthew went to Olive Garden. It was an icy day, and she was moved by how he gently took her hand to help her walk into the restaurant.

Jennifer knew she was having a girl, and so they discussed names she was considering, including Victoria.

"I've always loved that name," Matthew said. "You should go with that!" In that instant, Jennifer knew what her baby would be named.

Victoria was born at 9:46 p.m. on March 5, 2003, and twelve hours later, Matthew came to the hospital, where he met the baby and Jennifer's family for the first time. Someone took a photo of him holding Victoria, and he was smiling proudly—almost as if he were her father. "I can't say that heaven parted and the angels descended when I took her in my arms," he now says. "But it was a precious moment."

Matthew moved to Minnesota for his residency in anesthesiology, and Jennifer and the baby traveled from Michigan to visit him. Sometimes they'd meet him halfway, in Chicago. It was all so romantic, and by August, Matthew was ready to propose.

One day he put Willie Nelson's version of "I Can See Clearly Now" on his stereo. Victoria was napping, and Matthew asked Jennifer to dance. The dance felt awkward—Matthew was nervous—and so he aborted the dance and decided to just do it. He got on one knee, took Jennifer's hand, and asked her to marry him.

Matthew knew he was proposing to two people, of course.

When Jennifer's parents got news of the engagement, they told Matthew a secret: From the time their four daughters were born, they had been praying for each of their future husbands. "You're a man of integrity," Carol said to Matthew. "And we believe you were meant for Jen from the very beginning. I've got to tell you. I feel such respect for you, that you could look past Jennifer's mistakes and see the woman she is."

Days later, when Carol told Jennifer she wanted to take her to Becker's, Jennifer was suspicious. "If that's where Mom got her dress, they probably sell grandma dresses there," she told her sister Heather. But she agreed to go.

Jennifer felt embarrassed walking in, carrying six-month-old Victoria in a car seat. It was uncomfortable to tell Shelley and her saleswomen that she wasn't marrying the baby's father. But they were fascinated by her story. "Wow, your fiancé is a very special man," Shelley told her. "You're going to have a happy marriage."

Carol and Jennifer didn't want to buy a white dress. It seemed inappropriate. But they found a beautiful champagne-colored gown with a sprinkling of poinsettias on it.

The day Jennifer got married, her sister Heather sobbed all the way down the aisle. She was so grateful that Jennifer had finally found a safe haven and a worthy man. She felt renewed faith in her once-wayward childhood hero.

After they married, Matthew and Jennifer had two more children. Their youngest, Abby, born in 2010, has Down syndrome and a rare blood disorder; doctors say she will likely contract leukemia before age three. She's a beautiful little girl—they call her "the light in our lives"—but her health issues weigh heavily on the entire family. Abby ends up in hospital emergency rooms almost every other week. Jennifer says she appreciates her past struggles because they've helped prepare her for the struggles she's had with Abby. They gave her the courage to deal with what's ahead.

These days, the Ottos also find it helpful to think of all the tests and all the setbacks in their family history—from the day in 1929 when Great-Grandma Peggy ran away to the day in 2002 when Jennifer announced her pregnancy to the day in 2010 when little Abby was diagnosed. They got through all of it together, sometimes hand in hand, sometimes nose to nose. They'll get through whatever lies ahead, too.

Victoria, who was formally adopted by Matthew when she was a toddler, is now seven years old. From time to time, she'll look at that photo of Matthew in the hospital, holding her tightly, twelve hours after her birth.

"Your daddy picked you," Jennifer has told her. "That's a very special thing. And you know what? He picked me, too."

⌒

When Becker's Bridal hosts their "Blowout Sample Sale," Shelley and Alyssa never know who will show up, or what secrets they carry with them. The day can feel wild and exhausting, and all about making quick sales. But Shelley tries to keep in mind that even on these busiest days, in a store filled with frenzied shoppers grabbing at dresses, there are always families who've arrived here with a lifetime of bittersweet memories.

Shelley and Alyssa didn't know why Carol Otto ducked into that dressing room. They saw her crying, but couldn't tell if they were tears of joy or sadness. They didn't know the things on Carol's mind: thoughts of her late mother touching her face; of her grandmother, so late in life, rejoining the family; of her pregnant daughter's luck in finding a man of great character; of the health issues now facing her youngest grandchild.

And so all Shelley could do was to make pleasant small talk, and to joke about the naked mannequin. She thanked Carol for buying her gown at Becker's all those years ago, and for returning with her three older daughters.

Rochelle, Carol's youngest, isn't yet in a serious relationship.

"I hope when you're ready," Shelley said, "that you'll come back to see us too."

Jennifer and Matthew on their wedding day, with Victoria

Chapter Eighteen

Megan

*W*hen a bride and her family find themselves coping with an emergency that might lead to a wedding's postponement or cancellation, they don't immediately think to contact Becker's Bridal. In 1971, after Ashley Brandenburg's mother went through the windshield of her sister's car, needing 1,000 stitches, no one called the shop to let them know. Likewise, in 2010, Shelley never got a call about Megan Pardo's car accident on her way to teach kindergarten. The Pardo family was too overwhelmed to think of it.

The day of the accident, Megan's forty-eight-year-old mom, Laura, took five nerve-wracking hours to drive from Michigan to BroMenn Medical Center in Bloomington, Illinois. When she arrived, she was relieved to learn that Megan's injuries didn't appear life-threatening, but she was also overwhelmed by the magnitude of what had happened.

"Your daughter had her window open," a nurse said, and very quickly, Laura learned the ramifications of that statement.

Megan's decision that morning to roll down her window so fresh air might keep her awake had served to compound her injuries. When she

211

had jerked the steering wheel to the left, leading the car to flip, her face and right hand went through the open window, scraping along the pavement as the car rolled over. Her seat belt had saved her life, but any part of her body that went out that open window was battered and bloody.

Megan was conscious when the car landed in the cornfield across the road, but she was bleeding from both hands, her face, and her head. The largest laceration was above her left eye, but Megan's vision was OK, and looking at her right hand, she immediately knew that the damage done to it was severe. One finger was severed, and the others looked like raw hamburger. Her hand hardly resembled a hand anymore.

Though the pain was intense, she was able to press her damaged right hand against the horn while she frantically screamed and waved her left hand out the window. A young man driving a truck saw her, called 911, and remained at the scene to keep her calm. Her fiancé, Shane, then finishing his degree as an agricultural business major at Illinois State, wasn't contacted right away. It didn't matter. Megan was in such shock she couldn't even remember his cell phone number to tell rescue workers.

At the hospital, she was quickly taken into four hours of surgery in an attempt to repair the damage to her right hand and to take skin from the side of her body so it could be grafted on her face. Her left hand had fared better, but still had a broken finger and various scrapes and cuts.

For hours, Laura sat in the hospital waiting room with Shane, her twenty-three-year-old future son-in-law, a soft-spoken young man who was reassuringly calm. As the day wore on, Laura's good opinion of him was reaffirmed. If Megan made it through, Laura knew, Shane would be there for her no matter what.

Halfway through surgery, the doctor came out and spoke to them. Megan had told the doctor that she is right-handed, and he addressed that first. "The damage to the right hand is far more extensive than we anticipated," he said. He couldn't find bone, muscle, tendons or joints in her middle two fingers. Her pinky had just a few fragments, and the doctor said he was able to reattach the index finger up to the first knuckle.

"She's unlikely ever to be able to use the fingers on this hand again," the doctor said. "You should prepare yourselves for the possibility that we'll need to amputate her hand. She might be better off having a prosthetic hand with fully functional fingers than living with a hand that will basically be unusable."

The doctor returned to surgery to work on the skin grafts and to slowly remove the gravel that had permeated all of Megan's wounds. While Megan was in recovery, he returned again to the waiting room. "The next twenty-four hours are crucial," he said. "We want to see if the middle fingers on her right hand will stay alive." He was a straight-shooter: "I'm not optimistic. Only one blood vessel per finger is intact. I've been grafting skin around nothing—no bone. It's like a hot dog—loose skin just hanging there."

Megan's dad, Jack, who had been in Alabama on business, without easy airport access, drove to Illinois as fast as he could, but it would be ten p.m. before he'd arrive. And that tense, ten-hour ride to Illinois offered a terrible sense of déjà vu for him. In 1984, when his older daughter, Melissa, had fallen off a table while having her diaper changed, he had just left town on business; at the moment she fell, he was driving to Windsor, Ontario. Because he couldn't be reached by phone, state police were sent to find him on the interstate. They never spotted Jack's car, so he finally got the news when he checked into his hotel in Canada: His nine-month-old had fallen and was in a coma. Now again, twenty-six years later, terrible news about a daughter was reaching him. How many fathers, twice in their lives, get such calls while out of town on a business trip?

As Jack drove, he tried to stay positive. What good would it do to consider himself cursed? Unlike his wife and daughter, he was not a man of great faith. And so he didn't find comfort in considering the accident to be "God's will." Instead, he thought logically. "I've already been through the worst, losing Melissa," he told himself. "This car accident is awful, but the doctors say Megan's life is not in jeopardy. We've already handled the worst. We've lost a child. We can handle this."

By late evening, word of the accident had spread through Illinois, Michigan, and other places where people knew Megan. Online prayer chains were started, and Laura was advised to open a page on CaringBridge.org, the online site that helps friends and family remain apprised of a patient's health updates. In Laura's first CaringBridge posting, she wrote: "Megan slept fitfully throughout the night, as did her parents. We felt God's presence and the love of all of you as you prayed throughout the night."

On the morning after surgery, Megan's throbbing right hand was her alarm clock, and once awake, she had trouble breathing because her damaged nose was packed with gauze. "The doctor came in and shared the best news we could hope for," Laura wrote on CaringBridge. "All the fingers on her right hand are viable and have circulation. They were pink when he poked at them, and she let him know she could feel them. The doctor told her she's very lucky—a blessed girl."

In the days that followed, Laura used the site to chronicle Megan's progress, both medically and spiritually. It was therapeutic for Laura to write updates, and to read all of the supportive postings people were leaving in the online guestbook.

Wednesday, March 31, at 9:18 a.m.: "The doctor wants to build a splint for Megan's right hand. The goal is to get her hand and fingers to lie correctly. They need to elongate her fingers and keep them rigid. He wants the skin he has grafted there to become like an eggshell, so that when it's time for hand reconstruction, the fingers will be ready."

Wednesday, 7:01 p.m.: "The doctor and occupational therapist created a rubber 'banjo splint' today around Megan's arm, wrist, and palm. Each fingernail has been stitched to its corresponding finger and the ends of the stitches are hooked to rubber bands. Each rubber band is hooked to a peg on a loop. The purpose is to elongate her fingers and keep them rigid. It's awkward and uncomfortable, but she does have all four fingers and they look good. The only potential complication is that the index finger, severed in the accident and reattached Monday, is not looking healthy. Please join us in a powerful prayer for Megan's index finger."

Thursday, April 1 at 8:11 p.m.: "The doctor explained that plastic surgery can't be done on Megan's face for at least six months. The tissue he grafted has to become soft, with good blood flow. So for the wedding Megan will have makeup covering the scars. We hadn't really understood this, so it came as a shock. Meanwhile, because there are no bones, tendons, muscle, or cartilage in her two middle fingers, it will take a long time for them to be ready for additional surgeries, which will involve bone grafts with bone from her hip. Please don't stop praying, as the pain in Megan's hand is fairly constant, especially when the doctor tightens the rubber bands. We also anticipate some anxiety and frustration as she learns to live one-handed."

Friday, April 2, at 11:55 a.m.: "God is good! Megan is alive, she has normal brain function, no internal injury, her charming personality is intact, and she has Shane. However, she will no longer have the tip of the index finger on her right hand. The doctor has confirmed that the reattachment is not working. The fingertip is dying. She is scheduled for surgery Monday at 7 a.m. to remove the tip. At that time, he'll also make a decision about the pinkie finger (which is black) and the middle finger (which is turning purple.) Only the ring finger has a nice pink color. Megan's attitude remains good, as she realizes life with one hand is still a pretty good life."

Before the accident, Megan had believed she was in love with Shane. But it wasn't until afterward, as she watched him show his love for her, day after day, that she truly realized how deep the bonds between a man and woman can be.

"This is a test for us," Shane told people when they asked how he and Megan were doing. "Couples don't usually face a test like this so early in a relationship. But we're going to pass. Loving each other through adversity will make us stronger and closer." And it did. He actually realized that he loved Megan more every day, just seeing the courage with which she faced her predicament. In the days after the accident, Shane kept trying to reassure Megan by holding her less-injured left hand, to let her know he was there.

Megan and Shane two weeks after the accident

Early on, Megan told her doctor that her wedding was August 1, just four months away. "What will I look like then? Do we need to move our date?"

"Well, you'll still be healing," the doctor said. "We're going to be doing plastic surgery on your face, your hands. But you'll be able to get married. Don't worry."

Shane had listened to the discussion, and then somewhat softly, he offered a few words that filled Megan's heart, and her mother's, too. "Megan," he said, "it doesn't matter what your face looks like. I'll walk down the aisle with you today if you want."

When he finished speaking, Laura had to look away to compose herself. When the accident happened, this young man had been engaged to her daughter for just one week. He hadn't yet signed on to stand by Megan in sickness and in health. It would be understandable if he asked to postpone the wedding, or even if he was scared away completely. And yet here he was, saying all he needed to say in two sentences. That's the kind of love you wish for your daughter.

In the week after the accident, Megan cried at times about her predicament. How could she not? But mostly, she soldiered through. As Laura watched her daughter find ways to cope and accept, she was very moved by this thought: We might think we know our children's character, their inner fortitude and the limits of their resilience, but we can't fully predict how they will respond in a crisis.

Megan never asked, "Why me?" Instead, she said to Laura, "I'm pretty mad at myself, Mom. I can't believe I allowed myself to fall asleep while driving." More than anything, she'd say, she was grateful that "the grace of God got me through."

Laura was especially moved by Megan's attitude when she was told about the need for amputation surgery. Perhaps if the doctors had told her they needed to amputate on the day of the accident, it would have been more traumatic for Megan. But by the sixth day, given all the pain she'd been through, and all she had learned about herself, about Shane's love for her, and about the great concern displayed by so many people, she was able to accept the news. Besides, her fingers were turning black and ugly, with an odor that suggested death. "I'm ready," she said.

Before the operation, nurses asked her a number of questions, several of which were designed to gauge her awareness of what was ahead for her. "Do you know what the doctor plans to do today?" a nurse asked.

"He's going to amputate my dead fingers," she answered. She did not say it in an emotional way. She said it as if she had already detached herself from those fingers, as if she had already mourned for them and said good-bye.

In truth, Megan worried as much about her parents as they worried about her. "It's hard for them to see their baby girl in such pain," she told Shane.

"Just let them love you and be there for you," he replied. "It's helping them, especially your mom."

Her mother's hovering concern was often welcomed by Megan, but it annoyed her at times too. She appreciated that her mom was giving people updates, but wondered if all the gritty details were necessary. Her mother seemed eager to tell the world about Megan's hand, almost as if it would make it easier for Laura to wrap her own head around what had happened.

As Megan's recovery continued, the sites of her injuries throbbed for hours, and the pain medication made her vomit. But there were sweet moments too. One night, highly medicated, she was extremely loopy. Not much she said made sense. But then she turned to Shane, smiled, and told him, "I like you. You're nice."

Laura tended to the website. She went there not just to inform loved ones, but to grieve, to offer thanks, and to ask for assistance. She asked those reading to pray for the doctor's wisdom and diligence, for the skin grafts on Megan's forehead, for her colleagues back at Hope College, who were covering her classes, and most of all "for Megan's healing, both physically and emotionally."

On Monday, April 5, at 12:24 p.m., seven days after the accident, Laura wrote on CaringBridge about the amputation surgery on Megan's four fingers: "The tissue had died and was no longer viable. Dr. Allen also removed the dressing on Megan's forehead and found that a spot the size of a silver dollar had not taken the graft and would need to be re-grafted. Megan slept well last night (her mom, not so much) and was calm while we waited for surgery. Each of the nurses commented on her positivity and evident faith in God. She and I also talked about how she will be able to adapt. There are certainly worse body parts to have to live without."

Two days later, Laura wrote on the website: "The prayers we need now are for tomorrow, when the doctor removes the dressing on her right hand and Megan sees her hand for the first time minus her fingertips. Dr. Allen has warned us that it will likely be quite traumatic for her. Please pray that Megan will have the strength to face her hand."

When the moment came for the doctor to unwrap the dressing, Megan got queasy. Some of it was due to pain—the gauze was stuck to her wound in several places—but she also felt nauseated just looking at what had become of her hand. She couldn't tell how much of her hand was lost.

Everything was too swollen. But she knew she was missing a good part of each finger. "It's OK," she said softly, and then, "Thank you, Doctor, for everything you've done for me."

~

Megan remained in Illinois for several weeks, staying at a Holiday Inn Express near the hospital, where she underwent daily therapy. During doctor visits, Megan often felt great pain when her hand was undressed and debrided (the removal of dead skin). As he worked, her doctor encouraged her to look at her hand. "You need to grieve the loss of your fingers," he said, "to accept what your hand will look like." And so she would force herself not to look away as she kept her left hand in Laura's, squeezing tightly.

In physical therapy, Megan, the fledgling kindergarten teacher, became a student, learning to dress, write, and open get-well cards with her left hand. "Your writing looks like your kindergarten students' handwriting," her doctor joked. At night, Shane and Laura worked jigsaw puzzles with her, to help her improve her fine motor skills on her left hand. Soon, they started working with what remained of her right hand. Trying to touch her thumb to the stump of a finger often left her light-headed, but she persevered. Her therapist worked with her to try to make a fist, to grip a fork. The pain could be excruciating, but progress was made.

It was hard for Shane and Laura to watch Megan in such agony, and she was, understandably, very stressed out sometimes. "I'm sorry, I'm sorry," she'd tell them.

"It's OK," Laura told her. "We just wish we could take the pain away."

Meanwhile, the wedding planning continued. Megan and Shane worked on the guest list and planned their honeymoon in Mexico. They arranged to return to Michigan together to select a wedding cake. Megan also would need to go to Becker's for a second fitting. And as they thought about the wedding day, they decided that Megan ought to change the part in her hair and grow out bangs to cover the wound on her forehead. "You'll look great," Shane reassured her. (In the months ahead, her hair wouldn't always cooperate with the new part, but that was the easiest challenge Megan faced.)

Meanwhile, doctors kept finding gravel in Megan's wounds. All of that gravel could take months to work its way out. There was also nail tissue in the stubs of Megan's fingers. The nail tissue didn't know a finger was gone, and would try to grow a nail, which was very uncomfortable. Megan was told this could go on for the next thirty years.

On May 23, Megan agreed with Laura that it would be OK to post a photo of her right hand on CaringBridge, allowing friends and loved ones to better understand. Eventually, they'd all see the hand. Why put it off? "Megan told me to warn you in case you don't have a strong stomach!" Laura wrote. "I think her hand looks beautiful."

Megan was able to return to student teaching a month after the accident. She really had no choice. To earn her degree in early childhood education, she needed to finish her commitment to the school. But she felt very anxious. "Will the kids be afraid of me?" she asked her mom. "Will they not want to talk to me?"

Laura couldn't fully answer her. It's hard to know how children will react to something like this. But she did tell Megan: "The kids loved you, and you're still you."

It turned out, the children noticed the serious gash on her forehead first, and asked questions. She told them about the accident, how she was on her way to teach them when it happened. Her right hand was still bandaged, but the most curious kids asked for a look, and she obliged, unwrapping the dressing. The children stood around her, taking it in. Then one boy spoke: "At least you don't have to clip your fingernails now."

The other kids agreed: Here was an unexpected benefit! Megan had to smile. She let out a breath; it was a moment of appreciation and relief. For the rest of her life as a teacher, children would be looking at her hand, asking questions. But it would all be OK.

She pulled some strands of hair over the gash on her forehead, and led the children back to their desks.

Day by day, Megan tried to focus on what was positive. When people asked about her injuries, she'd tell them: "Early on, one doctor said I wouldn't have any bones in my fingers, but I do. He said I wouldn't be able to write with my right hand, but I can."

Eventually, Megan returned to Michigan to take care of wedding tasks with her mother. Everywhere they went, her mother felt obliged to tell acquaintances and strangers the story of the accident. Megan would have preferred to keep her hand out of view, to pull her bangs over her forehead and try not to call attention to herself. She thought of telling her mother this, but instead she mentioned it to one of her mom's friends at church. "Maybe telling so many people is her way of coping with what happened to you," the woman told Megan. And so Megan decided to just let it be, and to show her hand and lift her bangs every time her mother brought it up to a curious onlooker.

When they returned to Becker's for the second fitting, Shelley didn't immediately notice Megan's injuries, and neither did her salespeople. Megan was relieved at that. A bride wants to feel beautiful stepping into her wedding dress. She doesn't want to feel like an oddity, or an object of pity.

But Megan hadn't said anything about her urge to hide her injuries as she and Laura drove over to the store with Megan's sister-in-law and best friend. Once they arrived, Laura spoke up pretty quickly.

Gwen, her saleswoman, had been hovering around Megan, making small-talk. People's eyes don't immediately go to someone's hands, and Megan's hair had grown out and was covering her forehead pretty well. The injury on her nose was covered by makeup. Megan thought to herself: This is nice. No one is noticing.

Then, in the Magic Room, as Shelley got on her knees, ready to start hemming, Gwen said, "You look beautiful, Megan. You really do." That's when Laura answered, "Yes, she's looking so much better now. She's really coming along well."

And, of course, the saleswomen had to ask what she was referring to, and once they looked at her hand and heard all the details, a couple of them actually got teary-eyed. One Becker's worker had to walk away because she was ready to sob.

It's difficult for people to understand exactly how Megan's fingers were so damaged in the accident, and so she had to explain about the open window, and falling asleep while driving. Her mom even lifted Megan's bangs to show the forehead wound.

For a while, no one was talking about the wedding dress, and Megan had to stand there, patiently answering questions and accepting condolences. She didn't begrudge people their curiosity. It just felt deflating to discuss this while standing in her dress. When her mother was out of earshot, Megan said to her sister-in-law, "Boy, my mother sure likes bringing up what happened to me."

"I've noticed," her sister-in-law said. "Should we say something?"

"No, it's OK. I understand."

By then, Megan realized that her mother's response was a mix of her own nervousness and a maternal urge to protect Megan. Laura wanted to save her daughter the embarrassment of having her hand noticed, and it being the elephant in the room, with people afraid to say anything. In Laura's mind, there was another issue, too. She had been able to keep her own emotions in check when telling people the story of Megan's accident. But when Megan told the story herself, Laura often got choked up. Hearing her daughter so bravely explain her injuries, well, it was more than she could take. And so part of her chatter was proactive. She wanted to speak so Megan wouldn't have to.

Megan sensed all of this, and indulged her mother. As Shelley hemmed Megan's wedding gown, Laura talked. "We actually feel lucky," she said. "A lot worse could have happened. So many people have told us about a car rolling over and their loved one was paralyzed or had brain damage or died. Yes, Megan lost fingers and hit her head. It's been hard for her, for all of us. But we still have her. She's still Megan."

The last time Shelley had seen Megan in the Magic Room, she'd been engaged for just one week. There are photos of Megan from that day, smiling in her gown. Anyone who looks at the photos now can't help but notice her hands at her side, her fingers intact. They notice that her forehead was clear, that her hair was parted the way she'd always worn it. Those turned out to be her last photos before the accident.

Now Megan was back at the store, her new image repeating thousands of times in the Magic Room mirrors, her mother's words—"She's still Megan"—echoing in he head. "Come on downstairs," she heard Shelley say, "we're going to find you just the right headpiece."

Chapter Nineteen

Meredith

eredith Maitner never returned to Becker's to buy her gown, and never again saw that super-sexy number she had tried on there. She was one of the hundreds of brides-to-be who visit Becker's each year and leave without making a commitment.

The thing about Meredith: She has warm memories of that sexy dress and how sensational she looked in it. She's glad she has a photo of herself wearing it, taken in the Magic Room. But partly because she has spent these pre-wedding months very aware of her age—she'll turn forty just before her wedding day—she decided she needed to walk down the aisle in something more subdued.

She ended up buying her gown at a small, independent bridal shop that was going out of business. "The store was in this old, horrible-looking house," she later told friends, "and when I got there, I said to myself, 'They'll never have a dress for me.'"

In one bedroom there were racks of dresses, and in a second bedroom with green shag carpeting dating to the 1970s, there was a simple pedestal and a mirror. "The store didn't have a Magic Room, that's for sure,"

Meredith said, "but I found a magic dress. It works for my figure. It's cheaper. It's elegant. I love it."

Shelley never likes to lose a sale because someone can't find the right dress—that's one reason Becker's has 2,500 in stock—but like a fisherman resigned to letting some fish get away, she recognizes she can't snag them all. She tries to find it in her heart to wish all brides well, even if they don't wear a Becker's dress. That's harder to do, of course, with brides who waste her time trying on dresses they intend to buy more cheaply on the Internet. But for someone like Meredith, "I understand," Shelley says. "I hope she lives happily ever after and never needs to come back to look for another dress."

Younger brides are more apt to focus on the details of their ceremonies, dresses, receptions, and honeymoons. They walk around with thick "wedding notebooks" crammed with names, phone numbers, menus, gift registries. No one walks around with a thick notebook about how to prepare for a meaningful marriage. The marriage can feel like an afterthought.

But for Meredith, the months leading up to her wedding have been a time of introspection. Given her age, she has friends who've already bought wedding dresses twice in their lives. Some have found great happiness in their second marriages.

One of her friends married and had children very young; she and her husband didn't know what they wanted in a mate, or how to compensate for their differences. The marriage ended in divorce. The second time, this friend knew better what she was looking for. "It makes such a difference when you're with the right person," she told Meredith.

Because Meredith and her fiancé, Ron, are older and marrying for the first time, Meredith feels they're wiser, more settled, and more confident than when they were young. When she puts her life in perspective, she realizes that she may have skipped the "starter marriage" that so many women in her generation now have behind them.

"In all my years of dating, I went on a few runs of jerk, jerk, jerk," she says. "I also dated intelligent, genuine men who might have made good husbands for someone, but not for me. I just couldn't develop emotional feelings for them."

She also dated men who thought she was smart and fun, but they weren't attracted to her romantically. "There were so many times when I thought, 'Well, maybe there's something wrong with me.' But I came to realize that there wasn't something wrong with me, or wrong with the guy. There just wasn't a connection."

She is relieved that she never misstepped into marriage with one of the jerks—or one of the nice guys with whom she felt no passion. She recognizes the tradeoffs: It may be too late now for her to have children, given her age and that she has diabetes and high blood pressure. That saddens her. But mostly, she's decided, she's happy with where her life has carried her.

In her management role at a footwear company, Meredith earns significantly more than Ron does as a graphic designer. If they're able to have children, or if they adopt, he'll be the stay-at-home dad while she works. Meredith is comfortable with that. As she got older as a single woman, and very successful on her own, she realized that if she ever found the right man, it didn't matter if he was rich or had a high-powered career. And it didn't matter if he wasn't the stereotypical ideal on other fronts.

There's a lot of talk these days about the extended adolescence of single men; women complain that too many of them remain "pre-adults" into their thirties. There's a whole genre of movies—*Knocked Up, Swingers*—that showcase these guys. And yet, in ratios equal to women their ages, about 65 percent of single men in their twenties, and 40 percent in their thirties, say they want to settle down and get married, according to a 2011 Rutgers University study. The assumption is that these men are commitmentphobes who'd rather play video games than turn into responsible husbands and fathers. But from Meredith's vantage point today, the issues are more nuanced.

She has certainly seen plenty of boys inside the men she has dated, including Ron. "I prayed I wouldn't have a husband who sits around playing video games," she says. "But guess what? I've now got a forty-two-year-old husband who sits around playing Xbox with his friends. And you know what? Given all his other great attributes, I'm fine with that."

In essence, over the years, she was able to home in on what she needed from a man. Meredith is a chronic list-maker, and in her twenties, she'd list the qualities she wanted in a husband. She'd come upon her list and revise it, adding something, crossing something out. For a time, she thought she wanted a corporate executive, an accountant, or a lawyer. She thought she wanted an athlete. "I've always hated sports," she says, "but I thought I wanted a guy's guy with guy friends doing guy things. I didn't think I'd end up with a nerd playing video games all night long, like Ron does. Or that he'd be a 'foodie' like I am, someone who loves cooking, and watching the Food Network with me. But that's Ron. Who'd have thought?"

That "man-of-my-dreams" list, written and rewritten when she was a young woman, is now just a curiosity.

"I came to realize that, most of all, I wanted someone to support me emotionally—not necessarily financially," she now says, "someone to share a bowl of popcorn with, to go to a movie with, to share the responsibilities of caring for a dog or a home—or kids. I wanted to do the dishes in the kitchen and look out the window to see him cutting the grass. I wanted someone who could make the good times better and the hard times not as hard. I know, it's corny, but I wanted someone to grow old with me, and it's fine if he's playing Xbox some of the time. I feel so happy because I believe I've found that in Ron."

—⁓—

Three weeks before her wedding day, Meredith turned forty years old, and she and Ron were invited to her parents' house to celebrate. Her family had wrapped yellow police tape around the house that read CAUTION! 40TH BIRTHDAY IN PROGRESS. Her mother also had bought suckers that said 40 SUCKS! Everyone had their little joke that she was old, and then they had dinner.

"Overall, my fortieth birthday was pretty painless," Meredith says. "I was too busy with the wedding plans and the bridal showers, and I was just overwhelmed by the generosity of spirit that people were showing me. They know how long I've waited to marry. They know how much I've wanted it. They've given me such warmth and love. It's like I hardly noticed I was leaving my thirties."

Two days after Meredith's birthday, her sister-in-law hosted a bachelorette party, and Meredith's friends made gallons of sangria and played '80s music really loud. They also brought along a stripper pole, and though nobody stripped, everyone took a turn dancing with the pole. Her bridesmaids ranged in age from thirty-six to fifty-three, but that night, with those drinks and those songs and that metal pole, they felt young and uninhibited. Meredith did too.

Later that week, her father told her he had been thinking about something, and wanted to tell her. "Ron is a great guy, a great partner," he said.

"I know that," Meredith answered. "The most wonderful thing about him is that if I need his help, if I'm down, he'll be there for me. I can count on him. That's worth everything."

Her father smiled at her. "I just want you to know," he said, "that you've made the right choice."

Meredith didn't cry, but she felt her emotions rising. "I'm forty now," she thought to herself. "I don't always come to my parents with my problems. But it feels so wonderful to hear my father say that, to know that he approves."

Meredith also thought about how far she'd traveled—about how many wrong men she had dated, and how she had coped with the uncertainty of her life as a single woman.

"You know what, Dad?" she said. "At the wedding, I think I'm going to walk down the aisle really slowly. I've waited a long time for this. A really long time. So when I'm on your arm, in my dress, on my wedding day, well, please walk slowly with me. Let's make it last."

Chapter Twenty

A New Generation

*M*aybe Grandma Eva's ghost is here at Becker's, hovering and second-guessing the renovations. If not, and she somehow returned to the store after all these years, the place (and the brides) would feel pretty foreign to her.

One bride takes out her laptop, so she can use Skype to model her dress for her mother, vacationing in Portugal.

Another never-married bride stops by with her maid of honor and her fiancé's best-man: They're her daughter and son from a previous relationship, ages six and eight.

A third bride has come with an ice-filled cooler, sparkling wine, five bridesmaids, and her mother. This is the bride's sixth visit, and after nineteen total hours in the shop, unable to make up her mind, she has finally settled on a dress. "OK, I'll take it," she announces, and her mother and attendants start whooping so loudly that Shelley can hear them in the back office.

"That Cooler Queen finally picked a dress," says Shelley's daughter, Alyssa, who has just stepped into the office to deliver paperwork. Shelley and Alyssa peer out of the one-way mirror that looks over the sales floor. While the celebration continues, the saleswomen try desperately to resist rolling their eyes. It probably didn't take her this long to commit to her fiancé! In Grandma Eva's day, no bride would dare take nineteen hours to pick a dress. It would be the height of arrogance and indulgence, the talk of the town, a signal of near insanity.

There are other trends that would leave Grandma Eva mystified.

Since Eva's time, brides and their mothers seem to have developed superhuman abilities to notice even the tiniest stain on a dress; for some, a smudge can be a cause of great consternation and outrage. (In times of plenty, people find plenty of little things to get them down.) And it doesn't matter that, at their wedding receptions, some of these same brides will actually get on the floor and do the Worm. "You can just imagine what a dress looks like after a bride does the Worm," says Shelley.

Four brides trashing their wedding dresses

And here's where things have taken an even stranger turn.

Brides used to return from their honeymoons, dry-clean their gowns, and try to preserve them for eternity. But lately, Shelley and Alyssa have become accustomed to indulging a new tradition among brides, dubbed "Trashing the Dress."

In the weeks after their weddings, more and more Becker's brides have been getting back into their white gowns and ruining them by posing for photos in rivers, junkyards, Dumpsters, and pig pens. The resulting images are arresting reminders that marriages need humor, a sense of adventure, and a willingness to take risks and get dirty. (The concept was started by a Las Vegas wedding photographer whose dress-trashing photos went viral on photography websites in 2006. Other wedding photographers, especially those outside urban areas, saw the idea as a potential new revenue stream.)

Kelly Lynne Burke, a local photographer and a friend of Shelley's, often shoots weddings of Becker's brides. She says 30 percent of them now pay the extra $300 for the "Trash the Dress" option on their photography package. "It's a way for them to say 'I'm married, I'm done, I never need to get into that dress again,'" says Kelly. "These post-wedding glamour sessions are crazy and fun because the brides are so much more relaxed." Brides who felt stressed or repressed at their weddings—or who want to symbolically shake off traditions or push boundaries set by their mothers and mothers-in-law—feel liberated when trashing their dresses.

One recent twenty-two-year-old bride, Meggan Nielsen, decided to trash her bridal gown under a waterfall, to the dismay of her mother and grandmother. "They had an emotional attachment to my dress," she says. "They were with me when we picked it out. I had to help them understand the reasons why I wanted to trash it."

She told them that trashing her dress was an appealing ritual because it made a statement to her husband that she'd never again be a bride: She'd be married to him forever. "I have the wonderful memories of our wedding. I don't need the physical dress," she told her mom and grandmother. The trashing ritual wouldn't be mocking her wedding, she explained, "it'll be celebrating the finalization of it. It's a way of saying, 'The dress served its purpose well, but I don't need it anymore.' I don't need something that large and bulky taking up space in my closet. The photographs are enough of a sentimental reminder for me."

There was one other thing. When Meggan got married, she already had two children, a son and a daughter. She doubts her daughter will someday want to wear her dress. But trashing it removed the possibility, which also appealed to Meggan. "I want the experience of shopping for a bridal gown someday with my daughter," she says. "I want to again feel that bonding moment between a bride and a mother."

Her mother and grandmother didn't exactly give their blessings before Meggan trashed the dress, but they told her they were better able to understand her motivations. On the day she stepped under that waterfall and ruined the dress with dirty river water, she says, "It was invigorating. It felt like the right thing to do."

<hr>

At twenty-four years old, Alyssa watches all of these odd new wrinkles in the bridal world, and wonders what life at Becker's will look like a couple decades up the road, if she ever takes over the business.

Alyssa isn't sure yet what path she'll take. But she's open to the idea of someday accepting the responsibilities of keeping the store in the family for a fourth generation.

Unlike Shelley, who never went to college, Alyssa majored in apparel merchandising at Central Michigan University, and even spent a few weeks studying fashion design in Paris. Before graduation in 2009, she worked for a couture bridal designer in New York, helping with the production of gowns. "I wasn't good at it," she says. "I was doing a lot of pinning and beading, and I felt inadequate. Plus, the designer was always yelling at somebody. I realized I'm better suited for selling."

As part of her job description now, Alyssa has to tell brides that all sales are final. But unlike her tough great-grandmother, Eva, she tries to find friendly ways to give the news. "Well, here we are," she'll say, while taking a bride's credit card at the front counter. "You're buying the dress, so there's no turning back now. You're sure this is the right guy, right?" She says it all very lightly, but she's making a point that brides need to understand: no exchanges, no returns.

As Alyssa learns the business, she sees the need for the no-return policy. Still, her heart goes out to the victims of broken engagements. Often, they can't bring themselves to pick up the dresses they own but won't be using. They're too embarrassed, or it would pain them to see a new batch of happy dress-shoppers. Some just abandon their gowns to Becker's Dress Cemetery. Others send their mothers to retrieve them. "We'll try to sell it on eBay," a mother will say, as Alyssa gently puts an unwanted dress in a garment bag.

Now that she's working at Becker's full-time, Alyssa finds herself sorting through her feelings about love, marriage, and this line of work. Alone at home one night, she finds herself going through what she calls her old "box of love." It's a collection of letters, photos, and keepsakes she saved over the years. She has diaries there, too, from what she calls "the crisis years." Some entries detail her unhappiness over her parents' broken relationship, especially Shelley's decision to end the marriage. Other entries spell out her yearnings about love and her place in this world. "A girl's mind is a strange place," she thinks as she reads.

On January 24, 2002, when she was sixteen, she wrote about "what I want in life—the perfect wedding, home, children, husband. I want the kind of husband who will take me to an empty movie theater on our anniversary, and when we get there, our wedding will be playing on the screen. I never want to settle for less than love. But first, I need to slow down the pace and find myself. I need to get through my teen years and early twenties."

Nine years after writing those words, she says she's still has hopeless romantic tendencies, but her time in the store has given her perspective. She knows the statistics. Half the brides who buy dresses from her could end up divorced. Why will some make it and others won't? "I see a lot of brides who are young and naïve, but I don't assume that necessarily means their marriages won't work," she says. In the history of the store, she points out, thousands of brides arrived very young and naïve, including countless grandparents and great-grandparents of today's brides. Many of them ended up having successful marriages.

A greater issue, Alyssa decides, is an ability to communicate well, which she thinks her parents never fully achieved. Her father, especially, couldn't get his feelings out in the open, and retreated into alcoholism. Alyssa doesn't think that she and her boyfriend, Cory, are great communicators, but they're getting better at it.

Even though she grew up in a family focused on brides and weddings, or maybe because of that, Alyssa always has been somewhat conflicted about marriage. "My parents' divorce made me less idealistic," she says. "It's not that I don't think a happy marriage is possible. I'm just more cautious."

These days, spending long hours on the front lines of the wedding industry, Alyssa is often hyperfocused on business issues. How can she help her mother sell enough dresses to make the weekly and monthly sales numbers? And then, in the midst of that number crunching, existential thoughts will creep into her head. She'll ask herself: How did we all get here? Why do human beings even get married? Who first came up with all this wedding stuff? A ceremony, a ring, a vow, a dress, all of it?

And yet, seeing so many brides, it's easy for a young woman to get caught up in that urge to marry. Alyssa is not invulnerable to those pressures. A large part of her would like Cory to propose already. They've been together on and off since high school, and now that he works at Becker's in the back office, Alyssa has constant reminders that he's husband material. He's kind, hardworking, funny, romantic enough, and he'd be a caring, responsible father. He makes her life brighter. "I'm happiest when I'm with him," she says.

For his part, Cory says he loves Alyssa, but he wants to be careful and deliberate. He's getting his career established so he'll have enough money to buy a ring and start a life together. But more important, he wants to make sure that "everything feels right" before he takes any big steps. "I'm not prepared yet to get married," he says, point-blank. "Even though Alyssa and I have been together a while, we're still learning about each other."

Loved ones and friends are now pressuring him to "do right by Alyssa," and he's shaking off their advances. At his sister's recent wedding, it felt as if every guest was asking him about his intentions. During the reception, Hershey's Kisses were on all the tables, and one of his great-aunts used the foil from the candy wrapper to fashion a silver ring. "Go give this to Alyssa," she said. Cory smiled at her weakly and resisted.

Working at the store, he sees that steady parade of young brides, some in their teens, and he knows it's almost impossible that "they have all their ducks in a row," the way he's trying to do it. He knows some view marriage as something you jump into, that love conquers all. Sometimes that works. But he's not crossing any streets without looking both ways. This is sometimes hard on Alyssa, but he thinks patience will serve them well.

Alyssa (front row, on the left, in a black dress) used a cropped version of this photo as her Facebook profile picture.

While Alyssa waits, she's trying to keep herself in check. One profile picture she uses on her Facebook page addresses all of her emotions perfectly, and with a sense of humor. The photo shows her grabbing for a bouquet that had just been tossed at the wedding of one of her friend's. The look on Alyssa's face is this unforgettable, almost-possessed grimace. Is it a look of determination? Uncertainty? Terror? It takes a brave and self-aware young woman—especially when she's the heir to a bridal shop—to make such an image her Facebook profile picture.

Alyssa's father, Gary, worries that she overanalyzes her life. "She overthinks things, and that can make her nervous," he says. She's a lot like him in that regard.

Since Gary and Shelley divorced in 2000, he thinks a lot about the love he wishes for his daughter, and how it's different from what he wishes for his two sons. "With the boys, I want them to grow into men, to take care of themselves," he says. "But with Alyssa, it's like I want her to still be my little girl."

A large part of him wishes he could get a redo on some of the years when Alyssa was young. He still can't shake his memory of the night Alyssa won that cake at the Girl Scouts dance, and he drunkenly dropped it and laughed. And so he finds himself daydreaming about how he can make amends for such incidents. "I often think about what I could do at Alyssa's wedding to make up for some of the dumb things I've done," he says. He has considered buying a beautiful wedding cake, which could be an unspoken way of acknowledging and apologizing for that dropped cake from long ago.

Alyssa's hypothetical wedding sometimes plays out in Gary's mind—the ceremony, the reception, the words he might whisper in her ear or say publicly to the invited guests. "I don't want to do anything to ruin her day," he says. "I think about what I'll do and say. When I give her away, will I kiss her on the cheek or on the forehead? Will it be awkward? What should I say in my toast?"

Gary's awareness of the symbolism attached to weddings isn't surprising, since he spent fifteen years as a husband and son-in-law in the world of Becker's Bridal. But, of course, countless fathers outside the bridal industry mull over these same questions. Fathers who don't always know how to connect to their daughters often see the wedding day as a time to finally reach into their hearts and speak up.

Gary doesn't easily reveal his feelings to Alyssa, and he isn't adept at drawing out hers. He's stoic, and Alyssa is too. She's reluctant to talk about her toughest memories of family life because she doesn't want him to think she's blaming or judging him. She's impressed by the way he has pulled his life together, and prefers to focus on that. (Sober since 2002, Gary says he doesn't intend to drink again. "By age forty, I had more than drunk my lifetime quota," he says.)

After the divorce, Gary worked for a while in a car-bumper factory. He's now in charge of maintenance at an independent-living retirement facility in East Lansing. He lives in one of the units on the property.

Gary says he hasn't been on a date since Shelley left him. At age forty-eight, he's still handsome, and women do approach him, but he turns them away. He's aware that Alyssa and her two brothers have harbored fantasies over the years that he'll reunite with Shelley. "I admit that I have that wish, too," he says. "I do still love her."

He knows Shelley doesn't want him back; she is proud of him for his sobriety and forgives his worst behavior, but her life has moved on. "This may sound callous," she says. "I care about him, but my feelings are like those you'd feel for a brother who worked through his problems."

Given that she spends her workday with women and doesn't go to bars, Shelley doesn't always come in contact with available men. She has dated a half-dozen guys since the divorce, but doesn't expect to remarry. Her friends notice that she seems to be attracted to men with issues (she has never shaken her caregiver personality) or men who won't commit. "For some reason," she admits, "it's almost as if I don't think I deserve true love. So many of the brides in the store, they think they deserve love. But me? I'm always finding people who need to be healed first, or people who need me to love them but aren't great at giving love in return. What the heck is that all about? Why am I a magnet for these personalities?"

She doesn't expect some handsome, romantic, divorced fortysomething father-of-a-bride to walk into the store one day and sweep her off her feet. It certainly hasn't happened yet. "People say I'm married to the Becker's Bridal Building," Shelley says. "Maybe that's true." She admits she's lonely. And yet, returning to Gary wouldn't be the answer for her.

Gary hopes he's now a good role model for Alyssa and her brothers. His work doing maintenance for senior citizens in their apartments is more than a job; he looks after them, offers them company, keeps them safe. It's a high calling.

Gary spends much of his free time with his three children, and as Alyssa gets older, she's more conscious of how she interacts with him. When Gary is with the boys, they kid around a lot. They talk about sports. But with her, he's different.

Recently, just before Father's Day, Gary took her arm and said to her, "This is how I think I'll hold on to you when we walk down the aisle at your wedding." She smiled at him, but he was serious. "Maybe we should start practicing," he said.

He asked how she'd like him to dance with her during the father-daughter dance. What song? What steps? "It's OK, Dad," Alyssa said. "I'm not even engaged, and who knows if I ever will be?"

Actually, both Gary and Shelley seem to be making more efforts to show love to Alyssa, and she's appreciative. When she was young, hiding in closets to seek attention, they were more oblivious to her needs. Now they have urges to address them.

That includes, of course, her decisions about working at Becker's Bridal. These are questions complicated by Shelley's desires to have her remain in the business. Is Alyssa happy there? Should she make the store her career?

"I have to figure out where my life is going—marriage, kids, Fowler, New York, whatever," Alyssa says. "And so I find myself thinking: How will this work if I stay here forever? What will that look like?"

Alyssa is thrilled that her mother has built Becker's into a business selling $1.8 million worth of dresses a year. But the great majority of that isn't profit. Alyssa sees the pressure Shelley is under from brides, mothers, suppliers—and her $450,000 annual payroll. "I kind of absorb all of my mother's tensions," Alyssa says." I feel obliged to worry along with her. My mom's burden is my burden. Her stress becomes my stress."

Sometimes two days will go by and Shelley has hardly eaten anything besides a few crackers. Alyssa wonders: If she ever takes over the store, will she be so stressed that she'll forget to eat? Shelley understands this. She tells Alyssa, "I don't want you to feel confined by the walls of the store, or the limits of Fowler." But Alyssa knows her mother would love her to stay forever. Her father, too. He'd like her to be close.

She has a sense of how her life will likely go. "I guess my heart is here," she says. "This is my home. This is my legacy."

It's almost five p.m. on a Friday, and as closing time approaches, Alyssa and Shelley start encouraging customers to get back into their street clothes. As always, some aren't eager to take off their dresses. One has been walking around in hers for almost an hour. "Honey, we don't want to fray the bottom of the gown," Shelley tells her. "If you keep walking back and forth on this carpeting, that's what will happen."

The brides reluctantly take to the fitting rooms, and eventually head out the front door. After the store has emptied out, Alyssa says to her fellow saleswoman, Mona, "I feel like trying something on."

She gets herself into one of the store's priciest wedding dresses, and looks at herself in the old mirror by the front counter. Alyssa can be engagingly sarcastic. "Mona," she says, "will you marry me? No one else will!"

Mona just laughs and says she's done getting married.

Cory is in the back office doing the store's payroll. He looks through the one-way mirror and sees her parading around in the wedding gown. He reminds himself: He loves her, but he's not ready yet.

Alyssa isn't trying to subliminally suggest anything. Or maybe she is.

In any case, as she studies herself in the mirror, the expression on her face isn't the one from her Facebook profile photo—that crazy bouquet-catching grimace. On this day, she's smiling, and in this dress, she looks gorgeous. Cory ought to take a closer look.

If Alyssa ever does go dress-shopping for real, she thinks, she'll keep things dignified. She won't be one of those brides showing off her dress via Skype. She won't bring along an entourage of pals and a cooler of Champagne to indulge her for hours as she plays princess. She certainly won't make any plans to "trash the dress." After all, she knows well the painstaking, detailed beading and sewing that goes into each gown.

When and if she gets engaged, Alyssa assumes she'll just tour the floor after hours and easily narrow down the possibilities. She knows the stock. She knows what she likes. She imagines she'll try on a few dresses, make a decision, and then head up to the Magic Room with Shelley for a look. Maybe she'll ask her dad to join her in the Magic Room too. He'd feel touched to be invited.

A part of Alyssa, though, wonders if her time will ever come. After she gets out of the wedding gown, she plants herself in a comfortable chair on the sales floor, exhales, then tells Mona with mock exasperation: "Maybe my mom and I will be the last two spinsters in Fowler. We'll just live our sad little lives, and keep selling wedding gowns to everyone else."

In the back office, Cory is busy going through time-sheets and doesn't hear her. Neither does Shelley, over by the vapor iron.

Alyssa looks at the dress she'd been wearing, now back on its hanger. "I ought to remember this one," she says. "It could work. Someday."

Chapter Twenty-one

Julie

A s Julie Wieber's wedding approaches, she finds herself thinking about all the ways she can describe herself.

She is a nurse.

She is a widow, having lost her much-loved husband Jeff so suddenly.

She is a forty-five-year-old bride-to-be, after falling in love unexpectedly with Dean, her brother's friend.

She is a mother with a son and four daughters, all of them grieving, and all of them concerned—or angry—about her decision to get engaged barely a year after their father's death.

But Julie is also a daughter who remains incredibly close to her mother, Helen. And through her grief, and her surprising romance with Dean, she has been blessed to have her mother at her side, showing her love and trying to ease her pain.

Over at Becker's, Shelley thinks she understands some things about her friend Julie, including her great attachment to her mother and her urge to remarry so soon. "Maybe it's partly because you were born prematurely," Shelley tells her. "You were born with an extra need for nourishment. Pree-

*Julie with her son
and four daughters*

mies are fighters and survivors, but they often carry that need for nourishment the rest of their lives."

Julie's mom subscribes to the same theory. "Julie was born two months early, and weighed just three pounds, six ounces," says Helen. "Back in 1965, a lot of other babies born that small didn't survive." For the first thirty-one days of Julie's life, Helen was not allowed to touch her. "They say mothers need to bond with their children right away, but I couldn't do that. Julie was in an incubator."

In the first year of her life, Julie was sickly, and even after she began to thrive, she was a clingy toddler. "Maybe it was because she was the baby, my fifth child," says Helen. "But I think it was also because she was a preemie. She needed me. And for her whole life, I've never cut the apron strings. When the phone rings, I figure it's Julie. She raised her family in a home right down the street. She couldn't be any closer."

Recent studies suggest that people born prematurely are more apt to be anxious and prone to depression as adults. But preemies also grow up to be more risk-averse and more likely to heed their parents' advice and warnings. It's unclear whether this is because worried parents hover over their preemie children all through their lives, or because preemies grow up needing strong bonds with their parents. In any case, Helen believes that her close relationship with Julie is rooted in the circumstances of her birth.

Now seventy-seven years old, Helen has been in Fowler for almost six decades, ever since she married a local boy, Roy, who runs an excavation company in town. She has watched Becker's Bridal pass from Grandma Eva to Sharon to Shelley, and because she has seen this small town fade over the years—losing businesses, the movie theater, the hotel—she's grateful that Becker's remains. "It's a thrill when you drive down Main Street and see cars parked, and brides and bridesmaids walking around, smiling," she says. "It makes the town look happy—like we're busy."

Helen sees Fowler as a town with two faces. During store hours at Becker's, with young women populating Main Street, the community can feel young. But in truth, it is a town full of widows. When Helen meets friends for breakfast, she'll look around the table—seven or eight women, all senior citizens—and realize she's always the only one with a husband to go home to. One day she returned from breakfast and talked to Roy about it. "That's life," he told her.

"I know," she said, "but what am I going to do without you?"

On Friday, February 6, 2009, Helen had breakfast as usual with her friends. When she said good-bye to them after the meal, she casually added, "You know, when I'm in church, I always say a prayer for the widows." They thanked her. Later that day, Julie's husband, Jeff, the most loyal, fun-loving guy in Fowler, had his heart attack and died. "At the visitation, each of my friends reminded me of what I had said that morning," Helen says. "I didn't realize it, did I? Within hours, I'd be saying prayers for my own daughter."

On the first fitful night after Jeff's death, Helen didn't leave Julie's side. "I slept with her in her bed, the same bed where Jeff had slept the night before," Helen says. "I held her and I held her some more. And Julie just clung to me, the way she did when she was a baby. That's how we got through the first night and the second night."

⟞⟝

Helen lost her father in 1950, when she was seventeen. Her mother, then fifty years old, would live another thirty-three years, but never remarried.

On Sundays in the 1960s and 1970s, Helen would bring her kids to visit her mother, and little Julie was especially concerned for her widowed grandmother. "I don't like that we're leaving her alone," Julie would say as they drove away after dinner, her grandmother waving good-bye from her front porch. "Let's drive around the block and come back. We need to make sure she got in the house OK." (The empathetic urges that would make Julie an award-winning nurse were evident early.)

Julie only saw her grandmother on weekends. "But I'd think about her all week long," she says, "wondering how she was doing all by herself. How lonely was she? I felt so sorry for her."

Decades later, after Jeff died, Julie thought of her grandmother's many years as a widow. "We were sitting together, her head on my shoulder," says Helen, "and Julie said, 'I never thought I'd end up like Grandma, but I have.' I just held her and we cried."

Helen was glad that Julie and her kids found their way to counseling. They all needed it. For one thing, because Jeff died so suddenly, none of them were able to say good-bye. The pain of that cannot be underestimated.

One day Julie's therapist told her to get in her car and drive out of Fowler for a while. "Pretend Jeff is in the passenger seat," he said. "Pour your heart out to him. Tell him why you loved him, what you're sad about, what you're angry about. Scream if you need to. And tell him good-bye." Julie did that and found it helped, but just a little.

Concerned about her daughter's emotional and mental health, Helen was relieved when Julie became serious with Dean. She watched the relationship lift Julie from a very low and sad place. That's why Helen became such an advocate for her daughter when people said Julie got engaged too quickly after Jeff's death. And her advocacy was especially focused on Julie's kids.

As the wedding plans took shape, the kids remained ambivalent at best and, sometimes, openly hostile. Though Helen is very close to her grandchildren, now ages fifteen to twenty-three, she became fiercely protective of her daughter, just as she was when Julie was a three-and-a-half-pound preemie.

For a while, Helen listened to all of her grandchildren's complaints: "Mom betrayed us! She betrayed Dad!"

"Dad would want what's best for his kids, wouldn't he? And this isn't best for us. So Mom can't say he'd want her to be happy, if her happiness is making us unhappy."

"Why would she want to hang out with some guy, when we all need her?"

Over time, Julie's son tended to be the most accepting. But her four daughters would gang up on her, texting about her even while she was in the room, and lashing out at her, sometimes in public. When they were angriest and most disrespectful, the girls told Julie they hated her, that she was a terrible mother, and that their dad would never approve of how she was behaving.

"I've lost the ability to discipline," Julie admitted to her mother. Her counselor told her that's common in grieving families, because kids learn to manipulate a vulnerable parent. But that didn't make the pain and dysfunction any easier to handle.

Knowing that Helen's own father died when she was seventeen, the grandchildren expected her to be supportive of them, because she could tap into her own feelings of loss. But as twenty-year-old Lauren later explained: "It was the weirdest thing. All our lives, our grandmother had been someone we could vent to. And when we needed her, she was always there to console us. But in this case, she just laid down the law. She said, 'Your mother is my daughter and I'm standing by her! You can't talk to my daughter like that.' We'd never seen her act that way before. Never heard her raise her voice."

"In a way, I had to be almost cruel," Helen says, "and it was hard for me to do that, given how heartbroken the kids were." Still, she felt a need to encourage her grandchildren to reach outside of themselves—to help their mother, their siblings, and other people too. She talked to the kids about her own mother's many years as a widow.

"You know, my mother used to say that heartache isn't the worst thing. Sometimes you can take your heartache, and reach in deep and learn from it, and then you can use it to help someone else. Someday, people who are experiencing first-time sadness will come to you. And you'll see, you can be strong for them in a beautiful way because of what you went through losing your dad."

Helen explained that, starting when she was a young adult, she wished her mother had remarried. "She was alone a lot of years, and we worried about her, sitting silently in that empty house," she said. "Someday, you'll be very glad that your mom found Dean after your father died, that she has someone who cares about her. Life is for the living."

Helen didn't tell her granddaughters that she has a special bond with Julie, her little preemie grown to adulthood. She didn't talk about how her heart ached for Julie, maybe more than her heart ached for them. She just spoke to the kids with respect, and tough love, and hoped they absorbed some of what she said. Though they weren't thrilled that her allegiance wasn't with them, they assured her they'd gotten her message.

For her part, Julie tried her best to see things from her daughters' perspective. "It's taken me a while to realize that my kids lost something different from what I lost," Julie said. "They lost a dad to walk them down the aisle, to guide them through life. They lost a grandfather for their children. I lost so much, but maybe they lost more."

As the wedding approached, she tried not to talk about it too much, especially after her daughter Camie said, "What do you think this is? The wedding of the century?"

In calmer moments, though, Julie found herself giving her daughters this message: "I'll always love your dad. I love Dean, too, but he won't go certain places in my heart that remain reserved only for your father. I've started a new place, a different place in my heart, for Dean. I think Dad would understand this, and as time goes by, I hope you will too." She was buoyed when they said they appreciated her words.

~

As a process engineer at GM's Cadillac plant in Lansing, Dean Schafer is in charge of the robots used for the automated painting of all the cars. It's an exacting job, and he's good at it. He knows what he's doing.

On the volatile home front, understandably, he's less certain. He knows he's an outsider when it comes to the issues and animosities swirling in Julie's family. He's very much in love with Julie; that's without question. But how can he best support her? A couple times, he has reprimanded her children when he thought they'd been rude to her. There was a shouting match once. But mostly, he holds back. He's trying to build bonds with them, not turn them away.

Dean feels extremely lucky to have found Julie, and he's committed to finding the right way to build relationships with her family. He knows that will take time, partly because his journey has been different from Julie's.

Dean's first marriage resulted in three daughters, a son, and a lot of heartache. He remembers how much he loved his first wife, how excited they were when she went to Becker's to get her dress. But as years went on, his wife fell out of love with him, and her commitment to the marriage became an issue. The marriage eventually fell apart, and Dean endured a period of great depression. "I went through my own mourning process over my marriage," he says. "So I could empathize with Julie."

Dean didn't really know Julie earlier in his life, even though they had both lived in tiny Fowler. The crazy thing was that Dean and his first wife had bought their first home from Jeff and Julie. There hadn't been much interaction then, beyond pleasantries and a few house tours.

But once Dean and Julie began dating, he fell for her fast. Early on, he wrote her a poem titled "In Just Ten Days." That's how quickly he knew he wanted to marry her.

To his credit, Dean has completely accepted that Julie's bonds with Jeff remain unbreakable. "I know she's still in love with Jeff," he says. "Still is, and always will be. But I've also figured out that Julie has an amazing capacity to love. She has a heart the size of the Grand Canyon. And so I've told her: 'If I can have a little sliver of that heart of yours, you can keep the rest for Jeff.' Let me have just that small sliver, and I'll have more love than I've ever experienced in my life."

Dean's children are pleased to see him happy again, and they're glad

Dean and Julie

he's marrying Julie. But for them, of course, the circumstances are different. Unlike Julie's kids, they still have both of their parents.

A few days before the wedding, Julie invited her daughters, Dean's daughters, and her mother to join her for a group outing of manicures and pedicures. Julie was nervous. How would everyone get along? Would her daughters be friendly?

It wasn't a full-on, joyous get-together, but everyone was gracious and made polite small-talk. It went fine. "I know we're not as accepting as you and Dean would like us to be," Julie's daughter Lauren later told her. "We're going to try harder."

It meant a lot to Julie, and to Helen, to hear that. "I think I've gotten through to the kids," Helen said. "Or maybe they've come to an understanding on their own."

The day before the wedding, Shelley called from Becker's to say she'd made sure that Julie's simple dress with the brown sash was pressed and ready to go. "I'll come early to help you get dressed," Shelley promised. "You're going to look stunning."

A nurse. A widow. A mother. A daughter.

This time around, Julie knew, she wouldn't be just a bubbly, naïve bride, like she was in 1986. This time, guests might be judging her; wondering why was she remarrying so quickly. This time, nine extra people would be walking down the aisle ahead of her—her children and Dean's. And this time, everything would feel much more spiritual. Maybe her widowed grandmother would be there in spirit, waving to her from her front porch. And maybe Jeff would be there too, smiling that great smile of his, letting her know that in his absence, it's OK if she gives a little sliver of her heart to someone else.

Chapter Twenty-two

Ashley

*H*ere's what can happen two days before a wedding.

Ashley Brandenburg was in the car with her mother, running errands, when her mom just blurted it out. "You know," she said, "you don't have to get married if you don't want to."

Ashley looked at her for a moment quizzically. What should you say in response to such a statement?

"I mean," her mother continued, "you can call it off today if you'd like, and it's OK. Dad and I will understand. Everyone will understand."

"Why are you saying this, Mom?" Ashley had to ask.

"Well, it's nothing to do with Drew," her mother answered. "We think he's terrific. It's just that nobody ever said to me before I got married that I didn't have to go through with it. And I think a young woman should be told that she has the option to back out. That's all. If you don't want to get married this weekend, you don't have to do it."

Ashley, the PhD candidate in French literature, the valedictorian of her high school class, had, not surprisingly, already taken an intelligent, questioning look at whether marriage was right for her—and whether

253

Drew, the materials engineer, was the man for her. She did all that soul-searching around the time they got engaged. "Trust me, Mom, I gave it a lot of serious thought," she said. "And I'm at peace. I don't feel any pressure to get married. It's what I want."

Her mother was quiet for a moment, then figured she'd better explain.

"I'm never sorry I married your father," she said. "But I did feel like at twenty-two, that was too young for me to get married. I could have waited."

"Well, I'm twenty-seven, Mom," Ashley said. "I'm ready."

Later, Ashley ruminated a bit over what she would come to call "that weird talk." Maybe some daughters are desperate for their mothers to give them last-minute permission to run. They may need an exit strategy, a rescue, a reason.

And Ashley knows that each marriage has its issues; she's just decided that the issues between her and Drew are surmountable.

Like her father, Ashley is pretty close to being an atheist. (The wedding will be nondenominational.) But she has agreed to raise her kids as Jews because Drew's Judaism is important to him, not necessarily in a religious sense, but culturally. Ashley admits she's not fully comfortable with the rituals and the rules of the Jewish faith. She hardly recalls meeting a Jew during her childhood in central Michigan, and not all the people she's met at Drew's synagogue have been especially welcoming to her. She attends Passover seders with Drew mostly to be supportive of him.

"I had to think for a while before I agreed to raise the kids Jewish," she says. "But in the end, I decided it's important for children to be brought up having a cultural identity."

After Drew defends his dissertation, he and Ashley will be moving to Tempe, Arizona, where Drew has been hired at Intel Corp., the technology company. Ashley will be able to continue working on her dissertation from Arizona, and has more than a year before she'll have to defend it.

Ashley hopes to come back to Michigan each Christmas, especially once they have children. "Christmas, as my family celebrates it, has lost all its religious implications, but it's important to us," she says. "It's about gathering as a family, presents, lots of eating." She'd like her kids to be a part of that, and to have a connection to the Midwest sensibilities and rural way of life that she knew growing up. Funny, she thinks, how things that annoy you when you're young can seem so inviting when you're older.

Ashley also wants their offspring to receive a bilingual education. That idea seemed strange to Drew. But he was surprised to learn that there are more than a few French/English schools in the United States. And so he acquiesced on this point.

When two people commit to each other, Ashley is finding, there are a good number of issues that need to be discussed and decided on. They can't just be tabled. That's dangerous. And there have to be compromises.

That's true with wedding planning too. Too many brides have an attitude that "it's my day, so I want my way." Their parents, fiancés, and future in-laws often indulge them, just to keep peace. But it's often healthier, in the long run, if all the players respectfully hash things out. That's why some people say planning a wedding can be good preparation for living a marriage.

Ashley's biggest pre-wedding fight with her mother was over plans for a photograph. Her mother comes from a large family—fifty of her relatives will be at the wedding—and by tradition, a group photo is always taken at major family functions. Her mother was adamant about taking the photo right after the ceremony. Ashley knew it would be crazy trying to round up fifty people, including children, when there would be other things she'd need to be doing.

"It's not essential that we take this photo of this enormous crowd right then and there," Ashley told her mom. "Maybe we'll do it later at the reception."

Her mom didn't like that Ashley seemed dismissive. Ashley, already feeling stressed, didn't like that her mother wouldn't back down over "a stupid picture." What followed, as Ashley came to describe it, was "an explosion of words." Both she and her mother were being stubborn.

Later, when Ashley calmed down, she asked herself: Why didn't she just go along with what her mother wanted? Why did she put up a fight?

So what if the photo took twenty minutes to organize? How many of those fifty people won't be around in ten or twenty years? It would be nice to have one photo of them all together.

Ashley returned to her mother. "I apologize," she said. "We'll find a good time for that photo and we'll get it done."

So many brides and their mothers spend the weeks before a wedding discussing and debating every minute detail of the ceremony and reception. They trade thousands of words about issues that, in the grand scheme of things, don't really matter—napkins, place cards, tablecloths, photos, whatever.

Perhaps that's why Ashley's mother, two days before the wedding, decided to say something so unexpected: "You know, you don't have to get married if you don't want to."

Yes, in that moment, Ashley was taken aback by her mother's comment. But on reflection, she realized that her mom was trying to go beyond the surface conversations that mothers routinely have with brides-to-be. It's not just about the dress, the flowers, the reception. It's about the man and the marriage and the life that will follow.

"You don't have to get married."

The delivery of those words, Ashley came to realize, was actually an act of love.

Chapter Twenty-three

"I Do"

O n any given weekend, an average of fifty-four Becker's brides find their way down the aisles of Michigan churches, social halls, or country clubs. As Shelley and Alyssa go about their lives on a Saturday night, they sometimes look at the clock and think about which bride is saying her vows at that moment.

What happened to the accident-prone bride who feared she'd trip over her train and break her neck? Did that mother and daughter who argued bitterly in the store last week reconcile by the wedding? Did that bride who thought she'd collapse into a fit of giggles contain herself? "I wonder how they're all doing," Shelley will say.

Alyssa might venture a guess. Or she'll encourage her mother to clear her mind; the dresses looked gorgeous, the seams held, everything went fine. In all the weekends since Shelley began working at the store at age fourteen, it's been rare that she hasn't had a collection of brides on her mind. Sometimes, she wishes she could stop by certain ceremonies for a few moments, just to see the promises of the Magic Room come to life.

Danielle

Before Danielle's wedding, her grandmother, Cynda, visits the cemetery where Danielle's mom, Kris, is buried. She places a rose by the headstone, underneath the years of Kris's life: 1966–1999. "You did a damn good job raising Danielle," Cynda says softly. "You deserve to be at the wedding."

For most guests, the cemetery is on their way to Charlevoix, the resort town where the wedding will be held. One old friend of Kris's blows

Danielle and her grandmother Cynda

her a kiss as she passes the cemetery. Others see the tombstones out their car windows and silently reflect on that December afternoon when Kris was buried there.

Now it is five p.m. on a cold autumn day in Charlevoix, and everyone has gathered at a massive stone building called Castle Farms. Built in 1918 as a getaway for the president of Sears, Roebuck & Co., the castle has been converted into a banquet hall. Danielle and her fiancé Brian picked it after falling for the majesty of the place.

The wedding ceremony begins with Cynda and Brian's mother lighting two candles at the altar, after which Cynda places a calla lily on the table there; it was one of Kris's favorite flowers. After the bridal party enters to an acoustic version of Jason Mraz's "I'm Yours," it's Danielle's turn. She walks slowly, escorted by her grandfather and her mom's boyfriend, Ted, who carries in his pocket the handkerchief given to him an hour earlier by Danielle. It's embroidered with the words FATHER OF THE BRIDE, a gift of thanks to him for being there when her biological father was not.

Once Danielle and Brian are together at the altar, the minister, a woman named Glad Remaly, begins by explaining that the lily is in memory of Kris. "Even though Danielle's mother is no longer here physically," the minister says, "she is carried in our hearts as a source of love and inspiration. Danielle, your mom's spirit lives on in all fortunate enough to have loved her, and she is felt here today on this happy occasion."

The minister asks the couple to recite their vows, then leads them to the two candles. "At the beginning of this ceremony," she says, "Danielle's grandmother and Brian's mother came forward and lit their child's individual candle. Brian and Danielle, these two lit candles symbolize your uniqueness as separate people." She instructs them to use their individual candles to light a third candle together, "the unity candle."

She then asks Danielle to hold Brian's hands, palms up, "so you may see the gift that they are to you. Danielle, these are the hands of your best friend, the hands that will work alongside you, comfort you in illness, and hold you when fear or grief clouds your mind." She offers a prayer that ends, "May Brian and Danielle see their four hands as healer, protector, shelter, and guide." A minute later, she declares them husband and wife, and their friends and family applaud.

Cynda, in the front row, is wearing a gold bracelet with a small diamond that Danielle gave her the evening before, at the rehearsal dinner. "I had two of those bracelets made," Danielle explained. "The other one is for me." The diamonds came from Kris's most-cherished earrings. And so, on this wedding day, two simple bracelets speak to the love, past and present, between three generations of women.

After the ceremony, as the photographer poses the bride and groom with Cynda, Ted stands off to the side, observing. He's there with his wife, whom he met and married after Kris died. At one point, Cynda and

Danielle both start laughing. "Listen to them, it's the same laugh," Ted says. "And Kris sounded exactly like that. She had this loud, deep, let-it-all-out laugh that would light up her whole face." He pauses. "It can be painful when I hear Danielle laugh now. But it also brings back a lot of good memories."

He remembers playing checkers with Danielle and Kris, using the squares on his kitchen floor. He's thinking about Kris and Danielle, bobbing their heads together to Prince's "When Doves Cry," driving to the cottage in northern Michigan. Then a third memory comes into his head, of how he and Kris had a playful routine when he'd ask her to make him a drink. "No you make it," she'd say.

"No, you."

"No, you."

"No, you make it," he'd finally answer, "because you always put love in it." And she'd laugh that full laugh of hers.

Once his photo is taken with the bride and groom, Ted tells guests standing nearby that he always has premonitions about pregnancies. He can predict the gender of a baby. "I had a streak of sixteen correct predictions, then I got one wrong, and

Danielle and Brian on the dance floor

now I've been right six times in a row," he says. "Here's my prediction for Danielle: Her first child will be a girl, in honor of her mom."

At the reception, some guests choose not to mention Kris when they congratulate Danielle. They don't want to make her sad. But a few feel the need to articulate what they've all been thinking. "Your mom loved you so much," one says, "and she would have thought you looked beautiful today."

As for Brian, he picks his own moment to let Danielle know that he also misses Kris, the mother-in-law he never got to meet. The DJ plays Michael Bublé's "Everything" for the newlyweds' first dance, and there on the floor, Brian gently pulls Danielle toward him. "I've been wishing your mom could see us and how happy we are," he says in her ear. "But you know what? She's here. She knows. She sees us."

None of the people around the dance floor are aware of what he has said. They just see Danielle hugging her husband a little more tightly, as "Everything" fills the room.

Meredith

Though she turned forty a few weeks earlier, Meredith begins her wedding day as nervous as a schoolgirl on her first date. "I like to be nervous," she tells her bridesmaids. "It's my nature. If I'm not worried, there's something wrong with me."

They've spent the morning at the hairdresser, where Meredith has tried to settle herself down with a glass of Champagne. Her mind is racing with all the logistical details of the wedding. She's also thinking that she has spent her adult life as a single woman, and now, within hours, her status will change. The thought is more anxiety-provoking than she expected. She has a second glass of Champagne, which helps.

Now it is early afternoon, and she arrives at the church, gets into her wedding gown, and enters the sanctuary, where her fiancé, Ron, is waiting for her and their photographer. As she walks toward him, and he sees her in her dress for the first time, she notices a look on his face that she's never seen before. His smile, his eyes, his expression. "That's a look of love," she thinks. (It will be her favorite moment of the day.)

After the photos, time seems to accelerate. People had told Meredith that a wedding day flies by, and that she should try hard to pay attention. They were right. Meredith can feel the day speeding away from her.

As the ceremony gets under way, she's surprised by how anxious she feels. At one point, she and Ron are seated in the front pew while her uncle recites inspirational readings. "I'm going to pass out," Meredith thinks, and jumbled thoughts start piling up in her mind. "I have to leave the sanctuary and get fresh air. I can't breathe! But wait. If I leave, Ron will think I don't want to marry him. I do want to marry him. I do."

She hears the readings, but can't focus on the words. She's thinking: "I've waited forty friggin' years for this, and now I'm wondering 'What am I doing?' I'm one freaky bride, aren't I? I have to relax!" She takes Ron's hand, and that calms her down.

During the recessional, as Meredith walks back down the aisle, she remembers the advice she'd been given: "Pay attention." And so she walks slowly and looks at people's faces one by one. They're almost all smiling at her, two hundred of them. Applauding. Taking photos. Everyone who ever mattered to her is here: friends, relatives, co-workers. And lots of unfamiliar faces are smiling at her: Ron's relatives. "They seem happy for us too," she thinks. Unlike her parents, these strangers weren't waiting decades to see her married, but their smiles seem just as welcoming. Smiles without any baggage.

After a great many hugs in the back of the church, the wedding party climbs aboard a rented bus and heads to downtown Grand Rapids to have more photos taken in a park. Everyone is cheering, drinking, and blowing bubbles out the bus windows.

When they arrive, they see four other brides and grooms also posing for photos in the park. Meredith greets them all, wishes them well, and they say the same to her. "Each of these brides looks a decade or two younger than me," Meredith thinks, but that's fine. She *does* wish them well. And in a way, their youthful energy has enhanced her day. They've become snapshots in her mind, as she tries to hold on to each moment.

At the reception, Meredith's father says a prayer for her and Ron, and thanks everyone who tried to grow white pumpkins for the centerpieces. While planning this fall wedding, Meredith had thought white pumpkins would add a nice fairy-tale touch. She liked the Cinderella connection, though it wasn't necessarily because she felt like a bride approaching the midnight of her marriageable years.

She learned, however, that it's not easy to grow white pumpkins; their seeds often yield orange pumpkins. The quest for white pumpkins turned into what she came to call "the pumpkin fiasco." But then her parents found a friend who found a farmer who found a way to grow perfect white pumpkins in time for the wedding. Now here they are, forty of them, all beautifully carved with candles glowing orange inside of them.

Ron's brother, the best man, offers a toast: "I want to tell all of you that my new sister-in-law, Meredith, is one in a million. So it makes sense that it took Ron until he was forty-two years old to find her, because it takes time to go through a million people."

Everyone laughs, and Meredith thinks to herself, "They're laughing, but I actually did date one million men before I found Ron!"

At the end of the night, Meredith and Ron check into a hotel near the reception hall, and he disappears in the bathroom. Soon, he has prepared a bubble bath, and lined the tub with pumpkin candles he's brought over from the reception.

"It's beautiful, Ron," Meredith says, "but there aren't enough bubbles."

He adds more bubble bath, runs more water, they get in the tub, and very quickly, they're overwhelmed by bubbles. They can't see each other. It's like an *I Love Lucy* episode. "Honey," Meredith says finally, "to be honest, I'm just exhausted. If I don't get out of this tub I'm going to fall asleep and drown."

As they dry off and climb into bed, the anxiety that began Meredith's day seems like half a lifetime ago. She finds herself feeling extraordinarily lucky.

Yes, it's true that she may be too old to bear children. She and Ron didn't marry young, like their parents, so they may never see a fortieth or fiftieth wedding anniversary. Still, Meredith decides, after forty years, three weeks and two days of being single, after all her adventures and disappointments, after her personal million-man march, her journey has taken her to the right destination—right here, right now, cuddling with the right man, as they fall asleep together on their first day of marriage.

Meredith, Ron, and their mostly middle-aged bridal party

Ashley

In the days leading up to her wedding, Ashley has been able to set aside the work she's been doing to earn her PhD in French literature. But her fiancé, Drew, the materials engineer, can't take time off. He will soon be defending his PhD dissertation, so he's working feverishly right up until the wedding. He's literally taking a quick break to get married, and then he'll be back at work.

For most of her wedding day, Ashley, the pragmatist, isn't hugely emotional. She's surprised when she feels teary walking down the aisle. She didn't expect that.

The person at the ceremony who seems most moved, it turns out, is the local judge who is officiating. No one knew she'd be such a softy. She's so choked up that it's hard for her to get the words out. "I apologize," she says at one point. "I always get emotional when I do this."

Ashley can't help but smile. It's her wedding day, and yet she feels like reaching out to the officiant to calm her down.

Most of the guests are Catholic or Jewish, and they aren't accustomed to a nondenominational ceremony. But given that her dad is an atheist, and Ashley is close to defining herself the same way, she didn't want the ceremony to be religious. Her Catholic relatives would just have to understand. (Drew, being Jewish, wanted to incorporate one Jewish tradition at the end of the ceremony. Ashley agreed it would be meaningful.)

The couple put together the ceremony themselves, and the words spoken have been chosen carefully. "The union of Drew and Ashley brings together two family traditions, two systems of roots, in the hope that a new family tree may become strong and fruitful," says the sniffling judge. She turns to Drew's and Ashley's parents. "Will you encourage them in their relationship?"

"We will."

"Do you celebrate with them the decision they have made to choose each other?"

"We do."

"Will you continue to stand beside them, yet not between them?"

"We will."

After the vows, the judge reads: "May your house be a place of happiness for all who enter it, and a place where old and young are renewed in each others' company, a place for growing, for music, for laughter. And when shadows and darkness fall within its rooms, may it still be a place of hope and strength."

The ceremony ends with the Jewish tradition of the groom stepping on a glass, shattering it. The tradition has several interpretations. Because it recalls the destruction of the Temple in Jerusalem, it reminds the bride and groom that even in their happiest moments, they should recognize the heartaches life will bring. The broken glass also tempers the wedding celebration by symbolizing the fragility of marriage—the need for a husband and wife to treat each other with care and respect. And so the breaking of the glass is a moment that all at once encompasses sadness, joy, and responsibility.

When Drew steps on the glass, his Jewish relatives call out the congratulatory words "Mazel Tov!" The bride and groom kiss, then lead the recessional down the aisle.

During the reception, Ashley agrees to another nod to Drew's Jewish roots. The guests, led by his relatives, hold Drew and Ashley in chairs above their heads while they dance the Hora around them. It's a tradition that suggests a bride and groom are like a king and queen, held up by their subjects—at least for the duration of a song.

Ashley finds the experience kind of scary—she worries she'll fall at any moment—but she smiles through it, waiting for the song to end. Her response is appropriate: Millions of Jewish brides before her have felt the same way.

That mob-scene photo of Ashley's mother's family is taken during the reception, and comes off well. The fifty relatives smile, most don't blink, and Ashley's mom is grateful that time was carved out to get it done.

At times, Ashley feels like an observer at her own wedding. A wedding is a pageant. She accepts that. But she has no urge to be the pageant queen. "I'm in the dress and I'm the center of attention, by necessity," she thinks. "But I don't need it to be 'my special day.' As long as everyone else likes the food and music, that's enough for me."

Ashley's dad, not a big dancer, isn't gung-ho about the father-daughter dance, but he makes the best of it. As Elvis Presley's "Memories" begins playing, he decides this is as good a time as any to share words of wisdom. "Drew is a really nice guy," he tells Ashley while they dance. "I think you two are going to make it."

"Thanks, Dad."

"But you know what's most important in a marriage? Compromise."

"I know, Dad," Ashley says. She finds it cute. Not wanting to dance, not knowing what else to say, her father has picked this awkward moment to advise his strong-willed daughter. "Compromise is the key," he says, trying to make himself heard over Elvis.

Ashley smiles at her father. She and Drew have so much to do; their dissertations await them, their new apartment awaits them . . . their lives await them. In that sense, the wedding is a distraction. But in this moment, she realizes, she's content, holding on to her well-meaning dad, listening as he tells her things she already knows.

Ashley and Rick:
the father/daughter dance

Julie

As Julie Wieber's bridal party walks down the aisle of the Most Holy Trinity Catholic Church in Fowler, it's remarkable how fast everyone is moving. They're almost trotting, and there's hardly any space between all the bridesmaids and groomsmen.

Between them, Julie and her fiancé, Dean, have seven daughters and two sons, ages fifteen to twenty-three. While they all whiz by, guests might think the kids just want the wedding behind them, given the family friction. But actually, it was the priest who set the pace. Before the wedding, he was almost stern. "Everyone wants their wedding to be a show," he told the bridal party. "They forget the real marriage is with God; the uniting of two people. This isn't a show. It's a sacrament. Let's keep things moving."

Julie walks fast, too, but she looks elegant in a non-extravagant gown suitable for a woman entering a second marriage. (Shelley had come over earlier to help Julie get into her dress, and told her she looked even more beautiful than the first time.)

There are moments during the ceremony that lead people to think of Julie's late husband Jeff. One reading includes the words "Allow us to live together to a happy old age," a reminder that Jeff and Julie did not.

But there are also moments when the priest seems to be speaking to Julie's children, offering them the explanation that Julie and Dean didn't find each other as much as they were delivered to each other. "We may be tempted to think this is chance," the priest says, "but it is not. Julie and Dean never thought in a million years that they'd be here on this day, but God's providential love brought them together."

Julie's girls are trying to smile, but when the vows are recited, Camie, seventeen, lowers her head and her body actually starts shaking. Her younger sister, Macy, fifteen, and older sister Lauren, twenty, both put their arms around her. All are crying.

A heavy rainstorm hits as the ceremony ends, and the guests huddle in the church hallway, standing in line to greet the newlyweds. It's crowded, as people decide not to run for their cars until the rain eases. Dean is relieved when Julie's daughters each give him a congratulatory hug; he had worried that they might not reach out to him at all.

Later, however, at the reception, Julie's daughters can't fully contain how annoyed they are each time guests clink their glasses, encouraging Julie and Dean to kiss. Lauren and Stef do a lot of whispering and rolling their eyes at each other. "We shouldn't be here in these dresses," Lauren tells her sister. "Mom should still be married to Dad. Every-

Julie and Dean

thing should be fine, like it was. Not like this."

"And why does every kiss have to last like five minutes?" Stef asks.

"I can't even watch," Lauren says. "The only person I'm thinking about is Dad."

More clinking. This time, Dean actually tips Julie back to kiss her.

"This sucks," Stef says.

About sixty of Jeff's relatives are among the 260 guests. The wedding is bittersweet for them, naturally, but many tell Julie that Jeff would be pleased to know she has found a partner, and a way out of her grief.

Dean's four children spend much of the night smiling. They're glad to see him happy again; the kissing doesn't bother them at all. But as Julie's kids point out, the circumstances are different: Dean's divorce may have been traumatic, but not as traumatic as losing a beloved father suddenly.

As Julie's children see it, people just have to accept that they need time to adjust. Their grandmother, Helen, joins them by their table. "We could sure do with a little less affection from the bride and groom over there," one of the girls tells her.

"Well, if you're going to marry someone, and live and sleep with him, you have to love his skin, his face, his kiss . . . everything," Helen says. Her granddaughters interrupt. "You can stop right there!" says one. "Way too much information!"

Dean realizes that, as the years go by, he may end up being a part of the lives of Julie's children longer than Jeff was. He can see a time where he'll feel true love for these kids, and maybe they'll love him in return. Before the wedding, he had told people: "I hope their grieving will turn into acceptance. I hope I can be a positive influence."

Near the end of the reception, as Dean holds Julie's hand and thanks people for coming, his new stepchildren stand with their grandmother, off to the side, watching.

"I can see he loves her," Lauren says, softly and generously. "In a way, it's good that they have each other."

Her grandmother smiles. "Honey, that's how I see it too," she says. "This will be a good thing for your mom, and for you kids, too. I can just feel it."

Erika

Decades from now, Pastor Brad Klaver will look back and count hundreds of weddings that he'll have performed. But tonight, at Berean Baptist Church in Grand Rapids, the twenty-seven-year-old rookie pastor is officiating at the very first wedding of his career.

It's fitting that he's here for Erika and Reuben, the couple who waited until they committed to each other before sharing even a kiss. Erika's sisters, who started the family's non-kissing tradition, are the bridesmaids. And so there's a virginal feel in the air, from the tall, boyish pastor to the bride and groom to some of the young guests, who've made their own purity vows. It's a time of new beginnings.

Erika is preceded down the aisle by three flower girls, who haphazardly sprinkle fake snowflakes. Then Erika enters looking as lovely as she did in the Magic Room, holding the arm of her father, Vic.

When they reach the altar, Pastor Klaver begins: "The book of Genesis describes a time in the life of a man and a woman when they will leave their parents and cleave unto each other. They will begin a new home and family. We are here today to witness the establishment of this new home."

He introduces Erika's dad, who steps to the front, his voice cracking from the start. Vic quotes from Proverbs 22:6, which states: "Train up a child in the way he should go and when he is old he will not depart from it."

"Most people hear this verse and think the writer is talking about training of the law, morals, a good work ethic," Vic says. "But it's really telling parents to find out your child's individual gifts, the way they are wired. Help them to become the person God intended them to be. Reuben, over the past twenty-three years, Lynn and I have tried to know Erika's strengths, to help her develop them. As we have come to know you more, we realize that you have the strengths and desires to further that growth in Erika."

When Vic sits down, Pastor Klaver talks about the Bible's call to wives to "submit to your husbands." "'Submit' isn't my word," he says to Erika. "It's God's word. And maybe it would be helpful if I explain what this word doesn't mean. It doesn't mean you are less than Reuben, or that you don't have a voice. It means that you are making a choice to bring your life, your dreams and your will under the leadership of your husband. I know you wouldn't be here today if you couldn't trust Reuben to be the kind of man to whom you could confidently and joyfully entrust your life."

Pastor Klaver turns to Reuben. "Just as Erika is called to submit to you, you are called to love Erika. The word 'love' is one of the most misconstrued words of our time. We have reduced love to some euphoric feeling. Trust me, there will be times and seasons when there will not be feelings of euphoria. But in the biblical definition of love, love is action. It is the action of giving oneself for the greater good of another. It is laying down your life daily for the sake of Erika. Every day you are to delight in Erika, pursue her, protect her, provide for her, fight for her. Reuben, are you up for this?"

"Yes!" he says.

Pastor Klaver has another question: "Will you love Erika, comfort her, honor and keep her, in sickness and in health, and forsaking all others, be faithful to her as long as you both shall live?"

"I will," Reuben says.

For a first-time officiant, Pastor Klaver is impressive. He speaks with confidence and a smile, hardly looking at his notes. He concludes his remarks by speaking for everyone in the sanctuary. "Reuben and Erika, we are all rooting for you."

The couple kisses to applause and laughter, and as Sinatra's "Love and Marriage" plays as a recessional, one of Erika's sisters actually skips down the aisle. (Her husband, at her side, shakes his head and refuses to skip.) Erika and Reuben linger toward the front of the sanctuary, paying respect to their parents by offering hugs.

The dinner reception that follows is very low-key. No alcohol. No dancing.

Erika's mom, Lynn, is all smiles, but Vic is emotional. When it's his turn to talk, he keeps pausing to compose himself. "Erika, one of my fondest memories is taking you out for breakfast on your birthday each year. One birthday when you were little, I asked what you wanted to be when you grew up. You said, 'Either a princess or a McDonald's lady.' I understood the urge to be a princess, but why the McDonald's worker? You told me, 'Well, they get to talk to lots of customers and they all give them money!'"

After everyone laughs, Vic continues. "Erika, you have carried that happy, sun-is-always-shining countenance with you your entire life. As you have matured, you have also emerged into someone with great insight. On the dad-daughter trip we took when you were sixteen, you developed a list of ten character traits you desired in a husband. A list, so to speak, that could be used to filter out suitors before your heart started to fall for them. Holding fast to that list all these years never helped you get a lot of dates, but it has helped you arrive here today with Reuben. I'd like to read it again for you."

He pulls out that list she wrote at age sixteen and begins reading: "virtuous in character . . . humble . . . shows grace . . . displays awesome deeds . . ." When he finishes, he addresses Reuben. "I recall the first day Erika brought you to our house. She was on the back of your motorcycle, holding tight, with a giant smile. After you two left, Lynn said to me, 'Well, you just met your next son-in-law.' So, as a good dad, what did I do? Of course, I checked out your Facebook page! Here is what I read: 'I'm a United States Marine currently serving my God and Country. I am waiting for marriage to have sex, and am proud of that. I love beer in moderation. I am a country boy and I'm high on life! I love Jesus, my family, brothers in arms, friends, outdoors—and I will never grow up!'"

Vic looks up from his printout. "Right there on Facebook, we started to see why Erika was attracted to you. You had no intention of letting life pass you by."

He turns to his daughter. "Erika, from here on, your job is to stand by Reuben's side with discernment, support, affirmation, and prayer. Help him exemplify those character traits you desired years ago."

Reuben takes the microphone. At age twenty-three, he has returned from battle more mature, and the wedding guests who knew him as a boy can see this as he speaks. He graciously thanks Vic and Lynn for raising Erika well. He's earnest and serious. "Erika and I would like to ask all of you in the room to be part of our marriage," he says, "to be witnesses, to hold us accountable."

When he's finished speaking, a short video of the couple is shown: Photos flash by of Erika and Reuben growing up, while the couple explains how they fell in love. There are lovely photos of Erika and her three sisters, and several shots of Reuben with his comrades in Iraq. The highlight of the video is footage taken at the surprise family brunch when Reuben got down on one knee, pulled out a ring, and proposed. After Erika

Erika and Reuben

tearfully accepted, he stood up and took her in his arms. He leaned closer. He told her how much he loved her. And then . . .

He gave her the first romantic kiss of her lifetime.

In the reception hall, everyone watching the video breaks into applause at that moment, as Erika beams. Vic and Lynn, feeling grateful and proud, make eye contact with each other, but say nothing. Their own marriage has weathered a great deal; Lynn's memories of child abuse, the nightmares that followed, her early urges to abandon their marriage. But at this point in their lives, they feel very blessed—by their daughters, sons-in-law, grandchildren.

Three of their girls are married. Just one daughter, twenty-two-year-old Aleece, is left, waiting for her first kiss. As the night ends, Erika throws her bouquet and, in an obvious setup, Aleece catches it.

Of course, there's no need to call Becker's Bridal in the morning to get Aleece an appointment. For now, it's a matter of time, and more than that, a matter of patience.

She's got the bouquet. She's got the grounding of her faith and family, and a sense of life's possibilities. When and if the time is right, her kiss will come.

Megan

All the guests at Megan's wedding know her story. The accident that left her with a mangled right hand was only four months ago, so when Megan enters the church sanctuary, it's the first time some guests have seen her in a while. They take in the fullness of her arrival—her dress, her hair, her smile—but their line of sight soon goes to her hand, and to the "birdcage" headpiece covering the wound on her forehead.

During the ceremony, though, Megan gives them reasons to look beyond her injuries. There's the intensity with which she gazes into Shane's eyes at the altar. There's the ease with which he holds her hand.

For Megan's father, Jack, the wedding is far more emotional than he expected. He finds himself thinking about both the strides Megan has made since the accident and the long road ahead. He can't help it.

Some guests have talked to him in recent weeks, so they can sense what's on his mind today. "It's hard for me to think of her going through the rest of her life," he has confided to friends. "When I look at Megan's hand, I can't believe this happened. It would be one thing if she had all that surgery and would be done with it. But she'll need more surgery on her hands. She'll need plastic surgery on her face to make her look more normal. All the skin grafts from her hip, they're not the same color as her face. . . ."

But Jack is also feeling grateful to Shane, and impressed by the way he has loved and stood by Megan. At the time of the accident, the couple was engaged for just a week. Jack has been thinking: "Megan had such a strong desire to get married, to raise a family. She has such a love of children. If she had not found Shane before the accident, how would her life have turned out? Would she find someone else? There's no way to know the answer."

And so here, during the ceremony, Jack has an epiphany. Both Laura, his wife, and Megan adhere to the strict teachings of the Apostolic Christian Church. In the mid-1980s, Jack watched as Laura turned to the church for solace after the death of their nine-month-old daughter, who had fallen off her changing table. Jack understands why Laura and Megan have been drawn to the church, but his faith is not as absolute as theirs.

And yet . . .

Watching Megan and Shane gaze at each other at the altar, he feels as if he is in the presence of something powerful. The thought in his head is this: "They were brought together by God."

As the ceremony continues, Laura finds herself smiling; she hasn't yet cried and doesn't think she will. Unlike Jack, she's less focused on Megan's injuries. Instead, she's thinking: "For a mother to see her child so overjoyed, well, what more could I ask for? We're all very blessed."

At the reception, people notice Megan eating with her left hand. But they don't know that she can now grip a pen with her damaged right hand, and that she has an ambitious plan: After the wedding, she's going to write her thank-you notes with that hand. It won't be the beautiful handwriting she used to have; now her scrawl is closer to that of a third-grader. But she'll show everyone she can do it. Her effort will be a thank-you to her doctors and physical therapists, as well as to those who gave wedding gifts.

As the reception comes to an end, Laura thinks back over her own life. As a girl, she had fantasized about meeting the perfect guy, having the perfect wedding, embarking on the perfect life. What's the definition of perfect, anyway?

She learned as a young mother that terrible things can happen. Losing her daughter Melissa was a wake-up call for her, and it informed Megan's life too. Megan grew up knowing that babies can fall of changing tables and die. And so, Laura has noticed that Megan is entering marriage more realistically.

Watching Megan say good-bye to her guests, Laura feels a blossoming realization about what constitutes a perfect life. "Just because the accident happened during Megan's engagement," she decides, "that doesn't mean she isn't starting out with a perfect life. Perfect doesn't mean unflawed or without challenges or that bad things won't happen. Megan understands that. She accepts the idea that the life she has, that's the perfect life."

Megan and Shane are standing together, receiving everyone's well-wishes. At one point, as friends of their parents talk to them, they reach toward each other, almost absentmindedly. Very easily, they are hand-in-hand. The perfect life awaits them.

Shane and Megan

Chapter Twenty-four

Outside the Doorway

*I*t's Monday, nine a.m., and Shelley is about to leave home and drive the few blocks to the store. But first, as always, she takes a moment to light a candle. It's a quick, self-styled "gratitude ritual" she's been doing for years.

"Thanks for the week that just passed," she says softly. "Thanks for the week to come. Thanks for Becker's Bridal, for my parents' well-being, for my own stability."

She wishes health and happiness to the brides she'll meet this week, and to their families. Then she says Alyssa's name, and the names of her sons, hoping they will always know how much she loves them.

On this Monday, she adds a few extra words: "I know Alyssa is struggling with decisions about her heritage, about staying with me at the store and making Becker's her life." This isn't a prayer or a request to a higher power. Shelley doesn't ask that Alyssa remain at her side. Instead, she says simply: "I wish her well in her decision." After that, she blows out the candle and heads over to the store.

When she arrives, one of her saleswomen, Mona, is prettying up the

Magic Room; vacuuming the carpet, and using Windex to remove finger-prints from the mirrors. Mona has her own Monday ritual. She stands on the pedestal, looking at thousands of images of herself in all the mirrors, and as she hums a wedding march, she moves her arms as if she's conduct-ing an orchestra.

Alyssa arrives next. "Hi, Barbie," she says to her mother. Then she settles in for her Monday chore: listening to messages on the office an-swering machine to see if anyone reported a problem during a weekend wedding. She checks e-mails, too, scanning subject lines for complaints. "Nothing too serious," she tells Shelley, which is always a relief. (The worst report comes from a bride whose lining wasn't appropriately hemmed. Her bridesmaids rose to the occasion with needle and thread, stitching quickly and saving the day. It wasn't so terrible. It made the bridesmaids feel needed.)

At ten a.m., Shelley unlocks the front door and greets the week's first customer. Her name is Katrina, and she's a twenty-seven-year-old librarian from suburban Detroit. She's brought along her mother, mother-in-law, and two kid sisters.

As Katrina scans the racks, she talks to Shelley and Mona about her fi-ancé, also a librarian, and about what it's been like for her since her name-sake hurricane hit New Orleans. "I get tired of apologizing for my name," she says. "Everyone has a comment."

"We call her Katie," her mother interjects.

Katrina explains that she feels a special connection to the victims of the hurricane. Still, she has decided not to attend the upcoming American Library Association conference in New Orleans. "They give you a name tag and you have to wear it all day. I couldn't bring myself to walk around New Orleans wearing a name tag."

"Katrina is a beautiful name," her mother says, and then, almost apol-ogetically, adds the obvious. "Of course, we didn't know there'd be the hurricane when we named her."

Shelley listens and nods empathetically. There's so much parents don't know and wish they did. That's the definition of parenting, isn't it? Every parental decision, starting with the innocuous choice of a baby's name, can have ramifications in her life. Every choice we help our daughters make—about a childhood friend, a college, a career, a possible husband, even a bridal gown—has potential hazards.

Katrina doesn't like the first dress she tries on. "It looks like a wedding cake," she says. But the second dress, a $1,600 strapless gown from Spain with a bolero jacket and a sash along the waist, looks stunning on her.

"What do you think?" Mona asks.

"I think I love it," Katrina says.

"Well, come on upstairs," Shelley tells her. "We've got a special room. Let's see what you look like in there."

While Mona helps Katrina up the stairs, fluffing her train behind her, Shelley heads over to the counter to go over her schedule. She has fittings almost every hour until eight p.m. "A lot of time on my knees," she says.

Just then, a few quick bursts of light emanate from inside the Magic Room, as flashes from the family's small camera bounce off all the mirrors. Soon enough, Katrina's mom is crying the usual tears of joy, and Mona scurries out onto the sales floor. "I forgot to bring the tissues," Mona says, grabbing a box. "What was I thinking?"

Meanwhile, another bride-to-be has headed up the stairs and is now standing on the landing outside that old bank vault, with her mother at her side.

As they wait their turn, Shelley walks over to greet them. The young bride is fresh-faced and blond. She looks very much like her mom, who leans against the wall, holding two purses, her daughter's and her own. For now, Shelley knows nothing about this bride, nothing about her mother, nothing about their lives. She doesn't even know their names yet. But like the thousands of brides and their parents who've passed through Becker's Bridal before them, they have a story that carried them here, to this dress, this doorway, this moment.

"It'll be just a minute," Shelley promises the young bride. Then she turns to the bride's mother and smiles. "You're going to love how she looks in the Magic Room."

The pedestal in the Magic Room

Acknowledgments

*T*here were more than 100,000 Becker's brides who made this book possible.

Just as they are all embedded in that old mirror in the store, I also feel as if they're here in spirit, in the pages of this book. Though I'll refrain from naming them, I am grateful that over the last seventy-six years, they all made their way to Fowler, Michigan, to share their stories and find their dresses.

In a lot of ways, this book was a group project. Greatest thanks, of course, go to Shelley Becker Mueller for so graciously welcoming me into her bridal shop and into her life. It was an honor to share her story, and the story of the Becker family.

I owe heartfelt thanks to Shelley's parents, Clark and Sharon Becker, and to her daughter, Alyssa Mueller. And, of course, this book would not be possible were it not for the foresight and pioneering spirit of the family matriarch, Eva Becker.

I'm grateful to Shelley's former husband, Gary Mueller, her siblings Jenny Badgett and Tim Becker, her sister-in-law, Sharon M. Becker, and cousin Eleanor Klein, who shared their memories. Thanks also to Seth Kruger, Rev. Glad Remaly, Pastor Brad Klaver, Paul Fox, Pat and Ken Hafner, Clarence Simon, and Robin Jones Gunn.

The sales staff at Becker's was always helpful to me, even when the store was jammed with brides. I thank them for their observations and rec-ollections. Thanks to Mona Bryant, Bill Goldman, Gwen Seguin, Danyel Vining, Sara DeShone, Sandy Schmitz, Kay Sillman, Jan Burnham, Kim Thelen, Beverly Schaefer, Jennifer Scott, Jeff Seguin, and Cory Pung (who was still seriously dating Alyssa as this book went to press).

This book focuses on eight brides, their fiancés and their families. I am extremely grateful to all of them for bravely and passionately opening their hearts and sharing their happiest and hardest stories. I enjoyed getting to know all of them, including Danielle and Brian Wendell; Cynda Glynn; Ted Campbell; Holly Bysko; Jack and Laura Pardo; Shane and Megan Martin; Julie Wieber; Dean Schafer; Lauren Wieber; John Wieber; Helen and Roy Pung; Carol and Paul Otto, and their daughters Missy, Jennifer, Rochelle, and Heather; Matthew Sunderlin; Victor and Lynn Hansen; Er-ika and Reuben Burton; Andy and Leanne Blackmore; Gavin and Kayla Schutten; Aleece Hansen; Meredith and Ron Kauffman; Ashley Branden-burg; Drew Forman; Richard and Susan Brandenburg; Courtney and John Schlaud; and Susan Driskill. (You can learn more about these brides and their families at www.MagicRoomBook.com.)

Huge thanks to my agent, Gary Morris, whose storytelling instincts, publishing know-how, and daily bursts of humor helped me through every step of this project. I value his friendship.

At Gotham Books, I am indebted to Bill Shinker and Lauren Marino for their enthusiasm for this book, and for their careful and terrific guidance as it came together. Many thanks also to the always impressive Beth Parker and Lisa Johnson, who make the publicity process great fun, to Cara Bedick, a pleasure to work with, to Ray Lundgren for his beautiful design work, and to Laura Gianino, Casey Maloney, Jessica Chun, Helen Gregg, Mela-nie Klesse, John Cassidy, Kevin Che, Dick Heffernan, John Lawton, Susan

Schwartz, Melanie Koch, Sabila Khan, Julia Gilroy, Gail Schimmel Friedman, Sabrina Bowers, Elke Sigal, Glenn Timony, Fred Huber, Tim McCall, Kent Anderson, Mark McDiarmid, Katya Shannon, Chris Mosley, Diana Van Vleck, Harsh Patil, Melinda Hubik, Matthew Pavoni, Normal Lidofsky, Patrick Nolan, Don Redpath, Trish Weyenberg, Don Rieck, Sharon Gamboa, Richard Adamonis, Lisa Pannek, Andy Dudley, and Judy Moy.

Special thanks to Peter Jacobs and Amie Yavor, and to photographer Kelly Lynne Burke, Korey Tucker, Fred Siegel, Gayle and Nicole Goodman, Neal Boudette, Mike Radakovich, Jeff Bennett, Kate Linebaugh, Matt Dolan, Krishnan Anantharaman, and Mike Ramsey.

I thank my daughters, Jordan, Alex, and Eden, for their love and support, and for inspiring many of the questions I asked while researching this book. I'm grateful to them on other fronts too. Jordan helped come up with the idea for the lovely design on *The Magic Room* cover. Alex read every page, and I valued her encouragement, suggestions, and her eye for typos. Eden offered her smart thoughts about the book each step of the way. This book was a family affair. Early readers included my sister, Lisa Segelman, my mother, Naomi Zaslow, and my mother-in-law, Marilyn Margulis.

Without question, I owe my greatest thanks to my wife, Sherry. For months, I had been mulling the idea of writing a nonfiction book about the love we all wish for our daughters. I needed a place to set the book—a place with great emotion—and it was Sherry who suggested that I find a bridal shop. I'm grateful for her love, for our twenty-four years of marriage, and for those words she said to me as I first contemplated this book: "There's something about a wedding dress …"

Someday, perhaps, I'll have a chance to be a father of a bride. I know that when the search for a bridal gown begins, I'll think back to the wise advice I received from Shelley, her staffers, and all the Becker's brides and their parents. They taught me that a bride should make the final decision about which dress is "the one." What a parent thinks is secondary. My job as a father will be simple. My job will be to tell my daughters I love them.

Thanks to all of you for helping me understand this.